Biography

Priscilla survived her years of secondary school education (even achieving some A levels!) and went on to study music at the Royal Welsh College of Music and Drama in Cardiff. She then taught classroom music to primary school pupils in London and Devon.

Twenty-five years ago, Priscilla moved to live in a small village in France with her husband and nine children.

Comprehensively Failed was first published in 2023

This is the 2nd Edition. 2023.

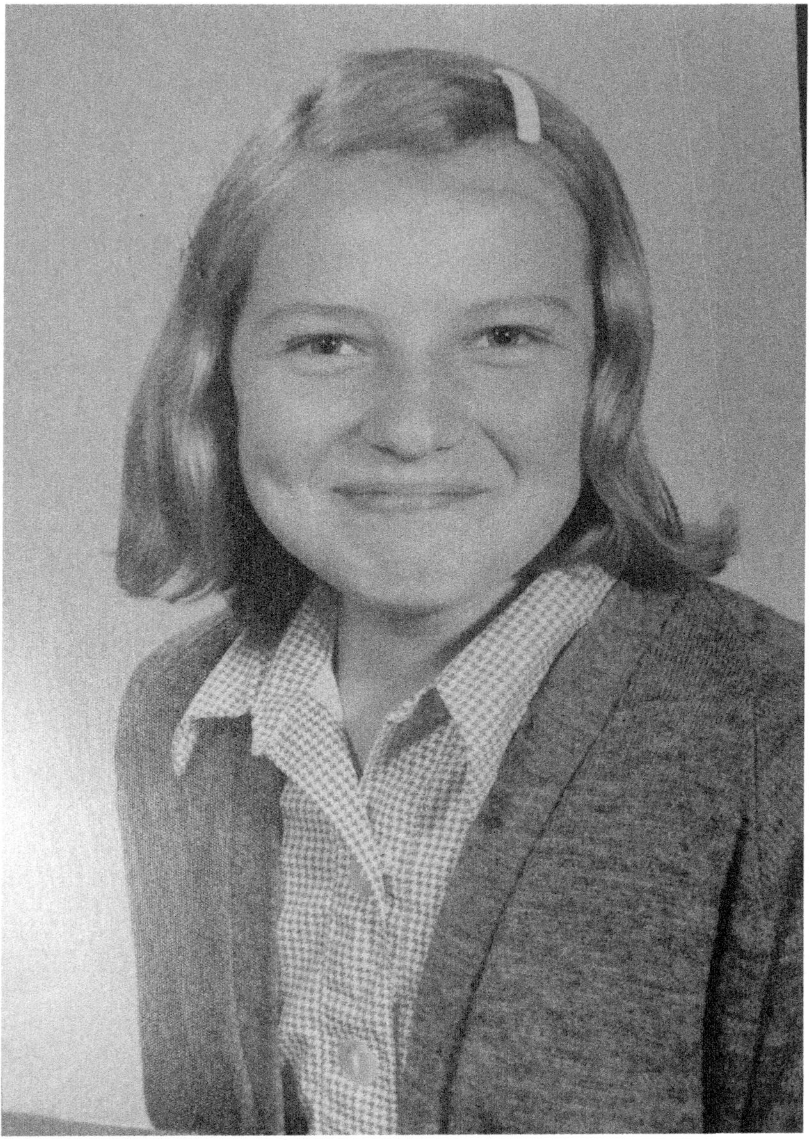

Thanks

Thank you to everyone who helped me. You know who you are!

Particular thanks to Gillard D (2018) Education in the UK: a history www.education-uk.org/history.

Disclaimer

Some names have been changed to protect privacy.

This is my perception of my lived experiences. It is my truth.

I accept that others opinions, perceptions and memories may differ.

Chapter One

June 1973   The day of the secondary school visit.

Here we all are, standing in the echoey, shoe-squeaking hall of our soon to be secondary school. This is the day of THE VISIT. Two hundred and ten of us from the several primary schools in the town that have now been orchestrated to be the new feeder schools, as well as the children arriving on buses from primary schools in neighbouring villages. I don't recognise the colours of their uniforms. An unprecedented large number of us for this first ever experimental mixed ability comprehensive intake.

I'm standing huddled with my class friends from primary school. Most of us are already eleven years old, the blasé top junior class! A lot of whispering, giggling, pulling up of our white socks and looking nervously around. Today we are going to tour the school, listen to the welcome talk from the headmaster and, most importantly, get assigned to our new forms for the September start of term and find out who are fellow classmates are to be for the next five years.

I am not quite as awed at being in this vast, reverberating hall as I think some of the others around me might be. With two older sisters already in the grammar school years (one just finishing A levels in the sixth form and one who will be in the fourth form (upper school) when I arrive in September 1973, I am familiar with the entrance steps into the school and the heavy, swinging doors leading into this hall. I have spent many evenings sitting here with my parents, watching my sisters perform in concerts or provide incidental music for theatrical productions. Just a few weeks before, the school had put on several performances of Shakespeare's 'A Midsummer's Night Dream'. Both my sisters had been in the orchestra providing the dramatic music interludes. I am well accustomed to the sudden expectant hush at the beginning of a performance when the lights are dimmed, sitting next to my mother usually in the front row, gazing wide-eyed up at the stage. The dusty, ripped black curtains pulled across all the windows. I notice, reassuringly, that even on this June morning, the curtains still hang ragged and limp, blocking out quite a bit of the morning light. Familiar surroundings and sensations.

I also have the advantage of being familiar with the layout of this building. Every Saturday morning, I come here to attend the music school offered by the county's music education department, open to all the town's talented youngsters aged from ten to eighteen. Arriving with my sisters, we then separate off to our various music ability graded classes and activities. I know the first-floor classroom where I go for theory of music lessons, the gym where I sit on a wooden bench for choir practise and indeed this actual hall where, between eleven o'clock and midday, I play the cello in the orchestra. The polished floor in this vast room always used to cause us young cellists concern that our pins would slip and slide on the buffed surface. Recently we have remedied this problem when the enterprising husband of my cello teacher designed the perfect cello pin holder. A small block of wood attached to a circle of rope. The rope we tuck behind the front legs of our chair, the wooden block lies perfectly in front of us ready to receive and hold firm the metal pin.

Quite a few of my friends in the top junior classes attend Saturday morning music school here too. A natural unquestioned continuation of the music education which had begun in our infant classrooms. How fortunate we had all been to attend a primary school tucked away in middle- class southern England where children were offered the opportunities to learn a musical instrument. Enthusiastic and patient peripatetic teachers came in to offer lessons on the violin, cello, guitar, piano, flute, clarinet and recorder. A primary school with a rich tradition of embracing all the arts steered by a forward-looking, culture-loving headmaster eager to pass on his knowledge and appreciation of the arts to all the pupils in his school. There was a little orchestra (one can only imagine how excruciating this was to listen to, as the eight, nine and ten-year-olds scraped, plucked, strummed and blew their way through simple pieces!). I was in a recorder group, the school choir, a string trio and a string quartet. There was a thriving and enthusiastic ballet group. A handful of top juniors also sang in local church choirs.

We were still practising hard for an end- of-summer term concert to be held the next month. Our farewell before we left the sanctuary of those sheltered years and moved on to secondary education in September. Our primary school was also always very much immersed in the musical activities of the town. Whenever the local amateur operatic society required children for their shows, they would ask our headmaster. Appearing in public performances required commitment and discipline as well as considerable musical and vocal aptitude. The ballet group had recently taken part in Kodaly's Hary Janos and I was still buzzing from my April six night stand of being an all- singing, all-dancing munchkin in the Wizard of Oz!

The grammar school years above me at my soon to be secondary school were also rich with a strong music and theatre tradition. In 1965, just a year before my eldest sister Rosemary had started at the school, a glowing review of their drama production 'An Italian Straw hat' had even appeared in the *Times Educational Supplement*. The school had only been functional for five years yet was already building up a reputation for excellence in the arts, sufficiently so to be picked up and commented on by a national newspaper!

When Rosemary and my other sister Catherine, three years older than me, were not in classrooms studying for O and A levels, their time was filled with choir singing, orchestra rehearsals, chamber music ensembles, county music festivals and inter school competitions. Only a few months ago I had been listening to Rosemary play the violin solo in Albinoni's Adagio in G minor with the upper school orchestra, sitting next to my mother in the front wooden pew of one of the town's many historic churches.

Following in the undisputed footsteps of my two sisters, it was simply expected by my parents that I would integrate fully and unquestioningly into the renowned musical environment of the school I was about to join.

I was looking forward to it.

However, standing with my familiar primary school friends around me, I am not thinking about music at this particular moment, just gazing in awe at so many children in this hall. A swirling, shifting sea of different coloured uniforms; mauve, azure, navy-blue, grey, emerald, lime- green, turquoise, brown. Dresses with stripes, dresses with chequered patterns, matching coloured knitted jumpers and cardigans, grey shorts, Clark's summer sandals. So many unrecognised primary schools represented here today.

It is strange, though, not to see any red uniforms, no crimson-coloured knitted jumpers or red-chequered, white-collared dresses. That popular primary school has now been placed in the catchment area for another secondary school in the town. This adhered to the new experimental directive to scatter pupils of all academic abilities equally between the three secondary schools. For many preceding years the '*red uniform*' primary school had been the principal feeder primary school for the selected first year intake at the town's grammar school, providing the majority of the eleven plus examination achievers. The former grammar school in whose hall I was now standing.

In 1966, the year my sister Rosemary started at the grammar school, almost fifty percent of the successful eleven plus examination intake had come from just two primary schools in the town. The red uniform school and the primary school that my sisters had attended and where I was currently in the top junior class. Of the 110 first year selected pupils in Rosemary's particular intake, twenty-nine had arrived from the red uniform primary school and twenty-one from ours.

The names of the children having passed the eleven plus and their primary school of origin were printed each year in the congratulatory '*welcome*' section of the grammar school's magazine going home to all the parents during the autumn term. This stopped suddenly in 1967.

Maybe coinciding with the first rumblings of the Local Education Authority's decision to contemplate a move to government desired education reform?

Nothing had been decided, but everything might change!

Certain successful primary schools would no longer have a monopoly on desired secondary school access. Catchment areas would be redesigned. If the county decided to accept government education policy change, then pupils from the town's various primary schools would now be automatically allocated, without a selection process, to one of the town's three secondary schools. One was a former grammar school, two had been secondary moderns. Were some parents already beginning to panic?

1967, Rosemary was in her second year of grammar school. She bought home the school magazine. An article read: ... *'in previous years we have published the names of the primary schools which send us pupils, but we can do this no longer because some misguided members of the public have attempted to calculate from the pages of our school magazine the percentage of grammar school places obtained by each school....'*
This was six years before I had even started in the first experimental comprehensive year at that very same ex-grammar school but were the worries about an imminent government directive on non-selected comprehensive education reform, and the town's proposed new secondary school designated catchment areas, already beginning? Were some knowledgeable, forward-looking parents already questioning the fact, that with the termination of the eleven plus selection process, the choice of primary school for their child would now be crucial for deciding which secondary school they would then be allocated to?

Quite a few of my Saturday morning music school friends attended the red uniform primary school. We sat together in our theory of music classes, puzzled over key signatures, cadences and modulations. Played our instruments in the orchestra. I had assumed we would be together for our secondary school years. Our shared love of music, our inquisitive quick minds, our creative aptitude would surely have united us through our teenage years, but, sadly, this wasn't to be. Their primary school and mine had not been assigned to the same secondary school. Looking around this hall now, seeing none of their faces, it feels a little disorientating and disappointing that they will not be accompanying me through the next five years of secondary education.

Summer rain starts to spit against the window. Behind the closed wooden concertina doors, the dinner ladies have started work, laughing, chatting, the clunk of refrigerator doors being slammed shut, a metallic pizzicato of kitchen utensils.
 The heavy wooden swing doors are thrown wide open and adults spill into the hall. I recognise the tall, bald grammar school headmaster and some of the other teachers from concerts and plays I have attended here. These must be our new form teachers. Catherine (who would be leaving behind the lower school years and moving up to the fourth form) and I had been guessing which of the school's teachers would be assigned to the first forms. The adults purposely do not go onto the stage but stand in front of us at the same level in a gesture of *'we are all together in this exciting new era of informal teaching....'*
An awed hush settles, the headmaster begins his speech.
"Welcome to the school ...."

He informs us that there are going to be seven forms each with thirty pupils. The biggest ever intake so far at his school. The most recent grammar school years above us had consisted of intakes of around 150 pupils each autumn, five first year forms of academically selected children who had passed the eleven plus exam. This was all going to change when we arrived for our first day at this school in September 1973! We were going to be part of the government's educational reform programme.
The increase in the number of pupils arriving was to comply with Labour's new theories that intakes should be as big as possible with up to eight forms of mixed -ability pupils. These large intakes would allow for the broadest possible range of all abilities to be incorporated in each year group. The anticipated 'more disruptive and difficult' children could then be spread discreetly around all the forms avoiding the scorned and feared *'bottom set'* which invariably clumped together the pupils with learning and behavioural difficulties. The average ability pupils would undoubtedly be content wherever they were placed, working at their own pace, but how much consideration would be given to pupils in the higher academic ability range? Presumably they would be recognised too and spread around the many first forms. Would any thought be given to their needs, allowing them to remain in

small, equally minded groups to promote continued mental stimulation, incentive and intellectual competition?
Unfortunately, I would soon discover that I was going to be denied this attentiveness. For the next two years my academic ability and musical precocity were going to be purposefully ignored and I would be subjected to enduring many hours of boredom and solitude. My disappointment and anger at being part of this experimental education reform was on the verge of being ignited and would consequently ruin the next five years of my secondary school life.

The headmaster, dressed in his baggy, brown -striped suit continues,
"We are a very *'special year'* because, of course, we are the first comprehensive intake".
The past eight years of academic planning, political debates, local education authority committee arguments and town reorganisation have finally come to fruition and culminated in such a large, unprecedented number of us standing in this hall this very morning. Some of the young teachers behind the shiny-headed headmaster are smiling, swaying, rocking like a gospel choir about to burst into a rendition of 'Oh Happy Day'. A couple of female teachers even have their hands clasped in front of them as if in anticipation of throwing them wide open to exalt this new 'Educational Coming'. I don't know whether all of us standing in the hall are sharing their enthusiasm. It's hard not to notice that a few older grey-haired teachers are standing rigid and unsmiling behind the zealous headmaster.
I stand close to my primary school class friends, Helen, Jane, Sally, Jenny, Katherine, Sarah. Most of whom I walk to school with every morning from the yellow-bricked houses on our housing estate. Girls who I have spent the past seven years with, in happy classrooms. Our Church of England primary school accepted the young children from the nearest housing estates, plus some children from houses in the town and, also a little bit further afield from houses on the affluent north of the town housing estates heading towards the city, if their parents correctly played the *'C of E religious card'*. After all, my primary school was desirable, having the reputation of being one of the successful key feeder schools for the grammar school, providing a significant proportion of eleven plus passes.
The girls standing around me shuffle and jiggle, we exchange excited smiles. We go to each other's birthday parties. We watch Blue Peter and Crackerjack together after school in each other's living rooms. Their houses are identical in layout to mine. Their mums provide me with meals of fish fingers or spaghetti hoops on toast followed by puddings of Arctic Roll with Ideal Milk, banana flavoured Angel Delight hidden under Dream Topping. We knock on each other's doors on summer evenings and play French cricket together on the green. We perform on our musical instruments together in the primary school's little orchestra, we sing and dance together in the playground.

Now the forms are going to be called out,
"If you hear your name, come and stand at the front" announces the still smiling headmaster.
The calling out of names begins. A boy with wiry crinkled ginger hair and so many freckles on his face it looks like a dot-to-dot puzzle turns and waves to us all and swaggers up to the front of the hall next to the new form teachers. Two girls with matching pale blue and white chequered dresses run up together. Another boy pretends to trip on his way to the front. Excitable giggles flutter around. An unusual but amusing surname produces a few titters but the boy, obviously used to this reaction, simply grins around at everyone and strides confidently towards the growing group of already selected children. Two girls from my primary school are called consecutively. They walk towards the front of the hall looking back apologetically at the rest of us standing there. That form is complete. Thirty names called, they shuffle out through the swing doors and disappear.
So, I wasn't in that form. I move a little closer to Helen and Jane. This is agonizing. I notice Sally and Katherine are holding hands. Now form 1G is going to be called. A group of three boys from my primary school class follow each other to the front. I throw a quick grin at my housing estate friend Paul as he passes. He would always try to catch just me during our playtime games of British Bulldog

and sometimes if he had been to the sweet shop, he would let me have one of his pineapple chunks from the small white paper bag.

No, I'm not in that form but that's okay. I didn't really know any of the girls who walked to the front of the hall.

Now 1W is being called. Three boys with identical blue and yellow-striped ties are summoned to stand next to the adults. They slap each other on the back, delighted to be together. Two girls in matching green and white swirly-patterned dresses follow them, running up to the front holding hands. The surname Drinkwater gets some muted sniggers.

Now 1R, I still haven't heard my name and the excitable, expectant atmosphere has noticeably diminished. The mass of children left is thinning out. Around me now are worried grimaces, nervous twitching, fingernails being chewed.

Sarah's name is called, my heart thumps. She gives me a little low wave and moves forward. Jenny's name is called next. She runs after Sarah, thankful to be back beside her primary school class friend. That group of thirty meander through the swing door being held open by their young auburn curly-haired form teacher.

Now the thirty names for 1Z are going to be called, I'm getting a bit panicky....

None of us in the hall that morning had any inkling of the preparation that had gone into fine tuning the organisation for this first ever mixed ability intake. Maybe there had been too much emphasis on the actual development of the new educational restructure and too little consideration given to the individualism of each pupil?

As the then Education Secretary of the Conservative Government, Margaret Thatcher had already pointed out three years earlier in her speech at Scarborough in October 1970:

'We must avoid becoming preoccupied with systems and structure to the detriment of the actual content of education.'

My soon to be secondary school had had the task of creating seven first forms of mixed ability from the recognised feeder primary schools in the town. Now, also included in their catchment area, were the schools in neighbouring villages from which, previously, only a small percentage of pupils each year had passed the eleven plus examination and appeared at the grammar school. Some of these villages contained housing estates built for the London homeless overspill after the Second World War. Up until now the inherent attitude and academic ability of most of the children from these estates were completely unknown quantities. What potential would be discovered in the teenagers living in the houses hidden behind the tall secretive leylandii hedges?

This reassignment of local primary schools into new catchment areas was to be an exercise in subtle social engineering under the scrutiny of, no doubt, everyone in the town. The social aims of these new heterogeneous classes had been promoted to the public as improving the development of self-discipline, social responsibility, self-confidence and a sense of community. It was hoped by the comprehensive education campaigners that the more able pupils would be better stimulated by the new social mobility, and the weaker pupils would be better supported.

For several months in the early part of 1973 selected teachers from my forthcoming secondary school had been visiting their newly designated feeder primary schools in the area. Their job as co-ordinators was to collect the lists of pupils, discuss discreetly with class teachers about friendship groups and basic academic ability. This academic ability was simply based on two verbal reasoning tests taken during the last year of primary education. Sadly, little consideration was given to documenting a child's other intellectual levels, musical ability or talent in any additional subjects.

Maybe some secondary schools around the country would even make the decision not to use this basic information from primary schools in order to ensure an unbiased approach to the potential of their new comprehensive pupils.

Almost exactly two years after my standing in that hall waiting to be selected for a mixed ability form group, a team of HM inspectors set out in May 1975 to examine how *'gifted'* children were faring in the comprehensive schools in England and Wales. Their findings made interesting reading.

In the report, a few comprehensive schools confessed to refusing to identify academic talent on the grounds that in a school which purported to be comprehensive, it was wrong to recognise a special category of pupils for whom some unusual provision might be needed. Paradoxically, some teaching staff, and it happened at my school, were still willing to recognise a remedial category which was then separated out for special treatment. This attitude would confound me for the first two years of my secondary education. I watched in amazement, but then also with increasing anger, as groups of academically struggling pupils were discreetly removed from my classroom and given extra tuition. Why was no *'extra tuition'* offered to the pupils at the other end of the ability spectrum? I certainly wasn't going to struggle with the level of work required but I was most definitely going to struggle with boredom, lack of stimulation and zero incentive. I was desperate to be recognised as someone who needed greater impetus, a faster learning pace, more difficult and challenging material. But for twenty-four months this wouldn't happen.

It was this deliberate unrecognition that confused and distressed me the most. It wouldn't be too long before my misery manifested into exasperation and petulance, particularly when I later discovered that from our very first day at the school, the teaching staff had been acutely aware of who the high achievers were. We had been secretly identified, the pupils considered to be in the top twenty-five per cent of the academic ability range and who would be amongst the future O level examination takers maintaining the reputation of the town's grammar school excellence. However, in those first experimental years of education reform, no research had apparently been done into the fact that these academically gifted pupils might resent being forced to sit uncomplaining and ignored through dull, unstimulating mixed ability classes.

With the imminent arrival of such a large, unprecedented intake it must have been a monumental job for the staff at my school to calibrate each individual child's ability, the verbal reasoning test results and potential. There was inevitably going to be difficulty in passing on and interpreting records from so many different primary schools of the town and surrounding villages.
It was probably realised early on that a random process would not ensure form groupings would be equal in either educational or social terms. Therefore, a bit of discreet 'tweaking' would be required to refine each class, juggling a reasonable mix of individual ability with friendship groups and social criteria.
Two hundred and ten names written on two hundred and ten pieces of card to be shuffled, rearranged, juxtaposed to achieve seven equal yet eclectic first form classes of wide spectrum ability.
I simply expected to be placed in a first- year form along with friends from my primary school class. They already unquestionably accepted my musical precociousness and I felt sure that some of them would want to continue to join me in participating in all the extra curriculum music activities in our new secondary school and around the town. I looked forward to being amongst new girls arriving from other primary schools who would share my desire to absorb everything and learn at a rapid rate, have our intellectual levels pushed to the limit. Maybe I could even become friends with other eleven-year-olds who attempted to fill in some of the cryptic clues in the Times crossword every day as I did. I'd even managed to work out an anagram from the challenging daily crossword that very morning: Moon starer? (10) .
Would we start the subjects of chemistry, physics, a second foreign language, maybe even Latin? The subjects I observed my older siblings learn.
My childish expectations were about to be savagely shattered.

I have to assume that the card with my name on must have fallen behind a radiator at some point and missed quite a few of the first stages of aptitude and friendship grouping, only to be rediscovered at the final stages when six of the form groups had already been selected and finely tuned. The remaining thirty disregarded, problematic names left heaped in a pile, mine amongst them, would then be unceremoniously lumped together to become the seventh first form. The *'what on earth are we going to do with these last thirty names?'* class selection!

How on else could there be any other explanation as to how, standing in that hall on that prophetic morning, I was minutes away from finding out that I was going to be assigned for the next five years of my life to a form group of particularly mix-matched youngsters! The fact that my class selection was going to be called out last just about summed it up. Our names weren't even going to be called out. We would just be the last pupils forlornly scattered around the nearly empty hall.

I would soon discover that there were no other girls of my academic level in my class. Not a single child from my housing estate. Not even a child from my primary school class.

However, I didn't yet know all this when the names for the penultimate form group started to be called out.

The headmaster's voice is becoming a little bit hoarse,

"Right, nearly there now", he glances around at the children left standing in the hall, "The next names called out are going to be in form 1F".

Two more boys from my primary school are called, they cheer and thump each other on the arm in gratitude at remaining together. Sally's name is called, then Katherine's. Helen's name, she moves forward leaving my side. Jane's name too…. Ah! this must be my new form class then. What a relief! I am going to be with my friends. We have been selected to be in a form group together.

"….and the last name for this form is …" I smile expectantly at my friends, ready to walk forward. I just know it is going to be mine.

But it isn't.

I can't believe it. I watch in despair as new form 1F (with all my friends) disappears through the wretched swinging doors. My throat tightens, my eyes blur.

It was plain that seemingly random selected classes could never actually be that. Adherence to respecting friendship groups, putting children together with similar academic abilities or social backgrounds meant that, inevitably, there would still be some first forms with clusters of higher intelligence despite all the efforts. Four girls from my primary school have suddenly disappeared and I am left standing in the hall. I think I have just watched the *dream form* vanish from sight, swallowed up by the murky corridor.

Now there are just thirty of us left. My heart is thumping in my chest, molto agité. I'm feeling abandoned and incensed. I look around in panic at the group of us standing pathetically in the hall spotting that the headmaster has somehow slipped away too, unnoticed. I recognise none of the boys. A couple of the girls' groups seem to be connected, they are standing close to each other, similar colour dresses. Must be from the same primary school. I spot one girl by herself. She was at my primary school but in the other top junior class. I don't know her. I have never talked to her. I think her name is Julie, but she is from another housing estate. I decide I should go and stand next to her. We smile warily at each other. A white- haired, bushy- eyebrowed man is approaching us all.

"You must be for me then, 1B." he chuckles. "Gather around".

This, I know, is the supposedly scary Mr Bradshaw. One of my sister Catherine's cryptic warnings on preparing me for life at her school flutters around my head. "You don't want to be in Mr Bradshaw's form" she had said, "He's very strict, all the naughtiest children get sent to him to be punished".

All my bravado at boasting to my friends that I was familiar with the school, the classrooms, has deserted me. My stomach is churning. What is this strange mix of children surrounding me? Why has the school done this to me? I am furious that all my friends, especially my fellow music friends, have disappeared off together into other forms. Suddenly I feel very let down by everything and everyone.

An ominous and caustic beginning to my years of comprehensive education.

Mr Bradshaw is talking to us. We will follow him for a tour of the school. I sidle up even closer to Julie. Some of the other girls look a little (as my mother would describe) '*rough*'. Julie and I exchange another shy, sidewards glance at each other. Two girls wearing dark-blue dresses are holding hands. They must be friends from another primary school. I'm not going to hold Julie's hand though. I don't know her at all.

A group of four boys is obviously having trouble standing still, jostling each other and, to my utter disbelief, are paying no attention to Mr Bradshaw. Such blatant disrespect for an adult is something I have not witnessed before.

Once the autumn term had begun it became obvious to me that a certain selection of disruptive boys and a particular group of girls with challenging attitude issues might just have been specifically picked to be in this first form under the watchful eye of strict disciplinarian, ex -RAF Group Captain Mr Bradshaw. He had the reputation amongst the grammar school pupils of being able to throw a blackboard rubber across the room with the precision of a military trained sharpshooter.

But why had I been placed in this form 1B? Separated from my primary school class peer group, separated from all my musical instrument playing friends, separated, even, from any other child coming from my housing estate. I just couldn't believe this was happening to me. Was I being punished in some way? Maybe it was some kind of test to see how resilient, or, on the other hand, how compliant I would be in this idealistic experiment of reorganisation to comprehensive education. Were they expecting me to settle down, be happy amongst this melange of mixed ability eleven-year-olds, be the perfect guinea pig to partake in the government directed exercise to improve my social mobility skills?

Oh dear, not a very favourable introduction to my next seven years of secondary education.

Chapter Two

1966

In July 1966 I was nearly five years old. Probably pushing a teddy bear around our leafy garden in a Triang toy pram and sitting by myself under the willow tree having pretend picnics with the plastic tea set laid out on a tartaned blanket on the lawn. Surreptitiously picked flowers on the plates and, if my mother hadn't seen me leaning precariously over the pond, there would be murky water in the cups. I was the last child left at home. My older brother already attended the renowned public boy's school in the town having won a scholarship place. Rosemary was in her last year at primary school and would be moving up to the grammar school in September having recently passed her eleven plus exam. Catherine was already at the primary school I would soon be attending. Sheltered, middle-class England, it seemed that everything would just keep ticking on its guarded, untouchable manner for many years to come.

But no, monumental changes for reorganising the education system of the county's schools were being planned. On 12th July that year, the Department of Education and Science appointed by Harold Wilson's Labour government, issued Circular 10/65 requesting Local Education Authorities in England and Wales to begin converting their secondary schools to the comprehensive system of education. For most of the country this would mark the abolition of grammar schools and the eleven plus examination.

This circular, initially drafted by Michael Stewart, was then issued to local authorities by his successor, the recently appointed Education Secretary Anthony Crosland. It began with the bold declaration that the government intended to *'end selection and to eliminate separatism in secondary education',* outlining the Labour government's opinion that the existing tripartite system of education was flawed.

This tripartite system had been introduced following the 1944 Butler Education Act. It was proposed there would be three categories of state-run secondary schools: grammar schools, secondary modern schools and secondary technical schools. From 1945, England's youth would now be entitled to a secondary education which most suited their needs and abilities, being believed at the time, that an IQ test (later the 11 plus examination) was the legitimate way of determining a child's suitability to a particular course. Now psychologists were seriously discrediting the theory of innate intelligence. Sociologists were arguing that the divided secondary education system discriminated against children of working-class origin which led to a vast waste of talent, the eleven plus exam separated children into academic and non-academic streams exacerbating social divisiveness, and that moving to a comprehensive education system would enhance social mobility and create a more egalitarian society.

The initial response to Crosland's circular 10/65 was mixed. Of the 163 local education committees, fifty were already planning for fully comprehensive schemes, around forty had set up working parties to produce plans and the remainder were unwilling to consider reorganisation of their secondary schools at that particular time. My town's local education authority began discussing the change to a comprehensive system in 1967. Whilst I was innocently absorbed by my days in the reception class of the primary school, enthralled by the adventures of Janet and John, it was being minuted during a June 1967 Education Committee meeting of the local authority that *'the council should consider whether to examine further the need for reorganisation, but that no changes would be introduced until necessary buildings were available'*.

Rosemary bought home the details of forthcoming changes in the school's December 1967 chronicle. Parents were being prepared, they read:

'At the time of writing, our local Education Committee awaits the announcement of the Secretary of State for Education and Science concerning the future of our county's secondary schools. It is likely that from 1970 onwards our High School will gradually change itself from a grammar school into a comprehensive school: the intake of 1970 may well consist of seven or eight forms of girls and boys, not specially selected. We are now in the early stages of planning the next phase of building....'

In a second circular published by the Department of Education and Science in March 1966 titled 'School Building Programmes', the government set out its proposals for the years ahead 1967-1970: *'The Secretary of State will NOT approve any new secondary school construction projects which would be incompatible with the introduction of a non-selective system of secondary education.'* Did the need for funding for building work result in some Local Education Authorities who were resisting the education reorganisation being coerced into changing to the comprehensive system?

In December 1968, Rosemary again bought home the school's yearly chronicle. There was an update for the parents concerning the proposal to reorganise the town's secondary schools. The parents of the current grammar school pupils were informed that *'The change will not occur in 1970 as originally intended and a new starting date has yet to be announced'* and they were also told the exciting news that the school had, indeed, been included in the government's 1969-1970 school building programme. *'This will give us a much-needed increase in accommodation and provide the first instalment of the conversion to a comprehensive secondary school'*. The proposed building extensions included a work and social centre for 200 sixth formers, more science laboratories, a lecture theatre, a sports hall and a much-anticipated indoor swimming pool which would also be open to the town's population.

Anthony Crosland didn't stay long in the position of Secretary of State for Education and Science. By August 1967 he had moved on to be the President of the Board of Trade. During his thirty months overseeing the beginnings of the country's immense education reorganisation, I had completed my first year of primary school totally oblivious to the monumental and, I think it's fair to say, devastating effect his Circular 10/65 would have on me during my secondary education years. Anthony Crosland (interestingly himself the product of an independent school education) died in 1977. In her book in 1982 his wife Susan repeated his now famous pledge: *'If it's the last thing I do, I'm going to destroy every fucking grammar school in England. And Wales. And Northern Ireland'*. Strong vehement words considering how much one man's emotional directive would drastically affect many thousands of children's lives and change Britain's educational landscape for ever.

Tuesday 6th September 1966. I started at my primary school along with 12 or so other four /five-year-old children from our housing estate. Holding my mother's hand we made the short walk along the pavement of our tree-lined road, turned right at the junction and the long, low, red-bricked primary school was just there, on the opposite side of the street.

The land for our housing estate had been bought by the then Ministry of Supply to provide houses for the *'senior staff'* at the new government-owned Atomic Energy Research Establishment. 140 three and four bedroomed houses were built in the middle 1950s within the grounds of an old manor House which had been demolished in 1953. A Norman motte was left preserved on the edge of the estate and parts of the Manor house's walled garden were sympathetically incorporated into forming the borders of certain roads. The houses were built amongst the many mature trees and lawns. My parents had moved here in 1959 upon my father's promotion attracted, no doubt, by the estate's low-density layout, generous open spaces and only seven houses per acre. Every house had a small front garden and a larger back garden. During the early 1960s, this estate became one of the important catchment areas for the neighbouring popular C of E primary school with its reputation for excellence in eleven plus results. (The results not yet hidden from the public!). The families in these 140 houses would inevitably provide a significant proportion of grammar school entrants.

Dressed in a black and white dogtooth patterned pinafore, knitted cardigan and a ribbon in my hair, I was permitted to have a teddy bear tucked under my arm for that one short journey to my first day at school. Walking through the wrought iron gates, pushing open the red doors, my mother marched me towards the first classroom on the right. My nose instantly filling with the exciting odours of fresh paint, polish, disinfectant. My ears picked up the yelling of the children already out in the playground at the back of the building, someone crying, muted voices, heels clacking further along the corridor.

I thought I was very special when the teacher, on being told by my mother that my birthday was at the end of September, remarked I would be one of the oldest in her class. This feeling was immediately quashed when she pointed to a blonde-haired girl sitting forlornly by herself in the book corner,

"That's Sarah, she's already five". How annoying to learn that Sarah's birthday had been on the first of September! I wondered if that meant she could already read and write too. Could she, like me, play simple tunes on the piano, sing back musical phrases in perfect pitch and recognise the works of several classical music composers? Did she play the same games with her mother, listening to the music coming out of the radio tuned to BBC Radio 3 and try to guess the country of origin. Could Sarah recognise the meandering, dreamy French music of Debussy and Ravel, the predictable waltzes in ¾ time of the Viennese Strauss family or the singing strings of Tchaikovsky's Russian ballet music?

I joined Sarah in the book corner. Ahead of me now lay years of blissful infant and junior education. The rumblings and reorganising plans of Local Education Authorities were unimaginable.

Every day for the foreseeable future I was going to be cossetted and charmed by the world of Chicken-Licken and his mysterious falling sky, build towers with coloured number blocks, drink milk in the morning playtime, get to grips with the loops and curls of Marion Richardson's handwriting style and marvel at the botanical and sometimes gory exhibits on the nature table.

In 1967, my second year of being in an infant class, the Plowden report was published. Commissioned by the then Conservative Government Education minister, Sir Edward Boyle in 1963, it had taken four years to complete. Being the first investigation and report into primary school education methods since the early 1930's, Lady Bridget Plowden's report encompassed a range of progressive recommendations that primary education could choose to adopt.

Her suggestions encouraged a more child-centred approach with individual learning, moving away from formal class learning to smaller group work and projects. She implied that the end of learning by rote would allow a more flexible, informal curriculum to be followed. No more streaming of

primary school junior classes. No top A stream, middle B stream and a doomed C stream. As Lady Plowden wrote,
'At the heart of the educational process lies the child.'

With adherence to her recommendations, my days at primary school just couldn't get any better! The little, red-bricked school already followed the principle of non-selected, non-streamed classes. Each junior year had two classes decided purely by age. One classroom had the pupils with birthdays September to February, the other, the spring and summer birthdays.

Catherine, three years above me in the school, was unfortunately still trapped in the uncertainty of a final date for the county's change to comprehensive education. The grammar school had sent out yet another update, *'we know now that the reorganisation of the town's secondary schools will be made not earlier than 1972, although it could be later. When the date is confirmed, we shall turn whole-heartedly to the task of creating as good a comprehensive school as we can……'* Catherine's primary school junior years were therefore dominated by preparation for passing the eleven plus. My mother purchased the practise booklet from W H Smith for extra tuition at home. Every evening became a fraught session of verbal reasoning exercises attempted by my sister, then marked in silence by my mother consulting the confiscated answer section pulled out from the middle. Times tables had to be recited. I remember one evening shouting out the answer for five times six before my sister could reply. Although my mother looked at me briefly, eyebrows raised, I was promptly chastised for interrupting!

Catherine did pass her eleven plus and headed off proudly to the grammar school with the other twenty-five percent of top ability pupils selected from the primary schools of the town.

My music-loving cultural-minded primary school headmaster certainly made sure his little school followed Lady Plowden's recommendations. I was ecstatically immersed in an atmosphere of self-expression, freedom of individuality yet discreetly controlled and disciplined learning. Music permeated the school, beginning every day with singing the hymn in assembly. Monday mornings saw us sitting at our desks in the classroom listening to the wooden-boxed radio tuned in to the BBC School Broadcasting series 'Singing Together'. Heartily singing away to the good old folk songs, Bobby Shaftoe and his bizarre fashion of silver knee buckles, the Skye boat song, getting that lad over the sea and back on dry land and there was always the repetitive problem of the matrimonially reluctant soldier and his cumbersome musket, fife and drum. Then there was the inhibition of the PE lessons in the hall. Directed by the voice from the BBC's ' Music and Movement' radio broadcast we gaily danced around in our vests and thick blue knickers attempting to represent swaying trees, flowing water, skittish animals, juggling clowns.

My two sisters already had violin lessons, so my mother put my name down for cello lessons with Mrs Hooton, the peripatetic music teacher who came in once a week. Following in the steps of my sisters, I had just started attending the attending the county music department's Saturday morning music school. My life steeped in and dominated by classical music was beginning.

My cello lessons took place in the primary school staffroom, up a twisting dark staircase to the poky low-ceilinged room tucked under the eaves. It was always a feat of physical strength and a lot of huffing and puffing on my part to manoeuvre my three-quarter size instrument in its soft leather case up the narrow stairs. The right-angle corner halfway up required a stop and some deft footwork to negotiate the heavy and awkward shape around the bend.

One particular morning, I was in mid-manoeuvre but still hidden from view when I heard male voices above me. The headmaster and the top junior class teacher Mr Clifford must have been standing at the headmaster's study door, the headmaster was speaking.

"So, I'm just asking you to slow down a little with those spelling tests, Edward. Nicola's mother has already complained to me about the length of the list her daughter took home to learn last week. No need to rush to the end of the book. You know we're all supposed to be relaxing on the testing a little bit."

"Yes, headmaster, I understand of course. It's just that with the return of a Conservative government and the good news of Mrs Thatcher's circular, who knows, we might be keeping the eleven plus after all. Good lord, we can't let the standards slacken!"
They guffaw together.
Suddenly behind me there is the rustle of silk-lined tweed, the cloying smell of Yardly lavender talc fills the stairway.
"Goodness child, what are you doing lurking on the stairs?" Mrs Hooton hovers behind me, "Hurry up and get your cello out of its case. We need to get the lesson started. Now, how did you get on with the first few lines of that Bach prelude?"

I'd sensed that my parents had been pleased when Edward Heath won the general election on 18th June 1970. My mother had uncharacteristically clapped her hands together on hearing from the BBC Radio 3 news announcer that the Conservatives were back in control of the country. Margaret Thatcher was appointed to the Cabinet as Secretary of State for Education and Science. She immediately caused controversy when, after only a few days in office, she withdrew Labour's Circular 10/65 without going through a consultation process. She drafted her own new policy Circular 10/70 which suggested that local education authorities were no longer forced to reorganise to a comprehensive system. Maybe one of the reasons my parents so welcomed the Conservative victory. The potential threat to the town's schools might have rescinded.
The wording of the circular 10/70 was purposefully ambivalent and unconfrontational. Local authorities would be *'freer to determine the shape of secondary provision in their areas'* and *'Authorities whose plans had been approved could go ahead and notify the Department of their wish to change them.'*
Margaret Thatcher was offering the opportunity for local education authorities to change their plans concerning secondary education choices whilst, at the same time indicating that her policy was not intended to stop the actual development of new comprehensive schools or discourage the practise of a comprehensive education. She diplomatically cited that her department would *'expect plans to be based on educational considerations rather than on the comprehensive principle.'*
During her four years as Education Secretary, Margaret Thatcher turned down only 326 of 3,612 proposals for schools to become comprehensive. The proportion of pupils attending comprehensive schools consequently rose from thirty-two per cent at the time of issuing Circular 10/70 to sixty-two per cent in 1974.
The future of my secondary education now lay in the impending decision of my local Education Authority. What would they decide? Would they continue with all the planning, all the building work aimed at making the schools better equipped to cope with the expected large intakes and head towards comprehensivisation, or would they decide, instead, to revert to the traditional selection process and the separate identities of grammar and secondary modern in their towns?
Six months after the re-election of the Conservative government and Margaret Thatcher issuing her circular 10/70, my local Education Authority had finished their discussions, their deliberations and had reached their decision on the future of secondary education in their county. In January 1971, a decisive county education committee meeting took place. The minutes of the meeting record that, after a lot of discussion, the *'argument against abandonment was stronger'*. The change to non-selective secondary education would continue and that *'current major building work was at an advanced stage and the schools would soon be ready'*.
The date of September 1973 was finalised for the changeover of my town's schools to comprehensive education. The very month I would begin my secondary education! The efficiency of the builders had sealed my fate!

Chapter Three

February 1971. As the 15th of February 1971 approached, we had an additional weekly BBC schools radio programme to listen to, sat at our wooden desks in the junior year two classroom. Our individual desks were now pushed together in informal rectangles of six pupils. Four facing each other making a compact square and two abutted at one of the ends. We had to time the lifting of our desk lids with precision otherwise wood banged against wood (that was fun) or fingers got painfully trapped (not quite so amusing!)

The local Education Authority had voted, just the previous month, to proceed with the reorganisation of their secondary schools to the comprehensive system. It was now confirmed that we would NOT be sitting the eleven plus exam in two years' time when we reached the top junior class. Our primary school teaching could therefore be much more relaxed!

This new radio programme was entitled something like 'Towards mathematics'. I never actually listened to the beginning of the broadcast or caught the introductory speech. I was far too busy chatting away with the five friends around me on our rectangular island. The young, mini-skirted teacher wasn't very strict. She often had trouble keeping control of the exuberant eight- and nine-year-olds in her class.

The purpose of the radio programme was to introduce us to the decimal currency, but we slipped effortlessly into understanding and handling the new system. I had hardly any knowledge of the 'old money'. At home, my parents dealt with anything in that domain. We didn't live on the sort of housing estate, where at nine years old, I would be sent down to the local chippie to get a couple of bags of chips and bring back the change or wait outside the off- license with some shillings for a packet of Embassy.

The only memory I have of playing with plastic thrupenny bits and sixpences is in the 'shop corner' of my infant reception class. The change to decimalisation had already been announced in March of that year and I don't recall ever working on maths problems involving pounds divided into twelve shillings, half-crowns or pennies. All the school maths textbooks must have been withdrawn and reprinted. The new decimal monetary system would have been drip fed to us year by year.

There was even a song to merrily join in with, every week during the radio programme. The devised words fitted so perfectly to the melody that, since then, I have never been able to listen to the Narcissus piece of music from the Water series op.13 by Ethelbert Nevin without involuntarily singing along!

The pound remains, the same as it was before....
This time, there are, one hundred new pence no more......

But the highlight of the radio programme was undoubtably the game of Bingo held in the last five minutes of each broadcast. Who would be the winner this week? Our cards having been placed in front of us as the teacher walked around the classroom. Each card containing images of the decimal coins. If we had the corresponding image of the coins, or amount made by several coins together, called out by the booming male voice, we covered it with a tiddlywink. A very effective way to install quick recognition into our young receptive minds.

I doubt the simplistic game or being the winner quite merited the excitement I afforded it. It was obvious I had never been in a bingo hall! Such innocent enjoyment until ...

Until my friend Sally let me in on her little secret. Sally's mum was friendly with someone else who was a primary school teacher. One morning Sally sidled up to me in the steamy, dark cloakroom area as I was sitting on the little bench under my coat peg changing out of my wellington boots into my plimsolls.

" Guess what, I've got a secret to tell you. Do you want to hear it?" Of course, I did. Sally gave a little authoritative shiver to let me know the importance of what she was about to impart, "You know those bingo cards? Well..." The word well was elongated for dramatic effect, "Well, my mum told me that the teacher knows which card is going to win every week. It's written in her pamphlet."
Devasted and cross! But it made sense of course, why hadn't I realised it! Always a different child winning every week. I should have questioned the mathematical probabilities in a class of twenty-six of a lucky person getting the winning card more than once!
I felt very deceived. My first experience of being hoodwinked by someone in the teaching profession. It most definitely wasn't going to be the last.

Chapter Four

My teacher for the top junior class, Mr Clifford, was someone my mother would term as 'old school'. A disciplinarian demanding constant high standards, it was his job to *'lick the ten/eleven-year-olds into shape'* and for all the previous years, prepare them for the eleven plus examinations. Although it was now known we would not be sitting this selection exam, there appeared little or no adapting to a more informal style in his teaching methods. We continued to learn by rote, all facing a front blackboard seated at individual wooden desks. Times tables were recited aloud until there was no hesitation. He even pushed some of us to learning by heart the thirteen to nineteen times tables. The weekly spelling tests were an agonising moment too, as we relentlessly worked our way towards the last page of the little red flame-motif patterned book; The Essential Spelling List by Fred J. Schonell. Committee was one of the words to be learnt on the last page. I practised the rhyme with my mother in order to spell it correctly: two m's, two t's, two e's!
One boy in the class struggled with his writing and spelling. Brian had recently joined the primary school. He must have moved to live on another of the housing estates in the town which were in the school's catchment area. In more recent years he would have been sympathetically diagnosed as dyslexic and offered extra help during the school day. In 1972, life was considerably harder for the sufferers. As he wasn't naughty or disruptive, Mr Clifford could only believe that Brian's failings in the three R's was due to laziness. If the boy had had a week to learn spellings, what possible reason was there for him to submit a page containing ten illegible words consisting of random letters strung together?
One morning, the spelling test included the word remember. My mother's rhyme: em- em -er got me through yet again! Brian couldn't manage it. Mr Clifford strode menacingly between the desks to stand over the cowering child.
"Why can't you spell this word, boy? Everyone needs to be able to spell the word remember." The spittle flew sideways from Mr Clifford's lips, his face was puce. "Don't you ever use the word when you speak?" The rest of us were silent, watching in horror the anger of our teacher. Brian remained unbelievably calm.
"I use the word recall."
Mr Clifford thumped the desk with his fist, but he had been beaten. The next playtime we gathered around Brian in a display of solidarity agreeing how unfair Mr Clifford had been. I wonder what happened to Brian. He moved up to the secondary school with us but disappeared after the first year.
Quite a few recommendations from Lady Plowden's report on primary education remained alarmingly absent from the classroom of Mr Clifford.

In 1967, Lady Plowden had stated that *'infliction of physical pain as a method of punishment in primary schools should be forbidden.'* Five years after the report was published, when I was in his top junior class, Mr Clifford was still forcing any misbehaving boy to stand on his wooden chair where he would then hit them on their bare legs with a ruler.

A few days before term finished for Christmas 1972, six of us girls were instructed to wait behind as the rest of the class filed out of the room at four o'clock. Mr Clifford handed us each a brown envelope. As he passed me mine, he looked directly into my eyes.
"I think your parents will be very interested in this. I understand there are still a couple of music scholarships up for grabs". The envelope instantly grew heavier in my hand. Something precious. As soon as Mr Clifford had mentioned the words music scholarship, I knew what lay inside. The details for sitting the Common Entrance exam for the public girl's school in the town.
Talk of taking the entrance exam and being accepted at the public school dominated the conversation at Saturday morning music school. My ginger-haired cellist friend, Patricia, who attended the 'red uniform' primary school, was certain she would be going. We chatted away, sitting next to each other in orchestra rehearsals every week. Apparently, Patricia's parents talked of *'nothing else'*. They assumed she would be offered a music scholarship and Patricia had already had a first measuring for school uniform items. How we had giggled together over her exaggerated descriptions of the unflattering grey pinafore and thick woolly grey tights! How I wished I would be wearing these clothes too! Violinist Alicia, in my theory of music class, would automatically be granted a prestigious place; her father was a vicar at one of the churches in the town. Another music school friend, flute-playing Fiona, would also be offered a place on the criterion of already having an older sister attending the school.
Going to this renowned girl's school in the town was my secret dream. I would be surrounded by like-minded girls, absorbed in a competitive academic world, encouraged to continue my music studies to the highest possible level. I knew I had the academic ability to pass the entrance exam, but to be granted a music scholarship would be the icing on the cake. Surely my parents would be so proud of me.
It had already been hinted by two influential adults in my life that my musical talent was of a sufficiently high standard to be granted one of the few sought after scholarships. With Mrs Hooton I had already begun practising suitable technically difficult and showy pieces for the audition. She told me somewhat cryptically that *'for my own sake, she dearly hoped I would go the girl's school'*. Whatever that meant! I didn't really understand her heartfelt gravity. The primary school headmaster had caught me by myself as I was packing my cello back into its case after performing a solo during a morning assembly.
"Well, thank you very much for playing this morning. It was lovely. We'll be losing you soon, but I do hope you will come back and play for us again sometime next year. I'll be talking to your parents of course, but we all know the best thing for you is to take the scholarship ..."
I did go back and give concerts. I never knew if he talked to my parents. I was never privy to such details. My parent's decisions would never include the consultations or opinions of an eleven-year-old. Obviously, my cello teacher and my primary school headmaster were acutely aware of what *'would be best'* for me considering what lay ahead during the next few controversial and exasperating years of my secondary education as part of an experimental government social reform programme!

I handed my mother the brown envelope as I arrived through the back door into the kitchen that afternoon. She ripped it open and scanned the letter then briskly refolded the piece of paper and pushed it back into the envelope. Her face was expressionless, eyes averted. "
"We'll see what your father has to say about that." Subject closed.

Apparently, my father didn't have anything to say at all. The possibility of me sitting the common entrance exam would not be mentioned in the house again. Absolutely no further discussion on the matter.

The day of the public-school exam arrived. Five other girls from my top junior class had gone to try their best. Five empty chairs to dishearten and frustrate me. Mr Clifford looked up quizzically at me, eyebrows raised in surprise when I shouted out 'Present' to his register call, but he didn't say anything.

The girls arrived back at school during the after- lunch playtime. I felt a little sick with disappointment and jealousy but dutifully joined the rest of the class in gathering around them, pretending I was just as eager to hear about their morning. Helen thought she had done *'really well'* but Judith wasn't quite so sure, she had messed up a page of long division. Jenny didn't care either way, she had only gone along because her parents wanted her to try. I suspect she just wanted to move up to the same secondary school as the rest of us and stay with her friends. Dorothy wasn't saying much as usual, a strange, introverted only child who lived on my housing estate. She was very clever in the classroom and would have passed for sure. She didn't turn up at any secondary school in the town in September though. During the summer holidays her parents had moved house. The three of them went to live in the neighbouring county, where the eleven plus exam and therefore selection to grammar school were being maintained. The fifth girl, Miriam, was apparently crying in the toilets.

Later that day, when I arrived back at my house, my mother was sitting in the living room listening to an LP of Tchaikovsky's first piano concerto in B flat minor. How I loved the opening bars, those majestic ascending piano chords would normally give me goosebumps. Today I felt nothing. My mother was working on the blue and white poncho she was crocheting for me. Catherine was getting a green and white one. The finished poncho formed a stiff square, there were no dainty, swirling tassels at the bottom. My mother had chosen wool that was far too thick and inflexible causing the four corners to twist stiffly in heavy spikes. It always felt awkward and uncomfortable, like an oppressive weight bearing down on my shoulders. I didn't wear it much, it never seemed to have the flowing elliptic curve of the more authentic shop-bought ponchos everyone else was wearing.

"How was your day?" asked my mother. How should I reply? That it had been upsetting, dispiriting and incomprehensible.

"Fine, thanks. Mr Clifford was very pleased with my diagram of the water cycle. We've got some vocabulary to learn for French. Oh, and by the way, those girls went for that common entrance exam thingy today." I hope I sounded sufficiently unbothered.

The crochet hook continued its relentless weaving in and out,

"Oh that!" My mother replied patronising. "Your father and I didn't want you trying for that. You wouldn't have fitted in there; we don't know any of the girls or their families…."

….. *Really? What was my mother basing her information on?* ☐Actually *would very much have liked to have had a chance to 'fit' in there and I did know quite a few of the girls who would have been in the same first year as me…..* But my mother hasn't finished her reasoning,

"Much better you go to the same school as your sisters. You can wear all their passed down uniform. We don't want to be out spending money on new clothes and other stuff. Besides, I heard from Judith's mother…."

…. *Hang on! when on earth does my mother talk to Judith's mother? …..*

"……..☐tháf they know you've sat the examination and you fail, then you lose the privilege of this catchment area and won't be accepted at your sister's school. You'll have to go to that ghastly secondary modern over on the North Road estate."

Too many excuses of course, but I innocently believed that rumour (lie) for many, many years. It wasn't until I was well into my thirties and reminiscing with my brother about school days that it suddenly dawned on me; I had been spectacularly deceived. My brother had, of course, gained a scholarship to the prestigious public boy's school in the town. I was telling him how much I had wanted to do the same, get a scholarship to the girl's school. He burst out laughing and informed me I wouldn't have had 'a hope in hell' of going to the girl's school! Didn't I realise that our father had been so stuck in his Victorian ways he didn't believe in girls following academic further education. A university place would never have been an option. Even though it was now the 1970s, for him, it was still only acceptable for girls to be secretaries, primary school teachers or nurses.

Chapter Five

My very last day at primary school, Friday 20th July 1973. The girls from the two top junior classes, me included, all seem to have been on a bit of an hysterical high for most of the day. The entire after- lunch playtime was spent spinning round in a large circle screeching the words of Jimmy Osmond's 'Long -haired Lover from Liverpool' and something about 'tying a yellow ribbon around an old oak tree'. I didn't know the songs or the words, just mouthed along. It didn't take long to pick up the gist of the repetitive words. Pop music had yet to filter into my life. At home, I was kept totally absorbed in the world of classical music. I had begun to realise though, that other girls in my class had more relaxed and modern home influences. At their birthday parties we danced around uninhibited to exciting, pulsating music pretending we were at a *'disco'* (whatever that was!). Birthday parties at my house involved sitting cross legged in subdued circles passing the parcel whilst my mother played Dvorak's Slavonic dances on her reel-to-reel tape recorder.

I had gradually become aware that my parents were a bit distanced and aloof, more old-fashioned, than the parents in my friend's houses I visited. My musical precocity and strict upbringing could easily have caused me to be shunned or ridiculed but thank goodness, during my primary school years this never happened. The strong music and art culture in our little primary school kept me bonded with most of the other children.

No doubt, the younger parents of my junior classroom friends were more welcoming and receptive to the changing trends of the 1970's. I watched in fascination the different home atmospheres of my peers. Their easy going, informal lifestyles, the music choices, the open conversations around the meal tables were all so different from the daily ambience in my house. I was gradually becoming aware, but still unaffected, by the contrasts I observed.

According to my mother, my father, a nuclear physicist, was the *'Head of a Government Scientific Department'*. Of course, I had no idea what he did when he left the house early every morning! He certainly travelled abroad a lot, giving lectures and visiting other scientific establishments. In reciprocation, visiting foreign scientists would be invited to our house for an evening meal prepared by my mother. My sisters and I had to be *'on our very best behaviour'*. My brother was now no longer at the house, studying for a master's degree at Oxford University.

The time spent sitting being seen and not heard at the dining room table always seemed interminable, knowing we were being watched by the guests. The atmosphere in the room becoming even more strained than usual and always absurdly unnatural. My mother's voice would rise by, at least, a major third, as she agreed with and gave a false tinkling laugh to everything my father said.

During a recent maths lesson on constructing block graphs, a top junior class survey had taken place. The question was *'What do you want to be when you grow up?'* There had been the usual choice of doctors, nurses, teachers and, not surprisingly amongst some boys, quite a few scientists, reflecting the influence of our fathers' careers and housing estate environment. I said I wanted to be a music composer! That only got one square coloured in, dwarfed by higher, more popular, more conventional column choices.

An exciting part of this Last Day of Term was being allowed to come into school wearing our own clothes. This would really show the younger children *'how important'* we were. The primary school headmaster had pretended to hum and haw over his decision, dragging it out over several days, purposely tantalising us. His last smidgeon of control over us before we left for secondary school. The morning had started sunny and bright. Not a hint of the ominous clouds that would arrive later in the day. I was wearing a vivid yellow and white tank top my mother had knitted, over a white short sleeved shirt. My matching yellow Ladybird -labelled trousers had the tiniest hint of a flare billowing out over my Clark's sandals. I thought I looked pretty good!

This final day of term was also the day you could bring in your own board games to play. The teachers were far too busy clearing the walls, tidying up, sorting through work folders to bother with lessons. Around me several Mouse Trap boards were being constructed. I had just finished a game of Frustration with Jenny, Helen and Sarah. Autograph books were being passed around. Not that there was much need to write anything cringingly immature to each other as a memento, most of us would now be moving up *'en masse'* to the secondary school in September. Five children from my class were going to other schools in the town. Their parents having chosen that they attend schools where they already have siblings. Apparently, none of the girls from my class were going to go to the girl's public school, I still secretly wished I was.

The morning playtime on this last day had involved the usual game of British Bulldog, attempting to get to the other side of the playground without being caught. We play in turns, the girls trying to run through a wall of boys, or the other way round. It wasn't so bad to be caught, made you feel a bit special. The usual punishment was to be dragged, seemingly unwittingly, by a group of boys through the boy's toilet block. A show of resistance was expected which involved a lot of pretending to be horrified and then harmless pulling, stretching the sleeves on our knitted grey cardigans. The boys obviously had the need for us girls to experience the stench of the stained porcelain urinals and the lingering smell of faeces emanating from the miniscule cubicles. Did boys really do a number two at school during the day? This was a revelation! And, if everything was going accordingly to plan, before you appeared back in the playground, supposedly distraught and shocked at the outside door of the boy's toilet block, it was fine to allow just one of the boys to give you a cheeky, inexperienced peck on the lips! I liked it when Paul, pineapple chunk boy, was the one to give the kiss. It goes without saying, none of these harmless shenanigans were ever mentioned to my mother. She would have been horrified!

No afternoon playtime today, it's the Final Assembly with everyone sitting cross-legged in the hall. Swimming, gymnastics and ballet certificates to be handed out. The headmaster talking. The last time I would hear him jingling those annoying coins in his trouser pocket. At some time during this farewell assembly heavy, dramatic clouds have bubbled up from the west. Distant rumbling heralds an approaching thunderstorm. We file back to our classrooms as an infant teacher plays us out with her usual rendition of Schumann's Soldier's March. My hands move in unconscious synchronisation. I'm learning the same piece in my piano lessons.

And that's it. That's the end of my primary school years. In just six weeks I will be starting at my secondary school. Rain starts to drum against the classroom window. I suddenly think of Julie in the other top junior classroom. She will be in the same form 1B as me in September. The shock of that visit day and the form selection has mercifully faded in my mind during the last few weeks of top junior innocent happiness but I decide I must try and catch her at the school gate as we leave. Although I don't know her at all, even know where she lives, maybe we could arrange to meet up in the holidays, go to the library together, go to Woolworths, something like that?

Going Home time becomes utter chaos. Torrential rain descending from black skies and rumbling thunder brings panic, shouting teachers and shrieking youngsters. What a portentous ending to my primary education. I linger around the coat-peg area, watching Julie's classroom door, hoping to see her. Sally and Katherine run out of the door together, squealing, holding hands and as it swings wide, I spot my mother standing on the pavement opposite, sheltered under an umbrella, anxiously scanning the school forecourt. I run out towards her,

"There you are, for goodness sake!", she wraps a red anorak around me and hands me a second umbrella. "I've been standing here for ages; couldn't you have been the first one out? You set off without a coat this morning. Now, let's get back home."

As we set off together, I turn back and catch a glimpse of Julie disappearing off, running in the opposite direction.

Chapter Six

First Year   September 1973

Tuesday 4th September 1973, the first day of term. My secondary education begins. Catherine has insisted she is not going to walk towards the building with me. She is, after all, now in the fourth form still in the grammar school section. I'm just the younger sister arriving in the first year! There will be six years of academically selected pupils above me. The school will be bizarrely divided, and I wonder how the majority will react to this big comprehensive mixed ability intake which will make up roughly one quarter of the entire school's population. 210 of us, around 700 of them! Are they going to be snobbish, belittling, rude? Will they try and trip us up on the stairwells, push us around in the concreted areas at breaktimes or will they just simply ignore us and treat us with a contempt representing their academic intelligence supremacy over us, the inferior intruders? How dare we arrive at their school without being selected to do so! I doubt we will even be worthy of their attention.

How I wished I was walking in as a grammar school pupil, but I had been denied that opportunity by being born just twenty-three days too late! The date for the education reorganisation in my county had been set as September 1973, for all the children beginning at secondary school that autumn term. Imagine if I had been born a few weeks earlier during the month of August instead and then I wouldn't even be in this situation. I would have been included in a completely different school year's intake. I would have started at primary school one year earlier. I would have been one of the very last children sitting the eleven plus examination. Hopefully I would already have been at the secondary school as an academically selected pupil! But it wasn't to be.

I had always assumed I would follow in my sisters' footsteps and set off proudly towards the grammar school each morning carrying my musical instrument, taking part in all possible extra curricula activities as I had observed Rosemary and Catherine doing. I wasn't to know yet, that ahead of me stretched five years of anxiety as to how I could actually get my cello into the school buildings without being seen! Although, since the shock of that initial *'welcome to comprehensive reorganisation education'* visit day and the eye-opening experience of the school environment I was about to be thrown into, I believe I did have an inkling that my life was going to drastically change, and I might have to acutely hide who I really am if I have any hope of fitting in.
.

I hitch the unfamiliar strap higher on my shoulder. The worn and battered satchel had been Rosemary's. She had now finished sixth form and was about to start at a teacher training college on the south coast. At the end of my road, I hesitate for a few seconds, hidden by the trunk of a tall horse chestnut, looking around to see if there is any sign of Julie. As she always disappeared off in the opposite direction from mine to get home, I'm hoping that her route towards the secondary school this morning might take her back past the primary school, across the top of my road and then along the pavement marking the boundary of my housing estate. I haven't seen anything of her since July and that four o'clock chaos of children hurtling out through the doors into the pouring rain. I see the backs of grey blazers, walking groups of varying heights but no Julie. At the road junction the primary school is on my right, I turn left.

The grammar school building is ahead of me. Nothing too unusual for me to make this approach. I do it every Saturday morning during term time to attend music school. Today something is glaringly different. During the last few weeks, the word HIGH has been surreptitiously removed from the wording on the front of the building. The six white letters of the word SCHOOL have been shuffled along the wall and reattached to cover the gap. Poignantly, the word HIGH can still very much be read. The missing letters appearing as ghostly pale traces on the weathered brick wall.

A strange, maybe unsettling, morning for the whole town. One former grammar school and two secondary moderns metamorphizing into three 'equal' comprehensive schools. But would they really be equal, I'm sure I was intelligent enough to wonder about all this? I was eleven, nearly twelve. Were the other children my age, the parents too, worrying about all this unprecedented reorganisation? It all seems very confusing and definitely a bit unbalanced. The new comprehensives now had their own dedicated catchment areas, designed to be as fair as possible a *'cross-section of the town and surrounding villages, socially and by ability'*. The first- year pupil intake should therefore be roughly comparable in all three schools.

Yet one of the schools (the school I was going to go to. How glad I was that my housing estate fell in the right catchment area!) already had six years of the town's selected pupils in the top 25% of the ability range. Accustomed to grammar education standards, it had the only sixth form facilities of the three schools. A thriving music tradition and a reputation for excellent theatre productions. It boasted an impressive and renowned modern languages department covering French and German and even offering the more unusual Russian and Chinese to A Level standard. This had been recognised as academically phenomenal and merited a BBC film crew visiting the school and producing a short feature film.

The other two schools had been secondary moderns accepting the pupils of the town who failed the selective process of the now abandoned eleven plus exam. Hardly an even playing field for the town to begin its auspicious experiment into comprehensive education.

The demands of changing the secondary schools to equal comprehensive establishments would be colossal. Nothing, of course, I could begin to comprehend but with my enquiring mind I was intrigued by the differences of the three schools in the transition. A mixed ability intake going into an established grammar school. Would the pupils be automatically pulled upwards by the inherent academic ability level? Top ability pupils going into a former secondary modern, would they suffer from a lack of intellectual motivation and resources in the years above them? Would the libraries in each school contain the same material, the same texts, offer the same access to research opportunities? One school had concentrated on O levels, the other two had pursued less academic, more practical subjects.

Was a former academically selected school going to be stricter in discipline than the other two? Would the grammar schoolteachers cope with less motivated pupils? I presume we are all going to be studying the same syllabi. I must ask my Saturday morning music school 'red uniform' primary school friends what they are learning at their different comprehensive school to mine.

SO much for me to think about. So much for me to silently observe. What monumental and uncharted years of education reform lay ahead of us!

In 1972, a year before my arrival at secondary school, my tall, bald-headed, soon to be headmaster was to meet Margaret Thatcher, the then Secretary of Education in Edward Heath's Conservative government. She was visiting the town's public boy's school my brother had attended, as well as being introduced to the headteachers of local schools. On being told that my headmaster was in charge of the local grammar school, going comprehensive, she leant towards him sympathetically and said,

"Oh well, you'll be alright then, because you're starting from a sound base."
A remark suggesting that even the government minister overseeing the country's monumental educational reform did not quite fully comprehend the enormity of the task facing the local Education Authorities. This would later be confirmed by reading the *Hansard* reports of parliamentary education debates taking place right up until 1976. Consecutive governments were blissfully unaware of the difficulties being faced in adhering to the demands of their various Education Bills and edicts. In the absence of a recognised national government policy, secondary schools attempting to revert to the new comprehensive education reform programme were being left to decide their own systems for placing pupils into suitable classes. No guidance on coping with the large intakes of mixed ability eleven-year-olds or recommendations on a suitable, universal curriculum. No advice on how to carry on preparing for the two parallel public examination syllabuses still in existence.
Was Mrs Thatcher implying that she believed the transition of an established grammar school into the comprehensive system would occur smoothly creating little problem for staff or existing pupils? Not much actual understanding of the difficulties and problems that lie ahead. No consideration given to the teaching staff who were having to juggle the demands of bigger heterogeneous intakes with maintaining the focus and needs of the existing grammar school pupils. No thought, either, for any of the pupils caught up in all of this. Since 1964, we have obviously just been the silent statistics manipulated by each elected government's projected social and educational reforms.

Up the few steps at the front of the school, walk under the archway, turn left through the swing doors and I make my way warily to the classroom assigned to my new form 1B. My years of comprehensive secondary education have begun.

Chapter Seven

We are sitting in our 1B form classroom up on the first floor. A wide, airy space with long metal-framed windows on two sides. If feels a bit like sitting up in a tree house as amber and copper-coloured beech leaves slap against the glass, tossed about by a squally September drizzle. Today we have all slunk back into the same chairs we occupied yesterday on our very first day in this form room. The individual plastic tables form a U shape, parallel to the exterior walls, facing onto the few tables grouped in pairs in the middle of the room. No one had wanted to sit at those middle tables yesterday morning. Far too exposed. It was the latecomers arriving in the classroom who had to sidle quickly into these, watched by everyone else.
I've established myself in a corner at the back of the room. Windows behind me on both sides, perpendicular to the tall, wooden-framed blackboard. Yesterday, our first day, I'd been one of the first into the classroom and had saved the table and chair next to me for Julie. She is sitting there now, but turned away from me, talking to the girl next to her. I think her name is Mary, I'm sure that's what I heard her say when we had to excruciatingly introduce ourselves to each other.
Julie and Mary have their heads together, animated babbling and giggling. I'm excluded. I hear snippets of girly chatter about a Donny Osmond and a song called *Young Love*. I don't want to break into their conversation, I wouldn't be able to contribute anything. I haven't heard the song, know little about The Osmonds or any other current pop music for that matter. My mother's transistor radio on the kitchen windowsill only ever had two settings, BBC Radio 3 or off. Classical music would always be playing at breakfast time and, in the afternoons when I arrived home from primary school, my mother would invariably be sitting reading and rereading her Agatha Christie paperbacks,

knitting or crocheting, or listening to her LP gramophone records on the HMV Stereomaster record player.

Watching Top of the Pops was never an option. Absolutely no question of being allowed to sit by myself in front of the television to view that *'dreadful rubbish'*. How very fortunate it was that the county youth orchestra rehearsals took place on the same weekday evening, Thursdays from 7 -9pm which became the perfect facade to cover for the fact that I was not allowed to watch the programme. I can always use that as an excuse, although sitting here surrounded by the other members of 1B, I get the feeling I won't be mentioning anything about cello playing or a county youth orchestra for quite a while yet.

For the moment I just need to concentrate on finding friends in this first form and *fitting in.*

Our form teacher, Mr Bradshaw is addressing us. We are to copy the weekly lesson timetable into our rough books. He gives the roller blackboard an almighty downward pull and with a shudder and rumble the already written timetable emerges from over the top.

I spot a word printed in quite a few of the squares: *Humanities*. That's a new word to me. Never heard of that subject before, but seeing the frequency with which it is written, I can only guess it is the new trendy, unthreatening word for the combined subjects of English language, English literature, history, geography, science and religious studies. This will be adhering to the new informal teaching ethos of integrating lesson material to form topics covering two or more subjects.

So, the six subjects are going to be grouped together, this sounds intriguing. Why couldn't they just be left as before in the same traditional, perfectly acceptable method? My sisters had studied them as separate lessons. The year above us in this same school were studying them as separate lessons for their grammar school curriculum. (The year I had wanted to be in!)

We had coped perfectly well in primary school, understanding the different subject material. Only six weeks previously we were deemed intelligent enough to recognise the particularities and skills required for each lesson. We had consulted the timetable taped onto the top junior classroom wall. We'd opened our desk lids and selected the correct textbook, the required exercise book. We were definitely capable, aged ten years old, of comprehending the diversity of the individual subjects. Why am I already getting the feeling that some sort of *'dumbing down'* is taking place?

In the excitement and enthusiasm for achieving success in this reorganisation to comprehensive education methods, it was anonymously recorded that *'some contended a slight reduction in academic standard was an acceptable price to pay for improved motivation and behaviour on the part of a majority of pupils!'*

The second day of my secondary education, filling in my timetable for this first year as part of an educational experiment, I'm feeling that the descent in academic standard requirement has already begun *poco à poco* (to use one of the Italian musical expressions I had recently learnt!).

As I continue to fill in my timetable, I notice something else. Writing the name of the teacher for each lesson, I am repeatedly putting in Mr Bradshaw's name. Well, I've actually stopped adding it, it seemed to be a waste of my Biro ink! It appears that over 25% of my weekly lessons will be taught by him whatever the subject matter during this year's ubiquitous *humanities* lessons. Thank goodness I chose a corner table with the opportunity to gaze out of the windows in two directions. I can do some birdwatching. It looks like I'm going to be spending an awful lot of time sitting in this classroom.

I've completed my timetable and, without realising, tune out of my surroundings and gaze out of the window to observe a kestrel hovering high up above a nearby tree, struggling to stay in position as it is constantly buffeted by the wind. Kestrel, I jiggle the letters around in my head. Skelter would be the perfect anagram……. helter-skelter: spiralling, circling. I'll have to work on writing some crossword clues. I reluctantly focus back on the room and look around. Julie and Mary are still chatting and haven't yet unzipped their pencil cases but a boy sitting by himself at a front table just beneath the roller blackboard seems to have also finished writing. He has placed his Gladstone -style brown leather briefcase on his lap and with his head down, is rummaging through the contents. I don't know him at all, but I'm impressed by how brave he is to appear with such a serious briefcase!

Is his briefcase synonymous with a desire to learn, a strong academic ability? Maybe we could become friends?

A commotion has broken out on the other side of the classroom. A blonde-haired girl with long plaits is beginning to cry. I can't imagine why; we are hardly being asked to complete a difficult task. Maybe it has to do with the blank-faced boy opposite her, rocking aggressively backwards and forwards on his chair, I'm sure Mr Bradshaw will sort it out. I notice that two cheeky-faced boys have not made any effort to produce pens or paper. They are just sitting, giggling together at their adjacent empty-topped tables. Mr Bradshaw chooses to ignore the 'Rocking Boy', walks straight past him and, approaching the two fidgeting lads, bends down to speak to them.

"Not to worry", I hear him say as he pats one of the boys on the shoulder. "I'll get you a xeroxed copy of the timetable from the lovely ladies in the office. They're very efficient on the mimeograph machine."

What is going on? Why can't these boys copy from the blackboard and write down the timetable? Have they both forgotten their reading glasses, their pencil cases, or is it something more serious? Surely, I haven't been put into a class with pupils who have difficulties in reading and writing? How incomprehensible this all seems to me with my sheltered middle-class upbringing. Why has the school done this to me? What an enormous exercise in developing my social mobility skills lay ahead of me!

Four weeks later and here I am again, sitting in a '*humanities*' lesson. Same classroom…same twenty-nine fellow form members. The only difference is that another teacher has arrived to take the class. I recognise him as my sister's O level English teacher Mr Sheenan. So, it would seem that Mr Bradshaw has already had enough of trying to teach us this bizarre, hotchpotch subject! I know he is a science teacher specialising in O and A level Chemistry, so I imagine he is somewhat relieved to revert to his true subject expertise and leave us motley lot to other members of the staff. Changes happening already. What has caused them to occur so quickly, after only a month into this experimental reform year? Are the teachers already struggling, or is it us, the pupils who are to blame? Mr Sheenan gazes around the room, eyes narrowed, forming a silent judgement of what awaits him.

At least it is sunny today. I can look out of my right-angle windows, and through the oranges and browns a crisp October blue sky is taunting me. Mary is sitting next to me for this lesson although sometimes I do catch her looking longingly around the room as if wanting to choose somewhere else to sit. I sense she is torn between responding obligingly to my pleading look for her to join me, when really, she yearns to break away from my side and cross over to the other side of the room. Consequently, it is only a tentative friendship that is forming between us. The conversation always limited to what is happening round us during the school day. It seems we are both still too shy and wary to open up too much to each other and reveal our true selves.

Julie has changed place. She now sits at a table on the opposite side of the U formation. I suspected her desire to distance herself from me and she now prefers to hang around with a group of girls who come in every morning on a school bus from one of the villages. I like to think that we did try to be '*friends*' for a while at the beginning of term but it was manifestly not going to happen, there was nothing whatsoever in common between us. She was in a different primary school class to mine, she lives on a different housing estate, she wants to be a hairdresser, she has no interest in classical music. I'm still incredulous (and annoyed) that for some incomprehensible reason, it was decided we would be the only two pupils from our primary school to be placed in this same first form. So much for the supposed criteria of trying to maintain friendship and social groups in each form. For the only two girls from the same primary school placed together in a first-year secondary education form, you really couldn't have picked two more dissimilar individuals.

I must concentrate back on the lesson. The new teacher Mr Sheenan is telling us that we can decorate our humanities exercise books as much as we like. He wants to see lots of illustrations; he wants to see the margins coloured in....

.... Goodness me, seems that art is now being incorporated into this confusing, all-encompassing subject as well!

That's fine by me. It will give me something to do when boredom sets in. I find I am often getting bored now. The tasks are not complex or demanding enough. I've inevitably finished what is required well before the end of the hour lesson and nothing extra is ever offered. Disappointment has engulfed me. After the first month, I'm already experiencing an acute lack of stimulation in class work for my academic ability level.

We are being told that today's exercise is to look at the person sitting next to us and write some sentences about their appearance. Apparently, we are going to use *'describing words'*. Surely the teacher means adjectives. That is the correct grammatical word we used in primary school. Mr Clifford had certainly drummed into us the various terms of the English language. Most of us could easily identify a verb, adjective, noun, adverb et cetera. Now it seems we have reverted to using childish terms so everyone in this mixed ability class can understand.

Now I am in a dilemma. How shall I play this? I definitely don't want to appear any different from the rest of the class. Shall I simply write a few banal sentences, carry on colouring in my margin and look out of the window, or shall I dazzle Mr Sheenan with a whole page of prose putting in as many compound adjectives as possible? But then what would happen if we had to read our work out loud?

Mary and I catch each other's eye and giggle. She is so pretty with her brown oval eyes and clear skin. The answer I pencilled into 5 down in the Times crossword that morning had been *'luxuriant'*. The clue had been a cryptic anagram; my favourite. *'Ritual nux embroidered and lush (9)'*. I could use that word to describe the texture and colour of Mary's lovely light-brown crinkly hair bubbling down from the central parting into two low bunches. What could she write about me? Another recent Times crossword clue, which had baffled me for a couple of minutes had been: *'One very happy to skip end of dance, being lonely (8)'*.

The answer being *'isolated'* of course. Easy once you had deciphered the different parts of the cryptic clue. Now, that was definitely a word Mary could use to describe me! What other words could she use.... perplexed, bemused, dispirited. I say nothing of course. We pick up our pens.

I choose the nonconfrontational option and write four mediocre sentences purposely adding some spelling and punctuation mistakes for good measure. That should make it seem like I am fitting in with 1B. I must not draw attention to myself, just appear to be the average mixed ability pupil.

I wonder what the 'Briefcase Boy' has written. As usual he sits by himself detached from the rest of the class. Which fellow class member would he have written about? Maybe he is in the same position as me and has been placed in this form group with no one he knew from his primary school. However, his tenacity and acceptance of the situation are intriguing me.

The pieces of work with our describing words are collected up and handed to Mr Sheenan who is now encouraging a class discussion to begin. "Right, you lot", he attempts to gain our full attention by slipping into a colloquial style of talk. His voice has the lovely lilt of southern Ireland. "I know nothing about you, so let's hear some of you tell me about yourself. Your hobbies for example.... Just put up your hands".

Oh, dear me, no! My hand won't be going up. Taking part in class discussions, talking about myself, is not something I will be doing in 1B, or 2B or 3B...or ever at this school. My refusal to participate in any classroom discussion would repeatedly infuriate the teachers for the next five years. It would be no surprise that I would soon be considered *'aloof'* and *'scathing'* by various members of the staff.

It was recorded by a team of HM inspectors sent out in May 1975 to examine how gifted children were faring in comprehensive school systems that:

'Some gifted children can quietly and unobtrusively accept teaching method and content which is inappropriate for them whilst others will struggle and resort to disruptive or uncommunicative behaviour.'

I have never been disruptive in my life, but sadly, I would quickly slip into the second category and become uncommunicative. After just a month at this school I was already angry and petulant. Why was I being expected to sit through hour-long lessons of inconsequential whole class informal teaching at an academic level I deemed an affront to my intelligence? I felt I was wasting valuable learning time and therefore, I wasn't going to participate in any banal, fatuous discussions. Could no one else in 1B or the entire first year comprehensive intake realise we were participating unwillingly in a vast experiment of social reform, hoping that the more able pupils in each of the seven classrooms would be an important factor in encouraging a stimulating, lively ambiance for the less able.

Would these mixed ability classes make the less academic pupils feel involved and challenged, excited to be part of a classroom atmosphere that had previously been denied to them?

Well, I certainly wasn't going to give the teaching staff the satisfaction of joining in, or contributing verbally, to any lesson. Who would have thought I had such an ill-humoured rebellious streak gnawing away inside of me! And was anyone else feeling as much distress and indignation as I was?

In a discussion paper by a working party of her Majesty's Inspectorate entitled: *'Mixed Ability Work in Comprehensive Schools',* which was to appear in 1978, it was noted by the HM inspectors that *'pupils of above average ability, particularly the most able, were at the greatest disadvantage in the circumstances generally encountered in the mixed ability classes'.*

Unfortunately, these observations wouldn't be officially recorded until I had already spent my first five frustrating years in the comprehensive education reform programme. For the time being, I am expected to sit obediently, silently compliant and unquestioning, through each day's tedious and unstimulating classes.

After just a month of sitting through lessons in this form room, I've already noticed how animated and excited the lesser academically able members of the class become when encouraged to speak their opinion and given the opportunity to talk in front of the whole class. Today it's the same. The boys with obvious, but never ever acknowledged, learning and behavioural problems jostle with each other to have centre stage, vie in their attempts to interest Mr Sheenan, try to say increasingly outrageous things, feel valued by his over-enthusiastic and (to me) cringingly patronising praise. Mr Sheenan replies with forced commitment.

"Well, that was grand, Matthew. Thank you for sharing that with us."

"Excellent, Kevin, how interesting that was to hear. We must discuss it again another time."

"Maybe you could repeat that again to the class, John, just without all the swear words this time..."

I watch the few boys thrive on the attention of Mr Sheenan. Their shoulders raised higher, grinning mouths on their shiny, flushed faces, arms exaggeratedly folded across their chests, leaning back on tilted chairs.

I'm not bothering to listen to what is being said, nor, looking discreetly around the room, I notice, are many others. 'Briefcase Boy' is sharpening a pencil, the shavings falling into his opened briefcase perched on his lap. He, too, has decided not to participate in this particular discussion. Julie and her new friends, the 'Village Girl' group, are giggling away over on the other side of the room. Lorraine and Michelle are surreptitiously flicking through pages of a magazine hidden underneath their adjoined tables. 'Blonde Hair' girl is staring up at the ceiling, twiddling one of her plaits.

Please, please let the end of lesson bell go soon, so I can be released from this mind-numbing hour. Lunchtime is next and I have an early lunch ticket so I can go straight in and eat in the first sitting. During the rest of the lunchbreak, it will be junior school orchestral rehearsal and I am so looking forward to being reunited with my music friends from primary school.

.
.

Chapter Eight

Nine o'clock. Register taken, we are instructed by Mr Bradshaw to sit and wait the arrival of the maths teacher.
My first maths lesson of my secondary school life. No need, of course, for us to change classrooms. We are going to have maths lessons sitting right here in our form room. I look down on the bobbing heads of an orderly file passing along under the window. I don't recognise the accompanying teacher and as the pupils are all walking so sensibly and purposefully, they must doubtless be a grammar school class! I expect they are going over to the newly built separate sixth form block and its lecture theatre. I envy them their freedom in roaming around the school buildings. For the first few days we have been confined to this one room. As lovely as it is to gaze out of the first-floor windows at the ever-changing autumnal colours of the leaves, I'm feeling somewhat claustrophobic being expected to spend so much time sat within these same four walls. To me, it feels like we are being deliberately confined, screened from the rest of the academically selected school years above us. Are we something to be ashamed of? Is this first comprehensive intake such an unknown quantity that there is a need to isolate us whilst they continually assess our disposition, our behaviour? Obviously, we can't yet be released from our first-year form rooms. I really don't like the overall atmosphere, I just want to break free, be given some independence and be reunited with my primary school friends. This classroom is so bland. I wonder what subject it is usually assigned to, there are no clues on the blank white walls. I allow myself a wry smile. An uninteresting, vacuous room designated to a similar disinterested and unmotivated 1B!
Mr Bradshaw is a chemistry teacher. He must have his laboratory where he spends his days teaching, somewhere else in the school. Heaven forbid that we first formers could be trusted to be let loose in a room full of Bunsen burners, iridescent chemicals in bottles on shelves and glass test tubes lodged in wooden racks on the bench tops. I would have enjoyed looking at posters and pictures on the walls. Something to study in the more boring moments. A wall chart of the periodic table would have been interesting. It would be fun to see how far I could memorise it. Some of the symbols for the elements I know already and use them to solve the cryptic crossword clues I love so much. I've just become fascinated with molecular formulas having been recently successful at home, making some soap with my Merit Chemistry set. The little instruction booklet informed me that soap was $C_{17}H_{35}COOH$!
Still no sign of the maths teacher. Around me are whispers, murmurings, muffled laughter. Mr Bradshaw strolls around the room and stops in front of the curly, black-haired boy who, yesterday, had been one of the two lads who didn't seem to be able to copy down the timetable. The table in front of him is empty again. No sign of a pen or pencil, a pencil case or a rough book. Mr Bradshaw doesn't bother to lean down to get closer to him for a more intimate conversation today, instead, he remains standing and towers over the sitting boy asking him in a voice, audible to everyone, to explain where, exactly, is his school bag, his pencil case, his exercise books?
"But sir, you see, shame innit! I left me bag on the bus didn't I". The 'No Bag Boy' grins around at us all. A group of three other boys, possibly his new accomplices, smirk and snigger, impressed by the bravado and audacity. Two girls on the other side of the classroom giggle conspiratorially. I now suspect they come in on the same bus from one of the villages. The bus that might, or might not, harbour the *'missing bag'*. Mr Bradshaw just shakes his head in a display of resigned disbelief and walks away.
Mr Bradshaw will, of course, cope admirably for the next three years with some of the more tiresome and demanding members of this form with their behavioural issues, learning difficulties and contrary attitudes. 1B does seem such a strange mix though, such a vast spectrum of ability and reaction. I've spent these first days observing and wondering if the more challenging and difficult children were selected to be with him. There do seem to be an awful lot in my form! Maybe the

younger, less experienced teachers were given thirty pupils of milder, more compliant aptitude. And what about the *'dream form'* with four of my friends placed together. There would be no adversity with that group of girls, and, why, oh why, couldn't I have been in that form? But I mustn't think about that now. The injustice makes me too upset and the anger will start surging through my body, curdling my stomach and ending up as flashing red strobes in my head, discordant and unresolving like a jarring Alban Berg tonal poem.

The solitary boy with the impressive briefcase on the floor beside him has his head down, studying his lap. I note that his rough book and pencil case are positioned ready on his table forming a perfect right angle. If only I had the confidence to start up a conversation with him.

The classroom door slowly opens, and we get the first glimpse of our maths teacher. A short Asian man with black, shining crinkly hair but everything else about him is brown. Brown skin, brown tortoiseshell- framed glasses, brown suit and shoes. This is the first Asian man I have ever encountered. As he introduces himself, I worry that I am going to have trouble understanding him. I do hope I get accustomed to his quiet lilting speech and nodding head. Although surely one doesn't need to have too much of a conversation during a maths lesson? I just want to be given some hard problems to solve. The classroom has fallen, unusually for 1B, into a stunned silence, probably sharing my initial reaction to Mr Khan. Even with my musical ear, I am struggling to follow his undulating voice. Did he just say that he will have to find out how much each of us knows?

Little surprise that a grammar school maths teacher would know nothing about any of our abilities to solve a numerical or geometrical problem in this unprecedentedly large mixed ability comprehensive intake. We've arrived here with, supposedly, only the results of two verbal reasoning tests to our name. Not much help for a maths teacher facing a class of new faces. I begin to feel a bit of sympathy for Mr Khan *'dressed all in brown'*. What a daunting task awaits him. He does seem a bit nervous, wringing his hands as he speaks. Imagine having to teach first year secondary school maths to a class of thirty when you have no idea whatsoever of their competence in your subject. No surprise then, that we will be doing the ubiquitous worksheets for the time -being so he can *'find out what we know'*.

I look around my fellow form members. Yes, what indeed do they know? What have they learnt in their primary school maths lessons?

During my top junior class, I had worked my way through the red Alpha Mathematics Workbooks. Far too many pages involving problems shopping with decimal currency. It got rather boring after a while! During the six weeks of the recently finished summer holiday, I had discovered negative numbers. I was SO annoyed at the world, but mostly my primary school teachers, for keeping their existence from me. Why hadn't Mr Clifford or my red Alpha maths workbook enlightened me that numbers didn't finish at zero? I felt I was now part of some secondary education maths club. I spent rainy August days alone, sitting at my desk in my bedroom, creating axis, plotting coordinates, drawing connecting lines from positive and negative numbers, there were patterns to be discovered, polygons to be perfected.

Another recent discovery had been prime numbers. Yet again, alone in my bedroom, I challenged myself to block in all the products of the times tables 2 to 10. This involved using copious sheets of my father's preferred IZAL medicated toilet paper as tracing paper over the same one hundred square grid. Some wonderful patterns emerged but some numbers didn't appear in any of the times tables. I researched these numbers in the town library.

Patterns, sequences, puzzles. My eleven-year-old brain couldn't soak them up fast enough whether they were either music or maths – Fibonacci or fugues.

I believed my most exciting maths project to date had to be my research into square numbers! The two- week family holiday to the Bed and Breakfast farmhouse in South Devon and the inevitable days of drizzle and Atlantic fog had given me plenty of opportunity to write endless columns of numbers in my Woolworths notebook. I thought I was on the brink of a major mathematical discovery! Did anyone else know that the difference between square numbers was rising odd numbers. How could this be? I needed someone to explain it to me.

I did have quite a few sneaky glances through Catherine's maths textbook if I spotted it in her open satchel left in the hallway. I stumbled across some basic algebra, had never seen that before, and I was instantly fascinated. Yet more enigmas to be cracked. What fun working out A and B or X and Y. Simultaneous equations, quadratic equations, factorising, expanding brackets. I loved it. However, not knowing the strict rules I resorted to solving them in my head or scribbling possible solutions on pieces of paper. I didn't know that the acceptable method was to get X on one side of the equation and then always do the same to both sides! And I wasn't yet to know that in future secondary school maths lessons or exams: *'Solve these equations showing every step of your working'* was to become one of the sentences I dreaded the most and would lead to a somewhat acrimonious relationship with future maths teachers. If I could do them quickly in my head, then adamantly (and, I admit, by the third year, rebelliously) I would just write the answer. This inevitably led to accusations of copying and a red cross. Sadly, never once during five caustic years of maths lessons did a single teacher treat me as an individual and find the time to suggest I work through and solve equations in front of their own eyes.

Fractions I adored. Working for my Associated Board of Music theory exams and playing instruments had given me much practice in the division of beats, note values and time signatures. Was a piece of music in simple time or compound time? I had to understand how to emphasise and phrase music in such complicated rhythms as simple triple, compound duple or compound quadruple. One semibreve equals two minims, four crotchets, eight quavers, sixteen semiquavers, thirty-two demisemiquavers, sixty-four hemidemisemiquavers...and I defy anyone to play triplets with one hand and quavers with the other at the same time at the piano keyboard!

One of the required exercises in the Grade Five Theory of Music examination was writing out in full the abbreviated ornaments written above the music stave. The trills, the acciaccaturas, the appoggiaturas, mordents and inverted turns all had to be meticulously divided up in equal measures. I had recently received a distinction in passing the music theory exam with the highest possible mark.

But no one else in this room knows any of that and, if I want to fit in here, I suspect that I will never talk about it to anyone either. Sadly, I am already sensing an enormous gulf opening between myself and the rest of the pupils in this form. I feel I don't have anything in common with any of them. Why on earth have I been placed here? My self-confidence is already evaporating, and I am confused.

Mr Khan *'dressed all in brown'* walks around the room, his tan shoes squeaking, putting worksheets in front of us on our individual tables. Most of us keep our heads down, a very subdued snigger bubbles up and then abruptly stops. Mr Bradshaw is still standing in the room, arms folded, surveying everything. Does he need to wait here to discipline us?

The worksheet, as I had expected, is ridiculously easy and unstimulating. So obviously starting with very basic sums and then getting subtly more difficult with each question. The typical aptitude test in disguise. Was it trying to fool anyone? It left me feeling frustrated and unfulfilled. Maybe I should have just messed up the whole thing as a protest to my incomprehensible situation? I wouldn't dare do that yet though, not during these early compliant but baffling months.

I finish the problems, zip up my pencil case, push the worksheet to the far edge of my table and look around. 'Briefcase Boy' seems to have finished too. I wonder if he will put his hand up or, like me, just sit quietly doing nothing.

Despite having been given a pen by Mr Bradshaw, 'No Bag Boy' hasn't made any effort to even look at the worksheet in front of him. It lies precariously, half hanging over the edge of his table untouched from when it was placed there. He leans back on his tilted chair, arms folded, staring up at the ceiling.

Forty more minutes before the end of the lesson. Through the window I watch a thrush hop from branch to branch. Forty more minutes of being bored. Maybe things will get better soon?

Chapter Nine

Music lessons with my form were so exasperating for me. The majority of my fellow class members had absolutely no interest in clapping rhythms, learning about crotchets and quavers or singing aloud. For them, the twice weekly lessons were simply the opportunity to have a riotous time, bang on the desktops in a pantomime of beating in time, throw the purple *Sing Together!* songbooks at each other and generally just laugh and mess around.

The music classroom at that time was still the poky garret-style room perched, seemingly precariously, on the upper floor of the school reached by climbing yet more stairs and walking along a short dark corridor. A new music block was in the process of being built next to the enormous new sports hall which was just completed. My school had certainly profited well from the previous six years of Labour Government with their increased spending on education projects and promises of providing money for new buildings to the Local Education Authorities who submitted plans for reorganising their secondary schools into the comprehensive system.

What a haven that new music block would become for me over the next few years. Many hours would be spent shut away in a practice room. Having a music lesson, practising by myself on the cello and piano, composing, rehearsing duets, trios and quartets with grammar school pupils. Increasingly though, my presence in those little rooms became less legitimate. Skiving a lesson, hiding away from the horrors of particularly bad days, often just sitting alone in desperation. I found an excellent hiding place in practice room n° 2 behind the upright piano. I would spend hours tucked away in the tiny, dusty space. Sitting, back against the wall, knees pulled up under my chin. Very often, silent tears dampening my cheeks.

But for this first year (and the second year as well) we must still use the old existing music room. High windows lodged under the ceiling make it impossible for me to look out. Very disappointing that even when we are released from our oppressive 1B form room to sit in another classroom I am unable to gaze out at the passing world. I have this burning desire to connect to reality, watch normal everyday events continuing outside of my classroom confinement. If I can look out of a window then I don't feel quite so trapped, so isolated in this baffling comprehensive experiment. Even if I can't see people at least I can observe the birds, but no birds can be seen from these lofty music room windows, just mote- speckled, diagonal shafts of light.

A few faded curling posters cling to the walls. A tableau of musical instruments grouped by families. A basic representation of note values. The obligatory posters of *'Famous Music Composers'* depict a Beethoven and a Mozart and a wild-haired, manic-eyed Berlioz.

I don't know how many of these music lessons I have endured now. Here I am again, sitting slumped at my individual wooden desk in acute discomfort feeling bad for Miss Gilbert, the young and enthusiastic teacher who, sadly, is unable to control the thirty mixed ability pupils in front of her. The only time form 1B fell into an uneasy silence was last week when Miss Gilbert ran out of the classroom in tears. I wanted to cry myself. I shared her pain and disappointment. Here was a trained musician trying to share her love and knowledge of music to a class who had absolutely no desire to learn or even show her the respect to listen. I was in that classroom. I was distressed, feeling wretched and sick to my stomach but I am learning to accept the fact that being part of this intake I must be silent, I'm a nonentity.

It would seem that like our maths teacher, Miss Gilbert has no background information on the mixed ability individuals sitting facing her in the classroom, just expected to teach 'music' to the thirty pupils arriving in her classroom. She is the lower school music teacher. Mr Digby is the upper school grammar school music teacher. Mr Digby knows me well, knows my musical capabilities, I encounter him every Saturday morning at the county run music school. He teaches me theory of music. He coaches me for string orchestra and quartets. Yet, for the time being, I am not to be recognised. The staff that know of my musical talent ignore me and, never mind the turmoil going on inside of me, I am expected to show absolute acquiescence sitting submissively in these first form lessons.

I look at my red-strapped Timex wristwatch. Still ten minutes to get through of this music lesson. We've done the tapping on the desks to learn a rhythm and we've pathetically sung along to *Donkey Riding*:
'Were you ever in Quebec, stowing timber on the deck….
Hey Ho, away we go'
I'm missing my primary school music friends. What a shame they are not sitting beside me in this lesson. We could have done some impressive vocal harmonizing during the singing. Maybe added a descant line, pitched some thirds below the tune or finished with a flourish, each choosing a different note to sing from the final F major chord!
Miss Gilbert announces there are some vacancies for violin lessons, if anyone is interested? This produces the anticipated sniggers; snorts of derision erupt from the boys sitting along the back row. I don't turn around but can sense the exaggerated miming of bows going up and down, the swinging elbows. The teacher suddenly pivots in front of the class tossing her mane of long black hair behind her.
"By the way", she addresses us, "just out of interest, does anyone play a musical instrument already?"
That absolutely confirms my theory that Miss Gilbert has no background knowledge of any of the pupils sitting in her classroom. Responding honestly to her question I slowly put up my hand. I notice a movement at a desk further along my row, a hesitant arm is being raised. It's Mary, I can't believe it! My heart does an exultant tremolo flutter. We've sat next to each for quite a few different lessons over the past weeks but why have we never discussed playing a musical instrument? I know so little about her, our conversations always timid and stilted. I know she doesn't live in the town but in a village seven miles away. She arrives on a bus every morning and disappears again at 4 o'clock every afternoon as soon as the last lesson finishes. She definitely hasn't turned up at lunchtime school orchestra or junior choir rehearsals. The five hours of lessons every day, mostly closeted in our unnatural 1B classroom environment, are the only time I see her. Quite a lot of the time we are forced to sit in silence, anyway, enduring intolerable whole class punishments. I wonder if Mary and I could be closer friends, united now by our music playing but I think I might have missed my chance. Already she is drifting towards other girl groups, preferring their company. Even arriving in this music classroom today she had shunned the desk next to mine and chosen to sit further along the row next to Julie and a tall, big-breasted girl called Linda.
Miss Gilbert reaches Mary first.
"So, Mary, what do you play?"
"The clarinet Miss". I strain to hear Mary's quiet voice above the rumble of chatter.
"How long have you been playing then, Mary?"
"Over a year now Miss, getting ready for my Grade 1 exam." I want Mary to look at me, but the intimacy of the conversation is taking its toll and she keeps her gaze fixed downwards on the scratched wooden desktop. Miss Gilbert walks over to me,
"Hello there, you play the clarinet as well then?"
"No, the cello Miss." She looks at me somewhat quizzically, probably wondering if I even knew what a cello was.
"Ah right, the cello." She turns around to address the rest of the class behind us…. I know exactly the very unoriginal comment coming next…."That's just a big violin to the rest of you." Thank goodness no one is taking any interest in our conversation. The end of lesson bell is about to go, chairs are being scraped along the floor, bags hauled up onto shoulders. I feel I must justify myself, "I started it at primary school".
"Have you taken any grades yet then?" Now I was in a quandary. I wanted Miss Gilbert to know of my musical aptitude, make her understand how frustrated I am having to sit in her lessons, but I

don't want any of the other class members to hear me talk about my playing. Such a turmoil of conflicting emotions. I so wanted the staff to recognise my musical talent and my academic ability but at the same time I don't want to seem any different to the other twenty-nine youngsters in form 1B.

I reckoned that there was enough bustle going on around us to continue the conversation. The bell was reverberating through the room, bodies were pushing past Miss Gilbert and myself, a bag hits me in the back as the rush for the door began.

"Yes Miss, I'm taking grade 6 in November." The music teacher's eyes fly wide open,

"Oh, I don't think you mean grade 6 practical, do you? that would mean you have already passed your grade 5 theory of music exam. You wouldn't understand all that….☐"

Actually, I did understand *'all that'*. I had recently passed my grade 5 theory of music examination. I could analyse chords and cadences, compose a short piece of choral music in 4-part harmony. I was able to rewrite passages of music in a requested modulated key, set a poem to music, write out in full abbreviated music ornaments and answer questions demonstrating a basic knowledge of music history, composers and their styles.

No one else in my new form 1B could possibly know what was going on in my head!

'Hey Ho, away we go, donkey riding, donkey riding….'

"Yes Miss, I've passed grade 5 theory. Working on grade 6 now at Saturday morning music school." Miss Gilbert is a bit shocked by this information. A brief narrowing of the eyes betrays the sudden annoyance at her ignorance of the individuals in her classroom. An immature smugness that I have surprised her with my secret musical knowledge is swiftly obliterated by a sense of sympathy for this young teacher. I don't want her feeling upset that, whilst she struggled to control the class, got us to tap rhythms, sing banal songs, she was completely unaware that a pupil in her class was cognizant to theory of music exercises recognised as roughly equivalent to O level examination standard. Every time Miss Gilbert had run to the piano to tap a key for the correct musical note to begin a song, I could have simply hummed the note out loud for her. I had perfect pitch. It hadn't occurred to her to ask.

She recovers well from her initial surprise and gives me a pleasant smile.

"Well, that's very interesting, well done to you. Why don't you bring in your Associated Board music theory practice workbooks and you could sit quietly by yourself in a corner and get on with it? I could always help you; you know."

I really doubt Miss Gilbert would be able to ignore the rowdy classroom and spend time with me during 1B music lessons and anyway I am never going to bring in my music books. That is part of my life that I intend to keep hidden. If I want to fit in with this class, I can't appear to be different. If I need to 'dumb down' to be like everyone else around me, then dumb down is what I will do. I will sit silently and obediently, suppressing my boredom and discomfort.

I watch Mary disappear through the music room door chatting with Julie and Linda. No chance to talk to her now. That was the last lesson of the day, she will vanish in search of her bus. Who will she choose to sit next to though, during all of tomorrow's lessons?

Chapter Ten

Wednesday 14th November 1973. Sitting as always in the form classroom waiting for Mr Sheenan to arrive and begin the humanities lesson. Normally we would have arrived back damp and red-faced from the sports hall having just had a sport lesson. Today was different. On arriving at the vast new sports building, we had been ordered to file into the big hall where the large wooden-cased television on stilts had been installed. No strenuous physical education for us, we were going to be allowed to spend the lesson time watching the Royal Wedding! Just as I dropped down to sit on the grimy floor, up on the screen Princess Anne was beginning her walk down the aisle of Westminster Abbey followed by a very earnest Prince Edward and Lady Sarah Armstrong-Jones.

This certainly made a pleasant change, sitting in the brightly lit and heated large sport hall watching television instead of being shouted at whilst pointlessly running up and down sheep-like, within the narrow white lines on the edges of the muddy sports field. My hockey stick rarely ever made contact with the ball. No surprise I was always sent out into the cold, foggy oblivion of being a little needed wing player, the coveted centre forward position being offered to much more popular girls! However, today, I certainly appreciated the nod to patriotism and absolutely wouldn't question the excessive use of all the electricity around me, despite Prime Minister Edward Heath's declaration, just the day before, that the country was now in a *'state of emergency'* and electricity was to be used sparingly!

Such a shame when the end of lesson bell clangs around the bare hall and we are faced with everyday reality, back to school life and the need to get our cramped leg muscles moving.

Mr Sheenan enters our form room and dramatically places a box on the teacher's desk. He turns around to face us with a broad smile, knowing he has aroused our curiosity. He slowly lifts off the lid to reveal tightly stacked, brightly coloured cards and makes the big announcement that today we are going to be working *'by ourselves'*. Apparently, we are going to be given a colour and we are to come up and pull out a card with that colour, take it back to our table and work through the questions. Why am I getting the feeling that I am back in a primary school infant class?

Some members of form 1B are looking quite excited. Something new, something different is going to happen. Mr Sheenan continues his spiel about *'how exciting this is going to be'* and *'what fun to be assigned a colour'* ....I wait for him to say it but he doesn't..... *"And what fun to be trusted to walk to the front of the classroom and be able to find the correctly coloured work card!'* I doubt the boy who continually rocks back and forth on his chair and is mostly switched off from the surrounding 1B environment will be able to participate in this new challenge.

My cynical mind begins whirling with questions. So, this is simply going to be an English comprehension lesson, and, with no trumpet fanfare or drumroll, a surreptitious shift has been made, moving away from whole class teaching towards individualised learning. Is form 1B ready for this experiment? I wonder if this is happening in the other six mixed ability first forms. I'm feeling slightly uneasy, almost as if I have been tricked. I've spent the last couple of months enduring unstimulating lessons completing average academic ability worksheets. Were we being constantly covertly assessed and now through the pretence of these new work cards, have they finally realised that it would be courteous to focus on us as individual pupils□withour very different academic demands?

Why else would there be different colour bands on top of the cards? Each colour will obviously denote a different level of ability, there will doubtless be subtle variations in use of language and pace of learning. Do my fellow classmates not realise this□too? I'm sure it won't be too hard to spot the contrast between the quantity of written text, the length of questions, the vocabulary used between the work cards at the front of the box and the cards nearer the back!

Far too much intelligent observation, too much critical analysis for a twelve-year-old to be processing. So many years at this school still lay ahead!

Mr Sheenan is calling out our names from a sheet of paper held in his hand and telling us our colours. Mine is going to be olive. I like that. Such an unusual and exotic shade and if you play around with the letters, you get the anagram voile which I know is the word for a silky, fine material and it has two meanings in French: veil and sail! Damn, I was so lost in my thoughts, I've missed hearing what colour 'Briefcase Boy' is getting. Mary is assigned yellow. Julie and Tracy get purple. As they are sitting next to each other, Mr Sheenan tells them they can work together from the same card. I didn't hear anyone else being given olive so I will have to pull out my work card very discreetly and walk back to my table with it held close to my body facing inwards. We walk up one by one to collect our colour. The cards with the olive-coloured strip across the top are, unsurprisingly, near the back of the box. OLIVE WORKCARD N° 1 it so helpfully informs me! I place it on the table in front of me and unzip my pencil case.

Just a simple exercise in English comprehension. I read through the passage and quickly answer the questions. Finished. The answers could all be easily found within the text. No need for me to employ any argumentative skills, step sideways into analytical thought or even include any individual creative flourishes. Yet again I have been left mentally unstimulated by a task requiring intellectual conformity and not intellectual curiosity. No demand for the more able pupil to engage in problem-solving exercises or further research.

OLIVE WORKCARD N° 2 completed and I'm about to start on N° 3. I'm challenging myself, how many work cards can I get through in one lesson! The passage to read through on this third card recounts a group of children trying to crack a code to get into a room. Sounds very pseudo-Enid Blyton to me. I'd avidly soaked up most of her books during primary school as well as those written by Noel Streatfield and Malcolm Saville. I've recently finished all fourteen of Willard Price's adventure books. Completely fascinated by the astounding geography and zoology details, these facts are now all stored away in my brain for future reference.... The usual length of an anaconda, the temperature on the equator, Bikini atoll is one of the twenty-three Marshall Islands situated in the Pacific Ocean. I'd dipped into my mother's collection of Biggles and Worrels but was not interested by the outdated subject matter. My understanding of everyday life at this secondary school needed to be decidedly more *Jackie* and *New Look* than Captain W E Johns.

During the six-week summer holiday I had been a frequent visitor to the town library, always now heading into the adult fiction section. I had discovered and was really enjoying the novels of Nevil Shute. I had also stumbled across the historical romances of Victoria Holt. My mother eyed my choice of books as I arrived home with the bag full for the week. I suspected the images of the voluptuous, doe-eyed and windswept females on the front covers might not meet with her approval. She nodded her head towards my pile of library books.

"Not my choice of course, you understand, but I do believe they are well written and accurate on historical facts". I think what she really meant was, *'It's good that you are reading these novels by yourself. Finding out about women's' feelings and 'all that nonsense'. This will do very nicely to replace any sex education talk I should be having with you!'* We had already endured together the acutely embarrassing moment of her opening the sealed brown envelope I carried home from primary school and passing me the pamphlet to be *'read at home'* entitled *'Peter and Pamela grow up'*.

If my mother thought I believed in love at first sight, innocent fainting women and being swept off my feet by chivalrous young noblemen, then sadly but inevitably, the chasm of understanding and dealing with current teenage life between us was going to grow ever wider. Goodness me, I was having to cope daily with being thrust into a school environment vastly incompatible with my home life. Everyday being surrounded by foul language, sexual innuendos and crude gestures, a completely alien world of social standards and behaviour that I had never encountered. Nothing I could ever explain to my mother. I kept quiet about everything of course. School life and home life were quickly becoming two very separate worlds.

My desperate need to cope and understand what was happening around me had led to some desperate, and I admit mildly criminal, measures. Two weeks ago, I had clandestinely taken *Valley of the Dolls* off a library shelf and let it fall into my opened rucksack. Now, that was an eyeopener, reading by torchlight in my bedroom every night! Maybe not that suitable for a naïve twelve-year-old but I quickly needed to broaden my mind, be more understanding and tolerable to the 1970's attitudes around me and clamber out of my blinkered upbringing.

The last question on Olive Worksheet n° 3 is about codes. *'Can you resolve this code and help the children get into the room?'*

GSV PVB RH FMWVI GSV NZG

Not too difficult. I quickly crack the code. For a few months now I have had fun working on the puzzle in the monthly magazine my father brings back from his office. An empty crossword grid with only numbers as substitutes for letters. I realised it was all down to letter frequency in the English language and enjoyed the challenge.

Work card n° 3 finished. Maybe I can make a start on number 4 now ....

.... suddenly, there is a commotion in the classroom. Mr Sheenan is raising his voice in anger, striding quickly between the tables. 'No Bag Boy' has scribbled maliciously in pen across a work card defacing it. Someone must have lent him a blue biro then! Mr Sheenan is having trouble comprehending this vandalism.

"Why, why?" he keeps shouting, waving the ruined card high in the air. Such an explosion of emotion. Everyone in the class is as shocked as I am. 'No Bag Boy' is shaking with frustration, purple-faced and defiant.

"I ain't doing no fuckin' crap like this no more. Gets on me bloody nerve all them questions. I'm finished with this shit", he gesticulates wildly at the work card still in Mr Sheenan's grip.

Future studies of mixed ability classroom teaching methods hinted that above average ability children were perfectly capable of working below their potential from lack of challenge or from personal choice and pass unnoticed, but that the slow learners could less easily disguise their inability to work at the level and pace of their fellows.

I watch Mr Sheenan in trepidation, an O level English teacher trying to control himself, faced with a classroom of thirty mixed ability pupils. Still half an hour of this wretched lesson to go. The usual gentle lilt has disappeared from his voice, and it has a harder, grating northern edge."

"Well, 1B, I'm very disappointed in the behaviour of your classmate over there. You will spend the rest of the is lesson sitting in silence at your tables."

No, no no. This is SO unfair. Another whole class punishment of being forced to sit in silence and do absolutely nothing. I'm fed up with being treated like an infant, being treated as just another unpredictable member of this strange, incompatible form 1B. My infuriation at not being regarded as an individual in this experimental intake is increasing, the acid scepticism curdles inside me. I didn't want to be part of this education reform programme. Has everyone had enough amusement now, watching me suffer in this social mobility trial? How dare they deny me learning time! I'm going to have to find an enormous amount of resilience to survive my school years here.

I look across at Mary sitting on the other side of the room and we share a brief smile. I throw a raised *'how ridiculous is this'* eyebrow movement in her direction. She covers a giggle with her hand, but I notice her eyes are moist and she seems as shocked as I am with the injustice of the situation. Julie, next to Tracy, seems unperturbed, both their heads lowered, rummaging through a makeup bag under the table. Michelle, seated next to them, is squeezing a spot on her chin. 'Blonde Hair' girl has her head down on the tabletop buried into her folded arms, is she crying, or asleep? I notice that 'Briefcase Boy' is scribbling something in his rough book and decide that I could do the same. I should be far enough away from Mr Sheenan for him to notice I am actually finding something to do for his ridiculous whole class punishment.

I place my blue rough book on the tabletop and open to a fresh page. I'm feeling defiant, I'll use this wasted time to do some composing. I lean low over the table surface and curl my left arm around the paper so no one can observe what I am doing. In my bedroom, I'm working on a sonata for cello and piano in my favourite key of E major – 4 sharps, but today calls for something more dramatic, more wistful. Maybe D minor? Then I can write a suspenseful, ascending melodic lane lingering between the B flat and the C sharp before resolving on a top D. Definitely need to get a poignant Neapolitan sixth chord in too, based around an E flat.

I draw the five-line stave roughly across the page. What instrument shall I write for? It feels like a melancholic viola sort of day. I write in an alto clef figuration at the beginning of the five lines.

The end of lesson bell startles me. I had been so engrossed in my music world that I had blocked out the negativity of the classroom atmosphere. We shuffle out of the room, directed by a dismissive hand movement from a still seething Mr Sheenan.

I don't think the colour work cards will ever be appearing again. I suspect the experiment into individualised learning has terminated for form 1B!

Chapter Eleven

December 1973. Something different is happening today. Instead of having the humanities lesson in our usual form room we are ordered to go and queue up outside the fifth-form common room. A large, usually empty and dark room situated on the other side of the school buildings. Getting there will involve a dash across the main courtyard dodging the icy shards of rain. "No running, no running", yells Mr Sheenan, somewhat in vain, as he holds his briefcase above his head and lunges after us as we hurtle through the double swing doors.

We line up against the corridor's flaking, white-painted bricked wall. I'm standing by myself in front of Julie, Mary and Linda. I hear them discussing a Gary Glitter song. They laugh together and begin to chant what I presume are song lyrics: *I love you, love, you love me too, love*....it all sounds very repetitive and juvenile to me, but they are having such fun, swaying together, arms around each other's shoulders and I feel jealous to be excluded from their moment of companionship. 'No Bag Boy' is jostling all of us in the queue, running up and down pushing bodies and thumping arms, wanting attention. I sense this change of routine is unsettling him. The 'Village Girl' group stand off to one side in identical positions of arms folded tight across chests. Lorraine is playing with 'Blonde Hair' girl's long plaits. The 'Rocking Boy' seems to have got lost on the short journey across to this different room.

The tall, bald-headed headmaster approaches along the dimly lit corridor, striding towards us. A distant but authoritative flick of his wrist gestures us to enter the room. He stops to talk to Mr Sheenan at the open door and then follows us into the gloomy room. My curiosity is aroused. What were they talking about? Why is the headmaster taking us for this lesson? Maybe in the staffroom, Mr Sheenan has related to the headmaster just what a dreadful class we are. I expect the headmaster has picked up on Mr Sheenan's desperation and simply wants to witness 1B for himself. Good luck with that! The usual despondency enfolds me as I enter.

This 'fifth form common room' no longer adheres to its name but now serves more as a meeting room for large gatherings or an overflow canteen. There is no formal layout of desks. Refectory-style long tables and high stacks of plastic moulded, thin metal-legged chairs line one of the walls. Ripped long dark curtains conceal the ceiling to floor windows and a third wall is made up of wood-panelled folded screens which now, pulled shut, conceal the once used food serving metal surfaces at the other end of the kitchen away from the main hall. Everything around me is so brown. Dreary and dark, dingy December.

The headmaster gives another commanding wave of his hand,

"Bring over some chairs." The ambiance up until now had been subdued, confusion about the change of classroom, but his directive unleashes the opportunity for some of the boys to take back control of their situation. A noisy eruption begins with chairs being reached down from the top of the stacks, passed from hand to hand, metal legs dragged, screeching across the wooden floor.

"Pick up the chairs for goodness sake." barks the seemingly already exasperated headmaster (welcome to 1B, I silently muse), "and quickly, come on now, make a semi-circle over here, in front of me."

Doesn't the headmaster realise that we are still too unprepared for this sort of informal gathering? We don't know each other well enough. Up until now, we have mostly been confined day in, day out, to our familiar classroom, tables and chairs in unchangeable positions. We are not yet experienced enough in the fluid social mobility expected from us. A ragged zig-zagged line appears facing the headmaster. Looking nothing like a semi-circle, far too many gaps between groups of chairs huddled together. Established primary school friends form small, enclosed clusters. Julie though, hopefully, places her chair behind the 'Village Girl' group. Mary follows her. Others, like me, sit by themselves. The headmaster surveys the scattered seating arrangement facing him but wisely makes no comment.

I concentrate on his talking. This is going to be an English lesson he is taking with us as our teacher today, (It's good for the clarification. You never quite know what the lesson will be with this bizarre conglomeration of so many subjects entitled *humanities*!), and most importantly *'he is here because he intends to spend a bit of time with each of the new first year forms in his school. Get to know all of us…..'*. An impossible task I cynically decide and what is the point if the staff then choose to ignore us all as individuals anyway? Get to know every one of the 210 pupils in this first comprehensive intake! Does he think we believe him when he says that? I must ask my primary school music friends if he has, indeed, taken their classes for an English lesson too. Did he give them the same speech, or is the headmaster, in fact, just relieving an extremely exasperated Mr Sheenan from an hour with 1B!

Apparently, he is going to read out loud a poem to us for which *'we must sit quietly and listen to very carefully'*. Yet again, I feel I am back in a primary school classroom environment. And then, *'we will have a class discussion on our thoughts and understanding of the poem'*. I'm disappointed. Such a shame the normal world is hidden from me by the heavy closed curtains. Nothing for me to look out at, no distractions to transport me from this claustrophobic dingy room.

The headmaster reads out the poem. It's about a cowboy riding out alone into the desert. The usual sniggering begins from certain boys. Did they hear a suggestive sexual innuendo? I certainly didn't, but now I've realised that this forced show of bravado and amusement is simply to hide the frustration and anger at not being able to understand the material being presented. It happens SO often now in 1B lessons. Some boys in my form cannot read or write. Of course, it is never mentioned but their inability to understand subject material, read texts, comprehend written tasks inevitably results in an immediate side-tracking display of disruptive derision.

"Right then, 1B," the headmaster regards us, "who wants to start off the discussion and tell me what they think about this poem."

'Briefcase Boy' immediately puts up his hand and begins to talk. He had enjoyed the description of the cowboy. He felt there had been powerful words to describe the heat of the desert. I notice other boys are fidgeting in their plastic chairs impatient to have their turn at talking, anticipating their moment of importance and acceptance. The headmaster is nodding animatedly. He must feel this discussion is going well. The lesser able in the class are obviously being stimulated.

It was expected by Government Education Advisors that academic levels of pupils in the lower ability groups would be boosted by the self-esteem and respect afforded to their inclusion in mixed ability classes. It was predicted that the brighter pupils would *'pull them up'* and therefore open them up to better social and employment opportunities over the coming years. The goal of the comprehensive education reform would be achieved.

As usual during class discussions, hardly any 1B girls are bothering to participate or show interest. I notice 'Blonde Hair' girl is lost in a trance of some complicated re-plaiting of her long tresses. Lorraine and Michelle are comparing the shades of their fingernail varnish. Julie and Mary are leaning forward on their chairs to peer at something one of the 'Village Girl' group is holding in her hand. Big-breasted Linda is blatantly adjusting the shoulder strap of her bra. Desperately hoping, I suspect, that all 1B are aware she is sufficiently well enough developed to have to wear one.

I have no intention of putting up my hand and becoming involved in a discussion for this particular lesson or any others, as my twice-yearly report would invariably point out:

'.........written work is of a consistently high standard, but she is much too reluctant to involve herself in class discussion......'
'.......excellent standard of work．More participation in oral work would be helpful to the class........'
'.........has done some excellent work this year. I would like to see her take more part in class discussions....'

The headmaster is asking a question,
"Does anyone know the meaning of the word 'zenith' which appeared in the poem?" Around me, only blank stares or shaking of heads. I know the meaning of the word. I pencil it into crosswords, code puzzles, use it in my own story writing. I had been amused to create my own cryptic crossword clue using the word: *Reached the zenith, but annoyed we hear! (6),* but I'm certainly not going to admit to knowing the definition of the word now in front of the rest of my form.
Suddenly the headmaster is pointing at me. "You there!" Does he mean me? Surely, he knows my name! I see him and his family regularly at all the school's concerts and plays and the town's music events.
"Yes, you there, do you know the meaning of the word zenith?" His finger remains outstretched directed towards me.
I'm shocked, intimidated and <u>very</u>, <u>very</u> cross. How dare he single me out in front of the class! I've just spent the last three months at his school coping with the painful realisation that since our arrival in the first form we are seemingly not going to be treated as individuals. Annoyingly, it seems the staff can only perceive us as anonymous mixed ability classes. It has been particularly distressing for me to deal with this deliberate non-identification when it is quite obvious that some teachers are actually perfectly aware of our academic capabilities and other talents. I think the headmaster has just proved my theory. Why on earth would he suddenly select me to answer his question when I was sitting silently, not drawing attention to myself, trying desperately to fit in as part of form 1B? He must be perfectly aware of my aptitude and was just attempting to goad a reaction out of me.

I felt the word zenith had been used in the poem to cleverly depict several meanings. The most obvious being that the sun was at its highest point overhead providing the time context of the middle of the day. The sun would be at its strongest causing the cowboy most discomfort. Why had he chosen to go into the desert at that particular time? Choosing the word zenith hinted to the reader that with the sun overhead there would not be much shadow. Did this make the cowboy feel more alone, give him a loss of self-identity? Was this the cowboy's deliberate last trip? What about the horse? What was his allegorical position in the poem?
The finger continues to point at me. The headmaster is waiting for my answer. I nibble on my lower lip. What shall I do? Do I admit to knowing the definition or do I lie? My intimidation wins and I mumble the correct answer. The headmaster narrows his eyes and gives me a long quizzical gaze, "Very good, but why didn't you put your hand up to answer?" I don't know what to say in reply, my face is burning, my heart thumping. Fortunately, it must have been a rhetorical question, he has mercifully turned away, distracted, flicking through his notes. Thank goodness the attention has moved away from me."
"Right, pay attention class. For the remainder of the lesson, there's a few minutes left, I want you to get into groups." Oh no! The dreaded phrase of *'getting into groups'*. Not a skill 1B has remotely accomplished yet. Pupil-chosen groups will simply involve primary school friends rushing to stand or sit together, invariably of similar academic ability and social level. Teacher-chosen groups will be unlikely to succeed during these first few raw months of mixed ability teaching. Still the incapability

to coalesce, swap ideas or listen. Head down, on the pretence of sorting through my satchel, I ignore the scraping chairs and moving bodies around me. Mercifully the end of lesson bell pierces the air.

Just as I am shuffling through the door, I hear my name being called. It's the headmaster's voice. Just as I had already suspected, of course he knows my name! Why though, this wretched unfathomable pretence that during form lessons in this first year of comprehensive education experiment we cannot be treated as individuals? Only three months at this school and already this is causing me much anguished confusion.

"Would I mind staying behind for a few moments?" He wants to have a word with me. Am I going to get into trouble, be admonished for non-participation during his lesson? I stand anxiously by the common room swing doors, the last of the class push past me. I hope I won't be late for the next lesson. Heaven forbid I will have to walk late into the next classroom. Everyone will look at me. I won't know where to sit, the girls will giggle. The headmaster takes his time to shuffle his papers, (*Hurry up, I want to shout at him*!), keeps one sheet in his hand, clips shut his briefcase and approaches,

"Thank you for waiting. I've been meaning to catch up with you for a while. I've got something to propose to you. I'm sure you know about our nine lessons and carols service." Was that a question or a statement? Of course, I know about the traditional church service held in the wide four-aisled town church on the last morning of term. Is the headmaster acknowledging then, that he is completely aware who I am, that I have musical sisters who have played in the orchestra, sung in the choir? He continues,

"Well then, you will know that it is a tradition for a first-year pupil to stand up in the pulpit and read the sixth lesson. The Luke chapter two passage? We've selected a few pupils who might be able to do this, and your name is on the list. I'm sure you'd like to give it a go."

I tune out of his talking for a moment. I'm wondering about the *'we'* he has just mentioned. Who are the *'we'* that have selected and identified possible first year intake pupils who might be intelligent enough to read coherently and confidently a biblical passage in front of the entire school and parents in a packed church? Is this the same teaching staff who refuse to recognise that some of us might, indeed, have a high academic ability but leave us, inexplicably, to sit in boredom during mixed ability lessons. Does this *'we'* consist of teachers who acutely know what we are capable of, but won't look us in the eye, expecting us to accept uncomplainingly their whole class punishments? The *'we'* who discuss our potential behind the staff room closed doors but continue to hand us banal worksheets in the classrooms?

Oh, this is SO hard to cope with. One minute recognised for who I really am, what I am capable of, the next minute totally unrecognised and ignored. Nothing has prepared my twelve-year-old self to deal with such conflicting and complex emotions.

The headmaster hands me the sheet of paper in his hand, completely unaware of my inner turmoil. "Jolly good then, have a practise of this and we'll hear the six of you in my study in a couple of days. Decide who we think will be the best one to do it". He sweeps past me, and I look down at the typed sheet:

'And it came to pass in those days, that there went out a decree from Caesar Augustus, that all the world should be taxed.....'

I'm feeling a bit nauseous, overwhelmed by the thoughts flooding through me. At last, I've been recognised, appreciated for who I really am, selected to do something special and yet, the next lesson I go to this afternoon, tomorrow, next week, it will be no different at all. I will just be back to being a member of strange form 1B. The headmaster's request is something secret that I won't discuss with anyone, but I will try for it. The excitement of being selected and the anticipation of performing in front of the whole school, for once, overrides my perpetual scepticism.

The usual childhood nostalgic build up to Christmas was beginning. Every afternoon when I arrived back from school my mother would be playing her King's College choir Christmas carol LP. Somewhat definitely it would seem, but never questioned by me, using 'unnecessary' electricity. Edward Heath's television addresses to the country informing Britain that we were *'facing a grave emergency due to the oil crisis, the miner's dispute and problems with the economy'* apparently falling on deaf ears at my house. My mother would never sacrifice her pleasure of having classical music always playing around the house. Even for a struggling Conservative government!

I had the school Christmas concert to prepare for. Always much anticipated by the grammar school music pupils in the years above me. I would be performing on stage with the junior choir and had a composition accepted in the lower school 'compose your own Christmas carol' competition. I would be leading the cello section for the lower school orchestra pieces. My sister Catherine would be involved in the upper school music performances. Away from the school there would be the county youth orchestra end of term concert to perform in as well as being part of an informal ensemble playing Christmas music in our local parish church.

As it happened, I didn't do the reading in the church on that last day of term, Friday 21st December 1973. Two of us first form girls had apparently been shortlisted by the headmaster and the incognito first-form teachers. Called to his study, the headmaster hummed and hawed somewhat embarrassed in front of us and said we were both excellent readers and performers and he couldn't choose between us. Thinking quickly that it would probably be for the best if I didn't make a spectacle of myself in front of form 1B, I suggested that Christine *'did the reading, I didn't mind at all...'* Christine immediately responded in the same fashion saying, magnanimously that I should do the reading. Therefore, the headmaster resorted to tossing a coin. I lost.

<u>On my report after the first term at my secondary school.   December 1973</u>

She is a pleasant, lively and enthusiastic member of the form who is working with a will and making excellent progress. She has a very enquiring mind and asks some very searching questions.
She participates very successfully in many school activities.
She has very good potential and <u>should do very well in this school.</u>

      Mr Bradshaw

Chapter Twelve

1973 ended with Slade singing Merry Xmas Everybody. The song hung around the pop charts for the New Year period and on into January. I doubt anyone else in my comprehensive intake had analysed the melody line, had noted the way Noddy Holder, during the last line of the chorus, separated the word *begun* into three syllables, raising the last syllable by a whole tone so the song finished with a major chord, a Picardy third.

January 1974 was a bleak month for the country trying to get to grips with the three-day working week and oil rationing. Television finished earlier at 10.30pm to conserve electricity, not that I would ever have been allowed to still be up at that time to be watching the last programmes. I listened incredulously to the conversations in my form room discussing the programmes watched at this late time. The television in my house wasn't turned on much. My mother watched a few favourite programmes which she had diligently highlighted in pen in the Radio Times: *Dad's Army, the Waltons, The Good Old Days.* Most evenings my father would sit at the dining room table writing notes for future speeches at scientific conferences or working on his stamp and coin collections. My mother would be sat by herself in the lounge engrossed in her crocheting and knitting. Catherine and I would be ensconced in our individual bedrooms spending the dreary winter evenings in solitude, curtains pulled shut, doing homework (mine didn't take too long, minimal answers) and music instrument practise. Absolutely no question of me bargaining a later bedtime with my parents. It was set at 9pm although I was allowed to read for a while.

Sunday evenings, I always enjoyed lying in bed listening to Alan Keith's *Your Hundred Best Tunes* floating up from the radio downstairs. An hour of classical music pure pleasure, obliterating the confusing thoughts about having to walk back into the school buildings Monday morning and begin another week of trying to fit in to form 1B.

A four-page typed bulletin was sent home with every pupil during January. It informed the parents that the school was receiving reduced oil supplies, *'providing the oil was delivered on time, it would not be necessary to close the school for the time being. If, however, circumstances changed…..'* Other paragraphs were much more upbeat, full of success and praise for everything happening at the school. The recent Christmas concert had maintained the usual high standard of music performance with *'over 200 pupils taking part.'* The six years of grammar school pupils above me were obviously doing a good job of keeping up the school's reputation for excellence in music and performing arts but I was chuffed that my entry for the lower school carol writing competition (years 1 to 3) had won first prize.

The reason for this self-congratulatory bulletin might have had something to do with appeasing the parents who were hearing and reading the murmurings amongst education critics and in the press about the current state of education in the country. Edward Heath's government was in difficulty and disintegrating. Panic measures at the end of 1973 had included a sudden £200 million cut to the education budget. Maybe the reason why the plans for the large indoor swimming pool on our school's premises had been dropped? The building now just an oversized echoing sports hall.

On the 21st of December 1973, the Times Education Supplement had declared that Britain's education system faced one of the grimmest years in living memory. It was all very sad, commented the local authority journal 'Education', because 1973 had begun *'full of promise for education'*. Edward Heath's assurances that his government were determined to do all in their power to give the education service the resources necessary had been exposed as an unachievable promise. Difficult times for my local education authority to smooth over the transition and maintain the acceptance and cooperation of all the parents during this first year of education reform in their county. Surely this uplifting, exhilarating bulletin would successfully quell any rumblings about problems and shortcomings currently occurring in the school.

I, however, was furious about this bulletin. A piece of writing I had submitted for an English essay classroom exercise had been included, printed without my knowledge, no permission asked. I should have felt so proud, instead I felt utterly let down by the staff and headmaster. How dare they print my personal writing in a school publication going out to all the parents without consulting me! I couldn't believe it when I spotted it. My cheeks burned and the blood thumped so loudly through my ears I was temporarily deaf to my surroundings. How betrayed I felt. Here I was, desperately trying to *'fit in'*, be part of mixed ability 1B, a nonentity. Not someone who was different and talented, a first-year pupil whose writing got printed in the school magazine.

The three examples of first form writing chosen to appear in that January bulletin were obviously from already identified top ability pupils. One of the other two essays selected had even been written by my music friend Jane! What was the school thinking of? Surely a mistake to choose pieces of writing produced by two pupils coming from one of the previous main feeder primary schools to the former grammar school. Hardly a true representation of the entire 210 experimental mixed ability first form pupils. How many parents would be taken in by this blatant pretence of: *'No need for worry over newspaper reports, read these examples of first year comprehensive pupil's English compositions. Grammar school standards are being maintained.'*

Not only had attention been drawn to my work by the teaching staff who were quite content to daily not acknowledge my academic ability and ignore my presence in their classrooms, worse was the revelation of my unsophisticated immature writing style based entirely on literary styles to which I was accustomed. I had written sentences such as:

'I had a thrill of excitement as I opened my eyes that morning in the dimly lit bedroom.......,' or *'as we talked our breath curled into smoky spirals in the frosty air'.* So embarrassingly infantile.

For many days after the distribution of that school bulletin, I was tormented by fellow form members especially 'No Bag Boy' and his little gang of followers, Kevin, John and Matthew. Boys sidled up to me and leeringly asked about *'my thrill of excitement'*. Even Julie egged on by the 'Village Girl' group felt obliged to giggle and sneer whenever I passed. It was an awful time. How I hated the school for doing this to me. My friend Jane had written a much more factual essay. She informed me she wasn't bothered by anyone at all.

The only relief I could find from this unwanted attention was when I escaped from the 1B form room and immersed myself in all the musical activities taking place during the lunchtime breaks. The junior choir, junior orchestra, quartet rehearsals and dance clubs. Then I could at least revert to being my normal self, surrounded by like-minded music lovers and instrument players, but how enviously I watched the second and third former grammar school pupils arrive at these rehearsals. So uninhibited in their friendship groups united by their musical talents, arms linked together, laughing and vibrant. An existence I was currently being denied.

When it was announced that the senior school (years 4-6) would be performing the musical 'Toad of Toad Hall' and needed first formers to act as animals, I was one of the first to put my name down. Another opportunity to be involved in a performing arts project with the older grammar school pupils. I couldn't wait to be absorbed in the ambiance of professionalism and be included in their high standards of performance. I would also be reunited with my former primary school friends, most of them girls from my housing estate, Jane, Helen, Jenny, Sarah, Judith, Sally and Katherine. They, too, had all chosen to be involved in the show. In fact, most of us mischievous stoats, weasels and ferrets had attended the town's feeder primary schools. After-school rehearsals and even some weekend ones meant that we could faithfully attend, simply arriving on foot. The reliance on school bus weekday schedules meant that pupils from the surrounding villages were denied the opportunity to fully partake in these extra curriculum activities. A gulf was already opening in the school's first unprecedented large comprehensive intake between the pupils who came from houses in the town and the pupils who came from the outlying villages, the new additional catchment areas. I wonder if this third unintentional division of the year group, not by academic ability or social status, but simply by location had been foreseen.

Robin Pedley was a university lecturer in education in the 1950s. His theories and advice on comprehensive education had received an enthusiastic following during the years of planning and transition under the former Labour Government's education secretary Anthony Crosland.

Pedley's vision for the new big successful comprehensive schools was that they would be the central feature of a *'happy, vigorous local community'*. He predicted united neighbourhoods would follow their children being educated firstly in their primary schools and then moving upwards together into secondary education. This secondary school would be the focus of the social and educational life of the community in which it was situated.

I could see this wasn't going to happen at my secondary school for the foreseeable future. The town's established social boundaries, now splintered by the reorganisation into new secondary school catchment areas, had become obliterated. The attempt to amalgamate new feeder primary schools, unchartered housing estates, unfamiliar villages in one large intake created too much social diversification, too many disconnected localities. Not much chance yet of a *'community spirit'* in these raw, experimental first years.

At the end of January my mother and I were planning to spend an evening sitting in the small but atmospheric Elizabethan-style theatre hidden away in what remained of the town's medieval abbey buildings. Singers and instrumentalists from the senior school were performing Henry Purcell's opera Dido and Aeneas. Catherine was playing violin in the chamber orchestra. I was already familiar with the aria 'When I am laid in earth' sung by Dido and had studied the Baroque use of ground bass. I was looking forward to listening to the opera in its entirety.
Arriving at the little building we began to climb the steep steps along the side wall searching for our reserved seat numbers. Suddenly Mr Digby, the grammar school music teacher bounded up behind us. He was the director of the production and would be conducting the orchestra and singers from the keyboard. He was in his usual flustered state, arms wildly flapping around.
"Ah, there you are", he announced. Well, yes, here we are! I didn't think we were late, still quite a few empty seats and I hadn't realised he would be specifically watching out for the arrival of my mother and me. We hadn't anticipated a personal welcome!
Mr Digby turns to address my mother. "Can I borrow your daughter please. You won't mind sitting by yourself?" No time for her to reply, he pulls on my arm, and I descend the precipitous stairs behind him at an alarming rate. What on earth is going on? We come to a halt beside the ornately decorated harpsichord nestled in the orchestra pit underneath the front of the stage. "I've been let down by my page-turner tonight. I've been waiting for you to arrive. I know you can do it, just sit beside me here and follow the music carefully. Turn the page quickly but keep looking at me as well, to make sure I have nodded to let you know I am ready for you to turn over. Sometimes the singers get it in their head to do an infuriating ritenuto!" He laughs conspiratorially with me. "Jolly good then!". My orders given, no time to say anything in reply, Mr Digby pushes me down onto the rickety wooden chair next to the more robust harpsichord stool and disappears off, climbing up onto the stage to sort out a more pressing theatrical problem.
The instrumentalists begin shuffling into the orchestra pit, settling into their places, arranging sheet music onto metal stands. Catherine walks by with her violin, spots me sitting obediently by the harpsichord, raises her eyebrows in surprise but gives me a big grin. I turn back around to scan the now darkened auditorium trying to find my mother, hoping she will be alright sitting by herself. We connect eyes and she gives a discreet low wave to let me know she has understood the impromptu situation. Then she gives me a quick wink. One of her special winks that I always receive when she is sitting in the audience, and I am up on stage about to perform. I'm not really performing tonight but I suppose my responsibility of following the music score, correctly turning the pages for Mr Digby as he plays the keyboard was quite an important role. I suddenly spot him waving frantically at me from the side of the stage as he attempts to attach his black bowtie around his neck.
"Quickly, give the instruments an A". I know immediately he wants me to tap the A key repeatedly so the chamber orchestra players can tune their instruments. I do as he asks and smile around at the senior school musicians looking expectantly at me, appreciating my help.
I'm in seventh heaven. Here I am, a first form pupil, accepted and integrated into the music world of senior grammar school pupils, respected, recognised and acknowledged. An evening of utter bliss which will inevitably be shattered at 9 o'clock tomorrow morning when I must re-enter the farcical, illogical, anonymous realm of the comprehensive education reform mixed ability classroom.

Chapter Thirteen

On the evening of 7th February, I sat with my parents in front of the television in the living room to watch Edward Heath address the nation.
"Who governs Britain?" he asked and announced a general election would be held on the 28th. Just three days before, on 4th February, the result of the miners' ballot showed eighty-one per cent in favour of a strike.
Harold Wilson, the leader of the opposition, began Labour's campaign by announcing the theme he would repeat over the next nineteen days. *'This election is not about the miners, not about the militants, not about the power of the unions'*, he said. *'It is about the disastrous failure of three and half years of Conservative Government which has turned Britain from the path to prosperity to the road to ruin.'* The polls expected a Labour defeat, but the result was a hung parliament. Labour gained seats but not enough for an overall majority. Heath sought a coalition with the Liberals under Jeremy Thorpe, but the two parties failed to come up with an agreement, Wilson became Prime Minister for a second time. He was to call another General Election held later in the year in October which gave him the desired Labour majority.
I could tell my parents were shocked when the Conservative party wasn't conclusively returned to power and that *'that wretched uncouth Wilson'* (my mother's words, taken in by his desired projected persona of a beer-drinking, pipe-smoking 'man of the people') was again going to be Prime Minister. The newly appointed Secretary of State for Education and Science, Reginald Prentice, wasted no time in announcing that Margaret Thatcher's attempt at stemming the tide of comprehensive reorganisation, her circular 10/70, would immediately be withdrawn and replaced by a new education directive; Circular 4/74. Entitled *'The organisation of Secondary Education'* this latest Labour circular reiterated the government's intention of developing a fully comprehensive system of secondary education and ending selection at eleven plus or at any other stage. Local Education Authorities should resubmit plans for comprehensivisation if there had previously been no reform.
Circular 4/74 also discussed the issue of the once held belief that comprehensive schools and the intakes should be large to incorporate the vast spectrum of mixed ability pupils from any one catchment area. This remodelled Labour government document stated: *'It is not essential for a comprehensive school to be of a very great size. There is no single ideal size for a comprehensive school. Experience has shown that some large schools work well but equally some authorities, teachers and parents prefer smaller schools...'* Was this a nod at the increasing criticism in the media that inexperienced teachers were unable to control or teach large unruly classes, resulting in a perceived decline in education standards throughout the country?
Big intakes, small intakes, large classes, smaller classes, Conservative principles, Labour visions. Nine years of continual government education reform ideas and experimental implication. Here we go again, I felt. Another government, different directives, new policies, and yet the secondary school guinea pigs remain helplessly trapped, always the silent pawns manipulated around the board in these political games.

The weeks of the Spring and early summer pass slowly by.
In humanities, during the wretched whole class teaching lessons (no chance of form 1B being allowed back to obvious individualised learning after the fiasco with those coloured work cards!) we learnt about Hercules and his twelve labours. Obtaining the girdle of Hippolyta was somewhat glossed over and, with all the regular disciplinary disruptions, there was no time left for getting the cattle of Geryon, the apples of Hesperides or capturing Cerberus. The lessons were tedious and puerile. I did a lot of colouring in of my margins and, after the recent betrayal of having my English writing printed in the school bulletin without my consent, made sure I made little or no effort in anything I produced or handed in. I did a lot of gazing out of the window and over a period of a week or so became enthralled watching a female blackbird feed her two fledglings as they flitted

inexpertly, immature wings flapping, between the branches. I played around with anagrams in my head and scribbled potential cryptic crossword clues in my rough book whilst Mr Sheenan's lessons droned on insignificantly in the background. Bald brick was an anagram of blackbird. All the letters of *watch the birdy* could be arranged into *thirty chew bad*☐...Now there was a crossword clue to be worked on!

Form 1B boys had loved the Hercules's stories of fighting, blood and death. A curriculum success on engaging the attention of mixed ability eleven- and twelve-year-old boys in this first experimental year. However, there wasn't much enthusiasm from the girls. Hardly the subject material to engage their interest. What they yearned for were the teenage love stories, the questionnaires entitled 'Who do you fancy?' and the pop group pull-out posters supplied in their weekly magazines, Jackie, Pink and Mirabelle. As Tracy so succinctly replied to Mr Sheenan after being reprimanded for not paying attention,

"Well, Sir, it's just all a load of bullshit really, innit? This old Greek crap don't interest us at all."

I practised for and passed another music exam; my mother was pleased. I became more and more silent, never talking about my days at school. The gulf between home life and school life grew ever wider.

Then it was announced that the lower school, years 1 to 3, would be putting on a play towards the end of the summer term. It was going to be Alice in Wonderland. I was so excited, a theatrical production involving working with the two grammar school years above me. Being back in the company of girls I knew from Saturday morning music school, school orchestra, the town's musical events. This was something I could do, perform on stage and be artistic. Goodness, I even wanted the part of Alice. After all, I had been one of only a handful of girls deemed capable of reading aloud, expressing emotion, yet maintaining a certain sangfroid, in front of a packed church for that Christmas service.

My audition went well, I read well, I acted, I sang perfectly in tune, I portrayed the right emotions. The O level English teacher Mrs Matthias nodded her head appreciatively when I had finished, shut her eyes briefly as if envisaging the result, smiled at me and made notes on the papers in her lap. The cast list appeared on the lower school notice board the next Wednesday morning break. We rushed to gather around. My name didn't appear anywhere. The disappointment engulfed me like slurry seeping through my veins. My body felt heavy, I couldn't move, I wanted to cry. Through watery eyes I watched Mrs Matthias approaching the noticeboard. She spotted me,

"Ah yes, you there." She waves her clipboard at me, peering over the top of her pink-framed glasses, "Excellent audition for Alice but you won't see your name on the cast list. We need you for the little orchestra of course......" and off she sweeps in a flurry of coloured silk scarves and swirling floral skirt.

Such puzzling emotions for a twelve-year-old to deal with. I feel like I have been punched in the stomach, winded and now breathless with disillusionment. There must have been discussion in the staffroom about me. Mrs Mathias has been informed that I cannot act on stage in her theatre production because they need me to perform the incidental music in the orchestra. The teachers (and the headmaster) how can they do this to me? They recognise me but refuse to recognise me. They talk about me, they know who I am, what I am capable of, one minute I am acknowledged but the next minute I will be ignored. How can I possibly cope with such painful disesteem? Do they not realise that my confusion and anger will only intensify into a swelling crescendo of petulance and then hatred for the way I am being treated?

The end of the summer term approached. Friday July 19th 1974 would be the last day of my first year at this school. I was crossing off the days. A few weeks before, I took home my end of first-year report. For every subject I had **A 1** apart from French. The teacher had awarded me an **A 2** commenting that *'although my work was always excellent and of a very high standard, she was disappointed that I never contributed to class discussions and oral work'*. I knew this French teacher from the town's musical events. Her daughter, Verity, played the violin in the county youth orchestra, was in my theory of music class at Saturday morning music school and, quite often, we were asked to rehearse together and then perform as part of a string quartet or string trio in school concerts, or for more intimate chamber music evenings entertaining visiting governors.

Verity's mother would rarely acknowledge me in her classroom at the secondary school. This was always hurtful, but sadly, now expected. Very often she would simply spend the entire French lesson coping with discipline issues, visibly exasperated and frustrated by the frequent interruptions. Of course, Verity's mother must recognise my face from music events, concerts, watched me play in small instrumental groups with her daughter. She would know that I came from a primary school that had offered its junior pupils several years of basic French lessons. She would know my capabilities; hence, I presume, the provocative grade **2** mark for effort.

But why should I bother to *'contribute'*? Be responsive and attentive, draw attention to myself when around me most of the class are being disruptive and disrespectful with no desire to learn a foreign lesson. I am simply too angry at my forced situation to rise above my immature selfishness and be cooperative and helpful to the French teacher.

My mother scanned critically through my grades, the teacher's comments, her right forefinger stopping to tap on the paper at the remark for the French lessons.
"This French **A 2** is somewhat disappointing. I think it's best if we hide this whole report from your father."

Chapter Fourteen

It has been decided that a Summer Show is going to take place. This will be an evening performance featuring acts by *'PUPILS IN ONLY THE FIRST YEAR'* the headmaster informs us, totally over-exaggerating as if we are still in primary school. He continues, "This is very *EXCITING NEWS ISN'T IT? LETTERS* will be sent home and he wants *ALL OUR PARENTS* to come and see what we have *BEEN UP TO!*"

"What a fuckin' waste of time that will be." mutters 'No Bag Boy' derisively scratching his scrotal area. He grins around at the rest of 1B clustered in groups nearby. No longer standing in the orderly rows initially created as we filed into the main hall for this first form assembly only five minutes ago. Two of his gang followers standing beside him snigger and try to imitate his cocky stance. It is surprising that 'No Bag Boy' has even deigned to appear in a morning assembly. Normally he arrives late, having missed registration, simply strutting unapologetically into the first lesson of the morning. The teachers no longer bother to comment.

'Village Girl' group aren't paying any attention to the headmaster, talking amongst themselves behind hands placed in front of their mouths. I look around at 'Briefcase Boy'. Head down as usual, he is studying his shoes. Julie and Mary stand together in front of me. I notice their jaws are synchronised in chewing illicit gum. Julie turns towards Mary and attempts a pink bubble which immediately explodes across her lips. They giggle. 'Blonde Hair' girl stands gazing up at the ceiling sucking on the end of one of her perfect plaits. The headmaster is still talking…

"This will be a *WONDERFUL OPPORTUNITY* to continue the tradition of showcasing all the music activities, the lunchtime clubs, the sort of event that always take place in this school". He concludes with an enthusiastic involuntary clap of his hands. *'So, if anyone has any hidden talents and would like to perform, they must tell their form teacher. He is really looking forward to listening to the choir, watching the lunchtime clubs perform….'*

I gaze at all the first formers around me. Most are not even bothering to listen to the headmaster and why should they? The majority have no interest in music activities or attending lunchtime clubs that take place in their secondary school. After ten months of this first comprehensive year, there were only six of us who attend the rehearsals of the lower school orchestra, being of a sufficiently confident music standard to play orchestral music. Mary had never yet shown up at a rehearsal. I don't mention it to her though, whenever we get the rare opportunity to be alone together. So only a mere 2% of us standing in the hall this July morning would be able to contribute to a Summer Show playing a musical instrument and, anyway, the *'lower school'* orchestra with its two years of grammar school pupils would not even be included in this proposed First Year only show! Twelve of us in this first year attended two different lunchtime dance clubs. Just under 6% of everyone standing around me. Did they really think there would be enough pupils interested in performing in this *'summer show'*? Surely it will just be the same few pupils appearing on the stage all the time……

Oh No! I suddenly realise where this is all heading, the usual nauseous abdominal cramp begin, and my breakfast of Golden Nuggets curdles ominously in my stomach. I will need to find a toilet very soon to relieve the now regular bouts of anxiety-induced diarrhoea. This is not going to go well for me and the rage at being put in such an unavoidable and uncontrollable position immediately surges though my body. How dare they do this to me! How dare they ignore me academically in every single classroom and then expect me to be an example of how successful the extra curricula opportunities, offered by the school during this experimental reform year, have been. Can no one else see what an absolute unsubtle publicity exercise this whole First Year summer show is intended to be? Will the spectators be taken in by what they see? Will this really be a true representation of the school's first year comprehensive pupil intake, I doubt it!

How long will this blinkered pretence of maintaining the standards of a grammar school continue☐and why does it seem that I am always involved! My English essay appearing in the school bulletin as an example of first year writing, being asked to read a bible passage during the traditional church service, performing on stage in music events during a summer show that will only feature a tiny percentage of the intake. Hardly an accurate portrayal of the mixed ability year group I am surrounded by.

I'll take part of course. I have no choice with the expectations from home and school. Trapped again. It certainly clears up a few recent unexplained and puzzling events. Why there was a sudden need to create a *'first year'* choir requiring separate rehearsals from the already established junior choir made up of pupils from years 1-3. I turned up for this new choir with some of my primary school music friends, but it was a somewhat unenthusiastic, straggly group of twenty-three girls and two boys who attempted to perfect the required songs. It explained, too, why Mr Digby had searched three of us girls out during a Saturday music school morning. We gathered around him, myself, my friend Jane from dream form 1F and Verity, the violin-playing, French teacher's daughter from 1S. Would we start rehearsing the first movement of a Haydn string trio for a summer concert? How special we had felt to be selected by him. We worked hard together. How betrayed I feel now, hoodwinked. Three first formers …how stupid had I been!

I glance around the hall wondering if I can catch the eyes of Jane and Verity but can see neither in the grey shuffling crowd. Surely, they will now also have realised the real reason for our sudden projection into the elite O level world of musical ability recognition.

On arriving at the school, the previous September, I had quickly realised that taking part in a lunchtime club or activity benefited me in three ways. I could participate unhindered in all things music based. I could meet up with my like-minded primary school friends and I could get an early lunch ticket! This much-prized pink bit of paper was the passport to sail directly into the dining hall. As soon as the lunchtime bell went, no need to queue, just hand this coveted ticket to someone at the door and you were in, first sitting. Fresh hot food, choice of all the daily dishes before the favourites ran out. Clean chairs and tables untouched by spillages, stains and putrid dishcloths.

How I hated that lunchtime queuing process, the bumping and jostling. The calling out *'save a place for me'*. The humiliation of the girl bullies pushing in ahead of you. The expectancy that you would submissively let them in ahead of you, I always did. Being in such proximity to some of the more degenerate, obnoxious first form boys was a daunting experience. Fumbling on the backs of the girls standing in front of them in the unsupervised queue and attempting to undo their bras had to be expected, was apparently amusing and could sort of be coped with. The day the boy behind me surreptitiously slipped his hand up my skirt, between my legs and into my pants was the moment I decided I was no longer going to stand in the lunch queue. A frightening experience which I didn't report to any adult. I was just relieved that it hadn't been a 'jam-rag' day.

Monday lunchtime was the Scottish Country Dancing Club with the gentle Mrs McGregor. Apparently, she was the *'remedial'* teacher. A word I had not heard before arriving at the secondary school.
It hadn't gone unnoticed by me that quite regularly over the last two terms some members of my class who struggled with reading and writing now disappeared for certain lessons and then re-joined us for others. It was all executed very discreetly but I think we realised that they went for 'help' with Mrs McGregor. It was exasperating for me to know that the teaching staff were willing to recognise a remedial category which they separated out for special treatment and yet there was no similar acknowledgment that pupils at the other end of the academic ability spectrum might appreciate getting special attention too. Could we not be 'separated' out as well and offered lessons of a more demanding standard? It was disappointing and hurtful to watch the less able being continually cosseted, catered for and encouraged, whilst the more able of us were simply left to cope, sit uncomplaining and compliant through boring lessons. How could I not be resentful?   Only specific categories of educational needs could be recognised in this experimental first year of comprehensive reform. Wasn't this at odds with the Labour Government's 1966 election manifest promoting the education reorganisation. In a section headed *'Educational Opportunities for all'* it had declared the intention to:
'ensure that those with special abilities have the opportunity to develop them to the full….'

Mrs McGregor was the quintessential genteel Scottish lady. Always unflustered, talking quietly in her soft accent. Her white hair immaculately permed into smooth waves. I thought she looked like the Queen. Invariably dressed in pale blue and grey arran sweaters and dog-toothed thick woollen skirts or swinging kilts, everything about her permeated utter unflappableness and calm but, my goodness, she could certainly get her *knaps* and *taes* up when demonstrating a new dance step during our Scottish Country dancing practices.
Throughout the spring and summer terms her club settled down to the same eight lassies turning up every week. It was fun to learn the steps, hear new rhythms, new chord sequences, whirling around in our figures of eight, laughing, back to being in physical contact with friends from my primary school. I doubt we ever reached Ceilidh standard, but we enjoyed pointing our toes, holding up our *heids* and learning the basics of the Gay Gordon and Strip the Willow.
Tuesday lunchtime was Morris Dancing club taken by my form teacher Mr Bradshaw himself. None of us were ever brave enough to ask him quite how it was he knew the choreography. We assumed it must be something he did in his spare time. Maybe, indeed, he was an actual member of the Morris dancing troupe which had a strong tradition and following in the town. Was Mr Bradshaw in fact a closet hankie waver and leg bell jingler? We would never know; he was never spotted in any photos of the troupe in the local press. We became ten loyal members, the majority being also Scottish Country dancers and we certainly saw a different side to Mr Bradshaw. More relaxed, humorous and 'human'!
As well as the obvious reasons of filling a lonely lunchtime and the early lunch ticket, Morris dancing was actually great fun. We laughed so much during the lunchtime practises. A whole new genre of

music for me to soak up too, the unexplored repertoire and technique of the accordion and concertina as well as the guttural, non-vibrato violin playing. A few weeks before the proposed bizarre summer show, Mr Bradshaw announced that, for this special occasion, we would be issued with white hankies to wave accordingly. It took us several minutes to control our laughter. Amusing to imagine a Mrs Bradshaw (if indeed there was one) sorting through and ironing all her husband's handkerchiefs.

The lunchtime clubs had been a perfect opportunity to seek out like-minded first formers. Our intake had been big and being so confined, so isolated, in our form rooms for most of each school day hadn't presented many opportunities to mix. A good example was violinist Verity who I recognised from Saturday morning music school and county youth orchestra weekly evening rehearsals. I had spotted her occasionally when her form passed mine, two grey reptilian columns slithering past each other in dimly lit corridors. But never any opportunity to stop and talk. In the Tuesday lunchtime Morris dancing club, I found two compatriots. Both had been at my primary school, but I hadn't been friends with either of them then and, since September, separated out into our seven first forms there would have been little chance of getting to know them anyway. Choosing to be in this lunchtime club had bought us together.

Emma had a genuine love and inbuilt intuition for Morris dancing. Her family were steeped in the town's dance tradition and male members of her family were presently in the troupe. It was exhilarating to be partnered with her, she was lithe and responsive, guiding me when I forgot the steps. Often, though, I was partnered with Big Pete. His persistence in attending the club was a mystery but he faithfully turned up every week. His large, lumbering body was more suited to being a tighthead prop on a rugby field than executing the quirky, gambolling dance steps, his hands would be wet and slippery, his face puce, but he seemed to enjoy it and we laughed together. Maybe he was just there for the early lunch ticket! Tuesday's menu was very often tomato soup and two cheese-topped scones. My favourite school lunch, maybe his too!

Wednesday lunchtime was junior orchestra (years 1-3) rehearsal and Thursday lunchtime was junior choir. How much I looked forward to these opportunities to be back amongst grammar school musicians. The last lunchtime was now, of course, taken up with rehearsals for the hastily formed first year choir. I observed the attendance and enthusiasm dwindle each week and felt acute distress watching the disappointed Miss Gilbert attempt to conduct us in preparation for performing.

It had been during a class music lesson that Miss Gilbert had first asked if anyone was interested in participating in this new 'first form' choir. No one had put up their hands. I was thrown into an immediate quandary. Do I put up my hand or not? Fortunately, I was saved by Miss Gilbert waving her Biro at me.

"You there, I'll put your name down of course….". Her eyes scan the classroom for Mary, obviously remembering their previous stilted conversation. "Mary, there you are. I'll put your name down as well, you playing the clarinet and everything. Are you still playing by the way?" 'Blonde Hair' girl and Linda giggle together and decide to put up their hands. Neither of them will ever appear at a rehearsal. Too much interaction between Miss Gilbert and certain girls in the music room, the boys of 1B can no longer accept their exclusion, and now need to regain dominance. They predictably begin to shout out to disrupt the lesson. Miss Gilbert risks a panicked glance at her wristwatch, how much more of this lesson left?

After only two weeks of standing together at the lunchtime choir rehearsal, Mary no longer turns up. I grab a quick opportunity whilst walking to the sports hall to ask her why she has stopped coming, "Oh God, I'm not wasting any more time with that rubbishy choir" she snaps back at me and runs on ahead to join up with Julie and the 'Village Girl' group.

One week before the summer show I notice Miss Gilbert approaching Mary at the end of a class music lesson. She had been sitting next to Julie and Michelle in a row of tables on the other side of the room.

"Just a minute, Mary," calls Miss Gilbert, "I've noticed you've stopped coming to choir. Any particular reason?"   Ah, this I want to hear. I slow down the process of returning the pens into my cloth pencil case. Each one suddenly takes an age to slot back in.

"Well Miss…" I can see from Mary's face that the reply has been practised, she doesn't seem as timid as usual and the defiant folding of the arms across her chest mirrors perfectly the permanent confrontational stance of the 'Village Girl' group.

"……the thing is, Miss, I come to school on the bus and there's no way me Dad is gonna drive me back into school for some stupid evening concert thingy here. My family just aren't interested in any of that sort of stuff, so there's no point me taking part in anything, alright?"

Miss Gilbert has no reply to that, speechless, her mouth is stuck in a small open circle. Mary had provided two different reasons, one to me, one to Miss Gilbert, for abandoning a school extra curriculum activity but they originate from the same problem. The impossibility to achieve Robin Pedley's vision of modern comprehensive schools reflecting united neighbourhood communities. The pupils in my year come from too many diverse social backgrounds, too many previously separated catchment areas, too many different established community enclaves whether local or further afield.

It's the last week of the summer term, the evening of the summer show arrives. It will be a busy evening for me. I am in every activity appearing on the stage. My resentment at being tricked into performing in this spectacle has been side-lined by the bustle and excitement of all the preparation. I will be lost in my familiar world of music. Singing as part of the choir, doing a little vocal solo, responding to Miss Gilbert's silent commands, interpreting her required tempo and dynamics. Demonstrating the choreography of Scottish country dancing and Morris dancing, waving white hankies! Playing our prepared string trio movement then a short cello solo…… nothing else will matter to me for the duration of the evening's performance. The hall isn't packed, quite a few empty rows of plastic chairs. My mother is sat in the front row. I doubt she will be able to give me a wink every time I appear on the stage. People around her will think she is suffering from Tourette's syndrome or struggling with something stuck in her eye. I'm sure she will save her special *'I am proud of you, just find it difficult to demonstrate'* wink when she catches my eye as I am poised, waiting to start the string trio performance, watching Jane and Verity, so that we coordinate our bows beginning the first crotchet phrase.

The evening is drawing to a finish. I am flushed, tired but exhilarated. The choir is now parading back on, in single file, to sing the two concluding songs. I walk out across the stage to take my position in the front row of the sopranos. A young girl's voice carries out across the expectant hush of the hall, "Look Dad, it's that bloody girl on again. She's been in everything…."

Second Year

Chapter Fifteen

At least the start of my second year heralds the return of recognisable lessons. We are now doing the separate subjects of English, History, Geography and Science. Different classrooms, different teachers, a welcome breath of fresh air after the claustrophobic conditions of our first year.
I presume that after one year of what seemed to me, (and did anyone else feel the same way?), a demeaning experiment to combine so many subjects under the umbrella term 'humanities', we are now considered mature enough to be able to grasp the distinguishing elements of English language, English literature, History, Geography, Science and Religious Studies. Will we still be allowed to colour in our margins though? That certainly kept me entertained during many hours of frustrating boredom! Maybe we will now be informed it is too babyish after all. After the first year of comprehensive reform at the school the teaching staff must surely be reassessing the successes, the failures of this education experiment. Will any consideration now be given to the particular academic needs of individual pupils? Being deliberately ignored and unrecognised during mixed ability whole class teaching had been, for me, the most hurtful and incomprehensible element of my entire first year.
The headmaster must think that we are now responsible enough to walk around the school buildings, negotiate the corridors without confrontation, cope with new classrooms and be receptive to different teachers. It certainly feels like the teaching staff have been handling us with kid gloves for our first year, unsure of how we would fit into their established grammar school dynamics. Now the second mixed ability intake has already arrived at the school. This time, next year, the comprehensive pupils will outnumber the entire secondary selected school years above them. An unstoppable tsunami of education reform.

So, now we are going to be walking around the school to change classrooms. I can well imagine a few of the more rebellious pupils might be tempted to become momentarily disorientated by all this heady second year responsibility and '*accidentally*' be unable to locate a room when necessary. Maybe they won't even bother to turn up. Who could possibly have imagined that I would soon be in this maverick category too, deliberately skiving lessons!
No doubt we will now have some lessons in the uninspiring grey terrapins which had been hastily erected around the edges of the playing field during 1972 and 1973 in preparation for the increased intake numbers. I had always thought the word terrapin referred to a reptile like a turtle but Mr Bradshaw, during our first day tour of the school, informed us that this is the term used for these ugly prefabricated buildings. They were the current 'quick fix' for schools needing to expand classroom space in a hurry. When Mr Bradshaw said terrapin, I immediately juggled the letters around in my head. The word would make a good crossword anagram clue: '*trip near and around this temporary building*'!
'No Bag Boy' has reappeared for this second year still with no school bag, exercise books or pencil case. The uncommunicative rocking back and forth on his chair boy is back installed at his table, shoulders hunched, fists clenched. He participates and contributes so little. Is he really going to be included as part of our form for another whole year?
I was pleased to see Mary again after the six-week summer holiday. We smiled shyly at each other as she sidled into the chair at the adjoining table. I notice she has completely changed her image. The middle parting and long low bunches have gone, her hair is cut short falling onto her shoulders in the popular layered style. She is wearing a longer swirling midi skirt, tan-coloured tights and high-wedged lace up shoes. She now looks like most of the other girls in the classroom. I've started this second year in the same hand-me-down grey skirt above my knees, long white socks and flat Clarks buckle shoes. Is Mary's fashion makeover a silent signal to let me know she anticipates rekindling her friendship with Julie, I must expect to be excluded and abandoned. Julie made her allegiance to the 'Village Girl' group very obvious. On this first day of term, she refused to acknowledge me. Same first-floor room, where one year ago I had saved her the table next to mine, this morning she entered, tossed her head affectedly to get attention, did a little wave to everyone (but probably not

me) and headed straight towards the girls sitting on the opposite side of the room. Message acutely and painfully understood.

'Briefcase Boy' is back, head down, looking at no one. His hair longer and greasier, still content to be by himself at the front of the classroom sitting under the wooden- framed roller blackboard.

At the beginning of the summer holidays, the last week of July 1974, I was so happy to be spending uninterrupted time back with some music friends. Jane and Verity from school orchestra rehearsals and our first-year string trio, Patricia and Alicia from Saturday morning music school who now both attended the public girl's school. For five wonderful days we were reunited by a summer music school for the town's newly created *'Junior Orchestra'*. I profited from days of rehearsals totally immersed with like-minded young musicians. It was as if the nightmare of being so incomprehensibly segregated at my secondary school from my friends and fellow music players for the last ten months had not really happened. Between scheduled orchestra rehearsals and string sectional practises we ate our packed lunches together sitting by the river, we laughed and talked nonstop together, we went swimming in the open-air pool in *'specially arranged for the orchestra'* evening sessions. Then we performed on stage a concert of Handel, Mozart and Bartok to parents and townspeople. I spotted several teachers from the school, even the headmaster's shiny bald head, sitting in the audience watching and listening to our playing. I assume the teachers and headmaster would have noticed my presence in the orchestra leading the cello section. I even had a small solo passage to play.

Apart from those few special music-filled days, I saw absolutely no one from my school year group for the rest of the entire school summer break. How strange the difference that one year can make. Before starting at our secondary school, we had always been a tight knit housing estate community. Children walking together every morning to the primary school, playing together outside every evening, the assumption that similar social acceptances and behaviour patterns of neighbourhoods would continue to bond the families as the teenagers progressed together through their local secondary schools. Sadly, this Robin Pedley vision disintegrated rapidly once we started in our comprehensive first year. Too big intakes forced the children from my housing estate to be disseminated between seven separate forms and for that first year we had been kept particularly isolated in our designated form classrooms. I felt the separation acutely, placed in a form with absolutely no one else from my housing estate. Predictably we grew apart. The Labour Government ideal of comprehensive schools embracing the communities in which they are situated and capturing the social characteristics of each catchment area seemingly impossible to achieve.

As we manoeuvre our way around the school from lesson to lesson with the exciting freedom of being second year pupils, through the dingy corridors, dodging groups of serious grey-clad grammar school pupils, I take great delight in looking through the glass-panelled top half of the classroom doors incarcerating the new wide-eyed first form intake.

"Get your crayons ready, suckers". I want to shout at them. "There will be a lot of colouring in to do!"

Our history lessons are scheduled to take place in one of the best classrooms of the entire school in my opinion. I do my theory of music lessons in this classroom every Saturday morning, so I already know and love it. The room is at the front of the school building just to the right of the bricked library wall forming a bridge over the three-step approach to the main entrance. Extensive windows face east, looking out over the small car park, the bus stop, across the main road and then onto my leafy housing estate.

Always so much light flooding into the room and so much to watch out of the window. Red double-decker buses pull up every thirty minutes on their journey north to the city. The people sitting on the upper deck can look in. I always look out at them, our eyes being roughly on the same level. Across on the other side of the main road mature trees hang over the remaining stone walls marking the boundaries of the grounds of the demolished manor house. Looking directly ahead out of the window a wide, tree-lined avenue, perpendicular to my history classroom disappears off into the distance. My primary school just visible at the far end. On one side of this road is my housing estate, on the other side is the council estate made up of older, smaller dark-bricked houses.

Mrs Parker, the dumpy, red-faced, lady who twice weekly 'did' for my mother lived on this estate in the downstairs flat of a house split into two. Occasionally I would accompany my mother when she visited Mrs Parker, taking with us surplus garden produce, a jar of homemade marmalade, a little Christmas extra that was supposedly from Catherine and me although I had no idea what was inside. It wasn't really something I enjoyed doing and I never felt at ease in the dark, poky kitchen. My mother and I would stand awkwardly in the cramped space beside the brown smeared enamel sink. There was only one chair at the tiny Formica table. I would be trying hard not to wrinkle my nose at unrecognisable strange smells. Always a relief when it was time to leave her house and cross back over the road into our familiar housing estate.

Children from Mrs Parker's estate attended my primary school of course. Bordering the buildings and playground it was one of the housing estates in the school's catchment area. We would have mingled naively in the classrooms unaware of social class difference although I was guilty of staring incomprehensibly at the yellow stains on their knitted grey pullovers and cardigans caused by being dried too close to an open fire. We had central heating, radiators in most rooms. In February 1972, I watched Blue Peter incredulous as John Noakes and Peter Purves explained how to keep Granny warm in bed during the power cuts: *'Pull apart your parent's newspaper'* they were saying *'and lay the sheets of paper between the blankets'* ……How little knowledge I had of living standards beyond my own sheltered existence!

Even though we sat together in the primary classrooms, we would invariably separate out at home time. Friendship groups still being mostly governed by the social divisions created by housing estate boundaries. Two different estates, two different social classes divided by one road. Before 1973, the vast majority of one housing estate moved upwards to the grammar school, the other estate's children expected to go to the secondary modern. A microcosm of the selected education system Harold Wilson's government was trying so hard to end.

The town where I lived, one of the oldest established settlements in England appeared outwardly to be the quintessential traditional southern England community with thriving small successful businesses. During the 1960's there had been one renowned public school for boys, one public school for girls, one grammar school and two secondary moderns catering for all the different education standards. The decision in the 1950's to build the new government scientific base nearby changed the dynamics of the town's population. Scientists with their families were drawn to live around the town in newly created housing estates. This created an unusual concentration of intelligent, aspirational families in small enclaves. The town became a much more multi-layered society with profoundly disconnected neighbourhoods. Now there were these new 'scientist' areas, there were the older large opulent houses in the north of the town on the way to the city. There were the recent and ongoing developments of modern smaller houses and bungalows and the existing council estates, a minority of which, unfortunately, had the reputation of harbouring social and behavioural problems. Just mentioning certain street names in the southwest of the town and an incident of trouble in the same breath would inevitably trigger an *'and what else do you expect?'* raising of the eyebrows.

Adhering to the 1971 decision of its local Education Authority to embrace education reform, this multi-layered town was now destined to be divided up equally between the three new proposed comprehensive schools. Since the early 1960s, certain areas of the town had always been the breeding ground for certain schools. Was it incredible enthusiasm for the move towards comprehensive education or unblinkered naivety by everyone involved to think that reorganising the town into new and unchartered catchment areas, far away from its well-established education and social formulae, would be a benefit for all?

Already recorded in County Education Committee meeting minutes was that the allocation of pupils to each comprehensive school had to adhere to three points:

- The wish of the parent
- The maintenance of a balanced spread of ability in the annual intake
- The convenience of access for each pupil

Under the new dispensation each of the three schools in my town were given a swathe of middle-class pupils as well as its share of adolescents from the more deprived areas. Included too was a proportion of youngsters with the undetermined quantities of academic ability from the surrounding villages.

And so, the carving up of the town began.

Did the LEA committee spend hours huddled over maps of the town and surrounding land, black pens in their hands, earmarking streets, circling around entire housing estates, crisscrossing areas with arrows? One can imagine the conversations:

"So, my fellow committee members, are we agreed then that this school gets this housing estate?"
"If the bus is passing through that village, it might just as well pick up the pupils from this one too. Good Lord! Let's keep the transport costs down."
"What are the academic statistics for these three streets?"
"Do we need more pupils of higher ability in that particular school?"

A magnificent game of unexplored logistics in which surely, the individuality and particular needs of each pupil was sadly neglected.

Eighteen months before I had even started my secondary education, eighteen months before the county began the comprehensive system experiment, it was recorded in the Local Education Committee meeting minutes of February 1972 that the headmasters of the three soon-to-be equal secondary schools in the town were already expressing concern that *'adherence to the agreed catchment areas might produce an imbalance of numbers and ability between the three schools'*. Had the realisation of the difficulty confronting them, dividing equally the vast academic and social diversities of the town, suddenly become manifest?

It was also recorded in committee meeting minutes that the headmaster of the present grammar school (my proposed secondary school) was unhappy about his school's allocation of two villages, wondering if their expected intake contained a significant proportion of pupils in the lesser academic ability group. He petitioned to the LEA committee that a particular area of middle-class houses on an affluent estate heading out north towards the city might be *'**better served**'* by his school rather than going to one of the two other previously secondary modern schools. A cryptic, but not undecipherable request!

His request was granted and the catchment areas for each school were again redefined and reorganised, still with little consideration for the individual pupils trapped in this education and social experiment.

Chapter Sixteen

Phew! I've managed to get my usual table next to the window in the history classroom. It's been a month now since we've been having these lessons in my favourite room. A blustery October morning, scudding white clouds race across the sky and brown horse chestnut leaves swirl in pirouettes up to the first-floor windows and then back down into the car park directly below.

Today we are plodding on with the Middle Ages, the villages with their villeins, the manor houses with their Barons, the use of the land and the feudal system. I know I have already studied all this at primary school and also read about this period of English History in my RJ Unstead book *Looking at History* which I chose, vastly guided by my mother, in the town's book shop, using the expected birthday book token from my godmother.

I doubt there will be anything new to learn in this lesson, at least I have the window to gaze out of, watching the outside world and normal understandable life. The half-hourly red double decker bus should soon be pulling up into the bus stop. I see there are two ladies waiting in the shelter. I doubt, too, that any of my 2B form mates will show the slightest interest in the 1300s. With the now usual disillusionment of my situation, I anticipate another wasted hour ahead of me.

I open my rough book and begin the regular ritual of drawing a circle. It seems I begin every academic lesson this same way now. I meticulously divide the circle into twelve segments. This is my strategy for coping with the boredom of each lesson. I colour in one segment every five minutes. It helps to relieve the monotony, gets me through the ennui of each hour.

Mrs Jacobi is walking around the classroom, placing worksheets in front of us on our tables. As she passes me her head is already turned away, her attention drawn to a commotion at the back of the room. It could only be 'No Bag Boy' who is informing the rest of us in his loud voice, that he has no interest in history whatsofuckin'ever.

"I ain't answering no dumb questions Miss. Who cares if summat happened in the bloody past. I ain't interested. They're all dead an' all anyway."

I have an interest in history though, I care, I want to learn more. So why am I inexplicably in this same classroom as 'No Bag Boy'? He grins around the room waiting for the usual appreciative sniggers from his band of followers. Some of the girls giggle too. I study Mrs Jacobi carefully. How will she deal with this situation. Outwardly she seems in control, but I notice a purple flush appearing on her neck and a slight tightening of her jaw. An *'old school'* (my mother's expression) O level teacher, more accustomed to being faced with curious responsive pupils. I feel sympathy for her. Can she keep control of this mixed ability class?

It was to be noted in a later HM Inspectors report that many schools reorganising to the comprehensive system had *'often underestimated the complexity and difficulty of successful mixed ability teaching'* and that as a future recommendation *'far greater care needed to be taken in the preparation, organisation of activities and evaluation of work for a mixed ability class'*. Mrs Jacobi would have been trained to push pupils to the highest standards using a basis of differential projects for individual learning. Now she was being required to adapt to whole class teaching methods pitched at average or slightly below average ability level. How could this possibly work? One worksheet for thirty pupils! Surely it was quite impossible for one ability level worksheet to cater for everyone, particularly not providing enough stimulation for the pupils at the top end of the aptitude range. I've already experienced a year of these frustrating worksheets but have never once been asked my opinion. I must presume the school just aren't interested in what we actually feel about being part of this experiment.

Mrs Jacobi is leaning low over 'No Bag Boy' muttering close to his face and I notice submissive nodding of heads amongst the boys seated in a row. A Biro is passed along the line and handed to 'No Bag Boy' so he could, in theory, write something on his worksheet. Mrs Jacobi's many years of teaching experience and authoritative demeanour have calmed the situation and she has taken back control of the lesson. I am so relieved. I just couldn't bear yet another wasted infuriating hour of whole class punishment always watching in silence, feeling trapped, my intestines writhing with indignation. Mrs Jacobi strides back up to the front of the classroom purposefully looking straight ahead to avoid the venomous stare of 'No Bag Boy' drilling into her back. This time, Mrs Jacobi has successfully quashed the disruptive infantile outburst. He is, after all, just a cheeky-faced, curly-haired, pre-testosterone twelve-year-old but how threatening and troublesome will he become once adolescent hormones flood through his body. The thought fills me with despair. How many more miserable years lay ahead of me, forced to be part of this education reform programme? How am I going to cope? How am I going to survive?

Finally, we are to begin the ubiquitous worksheet, but before we start Mrs Jacobi is telling the class that she will be helping anyone who is struggling with the answers. "All we need to do is put up our hands", she informs us with a patient smile, "although, of course, all the answers can be found by looking at the picture..."

The worksheet today is entitled 'Village life in the Middle Ages'. The picture filling the top half of the paper depicts a wattle and daub hut with a thatched roof. Smoke is curling up out of a hole in the straw. Two villeins stand outside. One is about to swing a crudely made axe above his head to chop some wood. The other holds a scythe. Typically, a female sits at the entrance of the hut holding a baby. If the picture supposedly provides all the answers, I won't bother to elaborate further on the agriculture methods of that period. I won't bother to include the word fallow and show that I have done extra background reading. What is the point?

I note with a wry smile that the artist has etched a brace of pheasants hanging upside-down at the doorway. Another bird from the same game family Gallimorphae, the ptarmigan, had been the answer to 1 down in the Times crossword that very morning which I had pencilled in before heading off to school. Always had to be in pencil of course, heaven forbid my father picked up the paper after his evening meal to 'finish off the crossword,' always disappearing into the downstairs toilet, and found an incorrect answer indelibly written in the grid. I had puzzled over the anagram, juggling around the letters of A TRAMPING until I realised the whole clue was hinting at a Scottish Highland bird. I stumbled a bit on the spelling of ptarmigan, not a word in most people's vocabulary, my departure for school somewhat delayed whilst I flicked through my parent's Birds of Britain guidebook.

I finish my answer to the final question deliberately pressing down hard with my pen on the last full stop with a grand flourish to emphasise my completion of the worksheet. Nothing too demanding. I simply looked at the picture and answered the questions with perversely short, banal sentences. No request for me to include any extra known historical facts. No opportunity for me to show what I was capable of. No window for the teacher to recognise if I had a particular penchant for history and would be a pupil to be encouraged further.

I look across at the clock circle drawn in my rough book. I haven't even blocked in the first five-minute segment. Ah, that's awkward! Now what am I going to do for the next fifty-five minutes of this lesson? Maybe Mrs Jacobi has a second, harder, more detailed worksheet for me to begin. I put up my hand, Mrs Jacobi approaches.

"Yes, do you need help?"

"I've finished."

"What! the whole worksheet, are you sure?" She studies me over the top of her heavy, black-framed glasses. "I expect you have just raced through it to try and be the first to finish. You probably haven't answered the questions properly."

I grit my teeth to control my anger and frustration. "I've finished."

"Hmm, let me see…"

Mrs Jacobi had taught O level History to my sister Rosemary and was currently teaching it to Catherine who was in her fifth-year class. Her husband worked at the same scientific establishment as my father. Several times a year social events bought our families together, an Open Day or cultural events in the town. I was acquainted with Mrs Jacobi from seeing her at the town's musical events. Her daughter one year older than me and in the grammar section of this school attended the same Saturday morning music school as I did, the same county youth orchestra, we played in concerts together. Just a couple of months ago I had seen Mrs Jacobi in the audience for our end of summer music course *'town junior orchestra'* concert, so why, now, was she so purposely not recognising me? Why is she pretending I am simply just another one of the exasperating 2B pupils presently occupying her classroom? Why, oh why, can't she give me the respect I surely deserve and appreciate that I have in fact finished the intended hour lesson plan in five minutes?

This continual and deliberate non recognition of my individual abilities, my potential, my achievements during mixed ability class lessons are getting too much for me to bear. The resentment and rage I feel against this school simmer silently but dangerously inside me. The most difficult and hurtful emotion for me to deal with has been the realisation that most of the staff are aware of my capabilities. This has been proven to me time and time again when I am approached individually, separated from my form.

Maybe I am just too sensitive, too temperamental! I must assume that the other sixty or so of us already recognised since our September 1973 first year entry as being in the top 25% academic ability range (this would be admitted a couple of years later) aren't suffering as I am. Are they content to sit through disappointing lessons? How on earth are they coping?

Since the start of our second year, we are now being taught quite frequently by grammar school teachers. Surely, they recognise pupils with a particular aptitude in their subjects. Does the teaching staff really not notice or have the time to care, how unstimulated, unsatisfied and frustrated some of the higher achievers are becoming in these experimental mixed ability classes?

Jump forward two years and I would still be sitting in this same classroom, following in both my sister's footsteps, preparing for O level History with Mrs Jacobi. I did love the subject of history but my choice of pursuing the lesson might have had something to do with being able to gaze out of the window of my favourite classroom!

In one of my Fourth-Year end of term reports, Mrs Jacobi had written that I had an *'imperious'* manner in her lessons. Her choice of word stung me and confused my parents. I didn't have the confidence to query her remark and my mother had long since abandoned going into the parent-teacher evenings. What was the point of discussing her daughter's education in a school system that according to the daily newspapers and BBC news had *'gone to the dogs'*. I was simply expected to attend school every day and, uncomplainingly, work towards passing an impressive number of O levels.

Imperious was not a word that described me at all! Many words would have been far more apt, soon to be used frequently by other teachers during my troubled fourth and fifth years: scathing, angry, critical and aloof.

I have to assume that Mrs Jacobi made a spelling mistake in her handwriting on that particular school report, she missed out a V and the word should have been impervious. Now that would have been spot on! I hold my hands up in guilty submission to that definition. That was absolutely me in 1976!

However, her next sentence written in my report got it exactly right.

*'Contributes **nothing whatsoever** in class but always excels in exams. She will achieve a good O level result.'*

Mrs Jacobi is glancing through my answers on the *Village life in the Middle Ages* worksheet. She seems a bit flustered as a commotion begins to rise in a crescendo behind us. A shrill voice is complaining, a chair being scraped across the floor.

"Yes, well, very good, that all seems fine to me. Why don't you go off to the library for the rest of the lesson. Find a book to look at or something. Just come back in and collect your things when the bell goes." She turns away, waving her hand at me to leave. That's it? I've been dismissed from the classroom. I'm speechless, in disbelief and feeling very let down. Normally unruly children get sent out of classrooms, why then, do I feel I am being punished for answering the worksheet so quickly? Am I now being castigated for being too clever during her class. How can I not be critical or scathing of what I see happening around me, of what I am forced to be part of!

I've been told to walk away from the rest of form 2B and go off to do something else more intellectually stimulating, work by myself. Separated from the class physically and mentally. What an accurate portent that would be of what was going to happen to me during my next school year, my third year!

Mrs Jacobi is already striding off down the room to deal with the latest disciplinary disruption. Has anyone else even bothered to answer the questions on the wretched worksheet? I no longer care. I get up slowly, push my chair under the table and walk out of the room quietly pulling the door to behind me. I'm panicking, I have a lump in my throat making it hard to swallow and my stomach has begun its usual anxiety-induced contracting cartwheels, I'll need to find an unoccupied toilet block soon. I stand outside the classroom for a while, my heart pounding. I can't just walk around the corridors. Catherine, sitting in a fifth-form lesson, might spot me as I try to slink past her half-windowed classroom door.

The library. Why on earth would I want to go into the library by myself? I certainly haven't got the confidence to do that. I've only been in the library once before during my entire time here. That was during Mr Bradshaw's tour on our very first day. Anyway, there is bound to be a lesson going on in there, as since the reorganisation to big intakes, existing classroom space has been limited and the library is now used as an extra teaching space. If I walk in, approximately sixty eyes will automatically turn to look at me. The library assistant will want to know *'what have I come in for?'*, *'what book am I looking for?'* or *'which teacher has sent me?'*

I suppose I could ask if they have the Times newspaper. I could continue with the crossword. I know 1 across begins with a P! No, no, I can't possibly do that, everyone watching me will think I am a freak. My only options are to hide myself away in girl's toilet cubicle for the remaining lesson time or run out of school. I wasn't intentionally skiving a lesson.... not yet. That would happen soon enough though! I had been ordered out of a classroom being denied the opportunity to gain fifty more minutes' worth of further knowledge.

Chapter Seventeen

Mrs Jacobi must be completely out of her mind! She is going to take 2B out of school for an afternoon on a history trip. Mr Willis, a sport teacher has been roped in to help as a second accompanying teacher. I admire Mrs Jacobi's determination and courage to continue to impart her love of history to her pupils despite the resilience and hostility she often has to put up with during second year lessons. I am really looking forward to the visit to a neighbouring village. Carrying on with the Middle Ages period theme, we are going to be walking around the village looking for examples of cruck-framed wooden structures, half-timbered houses and barns still displaying evidence of the two curved timbers leading up to the roof.

I hope I can somehow try and help make this trip be a success for Mrs Jacobi but as always, I am thrown into a dilemma. On one hand I want her to recognise that I am appreciating the experience, enjoying her effort, time and trouble for the trip out. On the other hand, I will have to appear just as uninterested and unimpressed as the rest of the class in order to be part of form 2B.

Second year and I still haven't found the formula of how I can ever fit into this strange form. It's like X and Y. I'm realising there is no algebraic solution, no possible merging, always destined to be separate entities.

I have already been spotted carrying my cello into the school on certain mornings however hastily I try to run in and dump it in the musical instrument cupboard next to the first-floor music room. Hopefully the separate new music block being built next to the sports hall will soon be completed and should make it easier for me to get in and out of school unnoticed. For the time being I have successfully managed to laugh off, or ignore, the very unoriginal comments about the case containing a machine gun. Thank goodness not many of my year group know exactly what a cello is or where you position it to play it!

With December only a couple of weeks away now, Mr Digby has already approached me (when I was by myself of course). Recognising me and my musical talents can obviously only be done when I am isolated, thank goodness, and definitely not in the classroom environment. He asked me if I will perform a solo in the end of term Christmas concert. It will be another busy music-filled evening and I will revel in being surrounded by the music pupils of the grammar school years. I will be on stage as part of the junior choir, then I have composed a carol to enter in the traditional carol writing competition. As well as performing the cello solo I will also be part of a string quartet. The second half of the concert will be the senior school choir and orchestra performing excerpts from Handel's Messiah. Remembering my previous successful evening, Mr Digby has again asked me if I will be his page-turner, sitting next to him as he conducts from the spinet. I just can't wait for this evening to arrive.

Waiting for the hired coach that gloomy November afternoon of the history trip was tricky. Who do I stand with? There's the usual threesome of Lorraine, Michelle and 'Blonde Hair' girl. Julie is with her new friends the 'Village Girl' group and Mary hovers next to them waiting to be included. Linda has her arm linked through Tracy's; they are wearing matching tartan scarves. Funnily enough, Linda doesn't seem quite so big breasted now, other girls seem to have caught up and have the same size mounds hidden away underneath their grey cardigans. Not me though, not yet.
I'll just stand by myself. 'Briefcase Boy' stands by himself too. I wish I had the confidence to start talking to him, but I can't possibly do that if the other girls are watching me. I open my satchel and pretend to rummage around in it searching for a specific something. Looks like 'Briefcase Boy' is using the same tactics. His head is down over his opened briefcase. I've noticed that this second year has heralded the start of using any bag other than a satchel or briefcase for bringing your books into school every day. The girls opposite me in the car park have a variety of colourful shoulder bags, tote bags and carrier bags. No doubt just the latest rebellious dig by the nonconformist teenagers against the previous grammar school regulations. How on earth am I going to ditch my scratched, shabby, seven-year-old hand-me-down satchel from Rosemary without my mother noticing?
Mrs Jacobi arrives in the car park and takes a rollcall. Halfway through she stops abruptly, a stunned silence. 'No Bag Boy' is not here. In fact, I realise he hasn't been at school for a couple of days now. With the run up to Christmas maybe he has far more important things to do. Off illegally cutting down fir trees somewhere with members of his family? Working on a market stall? I risk a quick glance at Mrs Jacobi. Do I detect a slight, surprised raising of her eyebrows? Other than that, her face remains passively professional, but I wonder if in her head she is secretly rejoicing, *Hallelujah*! This afternoon out with 2B is suddenly going to go far better than she could ever have imagined.

There is no sign of the 'Rocking Boy' either but then Mrs Jacobi, very subtly, hadn't even called out his name. There must have been an agreement that he wouldn't be included on this trip. So many secret decisions going on behind our backs... as if we wouldn't notice or question them!

The coach pulls in with bass rumbling and clouds of black exhaust smoke. The 'Village Girl' group push forward to get on first and bag the back seat. "Move the fuck up, girls" screeches Tracy, and she and Linda squeeze along the back seat too. Tracy sits on Linda's lap. Julie and Mary sit together just in front of them. I quickly lower myself into a seat halfway down the coach. Before the engine has even restarted, the excited girls behind me are swaying side to side and tunelessly singing Bay City Roller songs. I remain facing the front and don't join in with the shouted '*shalalas*' or the '*all of me loves all of you*'. Last year I would have turned around and shammed that I was singing. Now I don't bother. The pretence of being like one of them has finished.
Twenty minutes to reach the village, we stumble down the coach steps passing Mrs Jacobi who hands out worksheets. A trail is to be followed, looking at the buildings, answering questions, making sketches. I stride off by myself preferring to spend this afternoon alone. Already the twilight of late November is beginning to darken the sky, It's cold, grey and damp. I don't have a coat because I refuse to wear the babyish red anorak my mother suggests I put on every morning. No one else ever walks into the school buildings wearing such an unfashionable garment.
The worksheet isn't difficult of course but for once it's interesting and keeps me engaged. I find all the designated houses and barns, follow Mrs Jacobi's trail around the village and do some sketches of the roof and wall wooden frames. I stop to point out a building to Lorraine and Michelle, a barn they hadn't been able to find themselves, but I avoid any other groups standing clustered on the narrow pavements. Heading back to the coach involves crossing the green. I spot five girls standing outside the little bow-windowed shop, too late to change direction! They see me and wave

frantically, beckoning me over. I trudge through the wet grass, my flat shoes already soaked and my feet cold.

I know that none of these girls will have bothered to look at their worksheets. I presume they just want to copy the answers off mine. I'll let them of course, avoid any threatening stares across the classroom or nasty warnings about being beaten up after school. But no, they have something far more menacing to demand of me.

"Wotcha! We're playing a game. You're next. We dare you to go into the shop and nick summat. Don't come out until you have and then you shows it to us. OK?"

A sickening dreads floods through my body and immediately the familiar cramps of anxiety grip my stomach. I suddenly need to empty my bowels. This is terrible, I'm trapped. Tracy leers ominously at me waving a crumpled Curly Wurly wrapper in front of my face. "Go on, your turn innit."

I have never stolen anything in all my life, but I know I can't get out of this. I enter the shop, the bell above the door jangling, making me jump. My heart is thumping *precipitoso*. I attempt an innocent smile at the elderly lady sat behind the counter at the far end of the low-ceilinged, dimly lit shop. "Good afternoon", I call out. She looks up briefly from the magazine she is engrossed in, regards me with indifference and turns back to her reading. I edge towards the confectionery counter, feeling nauseous and shaky, and pretend to be studying the choice, my hand hovering low over the chocolate bars. I don't know the techniques for shoplifting but at least playing the piano has given me the ability to move my hands independently. I do some elaborate exaggerated gestures with my left hand, rippling arpeggios over various packets, whilst my right hand curls around a small tube of Rolos which I then try to push up my sleeve; the cylinder gets stuck on my watch strap, in desperation I just close my palm around what is still left in view and rush out of the shop *prestissimo*.

The gang of girls encircle me as I emerge.

"Wot you got then?" I show them the brown tube. "Bloody hell, she's fuckin' done it!" One of the 'Village Girl' group thumps me painfully on the upper arm. "Hand 'em over then."

I don't want their praise or admiration. I am never going to eat a single chewy Rolo ever again.

I wish I could end this chapter by saying that I never stole again, but I did. Just five months later in April of the following year 1975 I stole a fifty-pence coin from my mother's purse so I could go to Woolworths and buy myself my first ever pop music single. It was Abba's *I do, I do, I do, I do, I do*.

Chapter Eighteen

This second year I have started to learn the second foreign language of German. Everyone took home a form offering the choice of beginning German, Russian or Chinese, the languages currently being taught in the grammar school years. *'Put a tick next to German'*, my mother had told me *'Catherine already does it and you don't want to be wasting your time with those communist languages'*. I was quite attracted to the intricate artwork involved in writing the Chinese characters but German it was obviously going to be for me! This is the first time that pupils from the seven forms have mingled for a lesson if you don't count the remedial classes, but I think they were only ever small groups at any one time, not thirty pupils in a room together. This will also be the first time that I will be in a classroom, separated from the majority of 2B.

Finally, a recognition that some of the pupils might appreciate being further challenged, expand their learning experiences, move along at a quicker pace. Not everyone wanted to take up the offer of a second foreign language of course. For some, having to learn French was already traumatic and tortuous enough, maybe even a waste of time, so, having to study another language would be unimaginable! I wonder then, what these pupils will study during the extra lessons now scheduled into the timetable. Something less challenging perhaps, such as woodwork, cookery or parentcraft?

The best thing ever about taking German is that I am back in a lesson with two of my friends from primary school, Jane and Helen. I couldn't believe it, seeing them approach, as I waited in the queue outside the classroom. They too had opted for German. Big smiles all around, we raced into the room to bag three adjacent tables. So much for us to chat about. So good to be back together for a couple of hours a week. The elderly female teacher claps her hands for silence. She teaches Catherine O level German and sometimes I see her playing viola in the senior school orchestra. She won't acknowledge me of course and by now I wouldn't even expect it! Her grey hair severely pulled back in a low bun, she's always struck me as a bit *'mousy'* and her voice is almost a whisper. We all unconsciously lean forward to hear what she is saying. This will be her first experience at this school of teaching non-selected secondary pupils, but the fact that we have chosen to study a second foreign language definitely shifts the core ethos of the pupils in front of her. In her sotto voce, she mumbles to us that she will expect respect and hard work. Oh dear! She would soon be shocked by my impudence.

I wished we could have had textbooks to take home and then I would have been able to race through the pages soaking up as much as I could at my usual fast pace, but for the moment it seems we are bogged down with filling in worksheet after worksheet of repetitious undemanding tasks. The activities planned for this January morning lesson involve reciting aloud the vocabulary for means of transport: das Auto…..das Flugzeug……das Boot…der Zug…..der Krankenwagon…..Then we are to draw lines on the freshly -xeroxed, strong smelling paper placed in front of us, linking each written German word to the corresponding picture of a vehicle and then, if we've finished before the bell goes, we are, of course, to colour in the illustrations. Not very stimulating. Jane and I have finished quickly and start messing around, mispronouncing the words to each other, making them sound as ridiculous as possible. I'm just shouting out Zug (incorrectly rhyming with tug) louder than I realise as the room falls silent and Miss 'Mousy', Fraulein Farblos, is making a beeline towards my table.
"That's quite enough of your nonsense, young ladies. I won't have you disturbing my class. Take your worksheets with you and learn the words standing outside Miss Roseau's study door".
Miss Roseau is the much-feared strict head of the lower school. Positively *'ancient old school'* in my mother's classification. Chequered tweed suits, polished brown brogues and tortoiseshell framed winged spectacles. I've never yet given her an opportunity to chastise me and funnily enough I quite like and respect her. Exactly the sort of teacher I would have expected to encounter in a grammar school. I've met Miss Roseau often enough at upper school concerts and plays and, whilst standing obediently with my mother and sisters, she has always been most courteous, taking the time to talk to everyone, even me, the youngest family member. Her conversations were always intelligent and thoughtful. Just recently I had discussed with her such diverse topics as playing a stringed instrument, why did Shakespeare choose such a silly name for his donkey and French school exchange visits. She had noticed that our father's name had recently appeared on the back of the Times newspaper when he was a winner of their Saturday Crossword competition. I chipped in that I already tried to do the crossword myself. She nodded her head appreciatively, and smiling, told me she was more a Daily Telegraph crossword person herself!
So, Fraulein Farblos has sent Jane and me out of her lesson. Not the first time I have been banished from a classroom for finishing a designated academic task too quickly! Presumably the purpose of the punishment was hoping that Miss Roseau would come out of her study and question why we were standing there. Jane and I have no intention of complying, we must have just caught Fraulein Farblos on a bad day. We screw up our worksheets and deposit them dismissively in a rubbish bin as we run across the tarmacked recreation area. It's bitterly cold but sunny, the overnight frost still lingers in shaded patches. Jane shows me a secluded spot, a narrow gap, between two terrapins where we stand waiting for the remaining twenty-five minutes of the lesson to pass. We chat non-stop. What a wonderful punishment! How much I have missed daytime conversations like this,

perfectly at ease, immersed in my safe world of classical music. Jane tells me she is preparing for her next violin exam, which pieces she is playing, which scales she has chosen. Scales in a minor key can be played in harmonic or melodic form. For harmonic scales the same eight notes are played on the way up and down. Melodic scales require the sixth and seventh notes to be sharpened on the ascent and reverted to naturals on the descent. This form of the minor scale is more melodious and easier to sing.

Soggy tissues, crumpled chocolate bar wrappers and cigarette ends around my shoes tell me this must be a popular spot for skiving lessons. I'll add it to my list of possible places to hide when I can't face going into a classroom.

It's a shame that the German lessons are not more inspiring for Jane and me. Playing musical instruments means we are unknowingly already immersed in the rudiments of the language. The pieces we learn often have instructions for tempo and rhythm written in German: ein wenig, etwas, bewegt, schnell. Titles of works trip off our tongues without us even registering we are speaking German: Eine Kleine Nachtmusik, die Meistersingers and even the carol, Stille Nacht, which we had sung in its original language at last year's Saturday morning music school Christmas concert.

During the winter months, the afternoons when I arrived back from school, my mother had been playing an LP of Brahm's Ein deutsches Requiem, a German Requiem. The first time I walked through the back door and heard this music I was completely captivated by its beauty. On a leaflet included in the record sleeve was the text. In my W H Smith's exercise book, I copied all the words so that I could sing along. The fourth movement was my favourite: Wie liebich sind deine Wohnunge   How lovely is thy dwelling place.

It would be the beginning of my life-long love for Brahm's music. That fourth movement was written in the key of E flat. The first vocal phrase rising to the upper F, lingering there and then falling gently back down. I couldn't listen often enough to Brahm's beautifully crafted musical phrases. The rises, the poignant aching pauses, the resolutions like liberating releases of breath. The music could make tears fall down my cheeks. Obviously only when I was listening by myself of course. Did music make other girls cry too I wonder? Did lyrics of pop songs emotionally affect them? This was something I could never discuss with anyone.

I expect I was just getting far too hormonal. Weren't some of the books I read full of emotional women frequently bursting into tears, unsure of their feelings, confounded by new reactions. The start of menstruation surely couldn't be far away now. I've spotted wispy hairs appearing around my body in strange places. Little buds of breasts beginning to swell, so painful if knocked by accident, or purposely and clumsily squeezed by annoying boys. My hair's getting far too greasy and washing it every night is not an option, so I resort to puffing on some talcum powder to cover up the lank parting. Hide n'Heal borrowed from Catherine's dressing table inadequately disguises the increasing facial blackheads.

In the classroom I listen intently to the other girl's pop music discussions. The Bay City Rollers were unsurpassable, but please, no one look in my direction and demand which one I like best! David Essex is growing in popularity. Lorraine's older sister is manic about Mud. In Woolworth's I linger to gaze up at the posters, the pop chart board. What single is number one? In WH Smith I read the fronts of the magazines, memorize the names of the more obscure pop groups.

I was now secretly listening to some pop music at home but the songs I liked were invariably never the ones the other girls talked about. I loved John Denver songs and was teaching myself to play his chord sequences on my guitar. I enjoyed the piano playing of Elton John and adored every song that Abba released. My Christmas present from my parents had been a little Sony cassette player. My mother thought I should start recording myself playing my cello pieces and then I could listen back, spot my mistakes and improve my performance. I had other ideas what I might be recording. Now I could hide myself away in my bedroom every Sunday evening with my transistor radio turned down low. Rosemary had let me have her old one when she left home and headed off to teacher training college. A tape slotted in ready, cassette player positioned in front of the radio, all I needed to do

was press *record* and *play* simultaneously during the BBC top 20 countdown to illicitly capture the songs I liked.
Sadly, still such a clandestine activity, pretending I was, in fact, doing my cello practise. If the countdown arrived at a song I didn't want to record I would quickly settle back seated with my cello and loudly run through some scales, both harmonic and melodic of course!
The only time my mother ever even acknowledged that a pop chart existed was when Rosemary had informed her that a piece of music she liked from a television detective series was being played in the '*top ten'*. That was back in 1973 when Simon Park and his orchestra made a surprise entry onto the pop scene with 'Eye level', their theme music to Van der Valk.

Chapter Nineteen

January 1975. I've stopped going to most of the lunchtime clubs. The dancing clubs no longer take place anyway through lack of interest so now I just go to junior choir and junior orchestra. The other three lunchtimes I hurry away from the school buildings as soon as the last morning lesson is bought to an end by the bell. I expect junior orchestra will soon no longer exist either. Hardly any new instrumentalists have arrived at the school. The word 'orchestra' will soon be a misnomer as the numbers of musicians dwindle. It's getting to be more like a string group lamely coupled with a wind band consisting of a few flutes and clarinets and one trumpet. What a mismatched disharmonious sound we must produce. The reputation of musical excellence and proficiency of the former grammar school has definitely begun its diminuendo.
It seems that the whole atmosphere in the school has shifted too. It feels like the initial enthusiasm and efforts being made to embrace the first years of reorganisation have already become jaded. Is it only me that senses the tempers of the teachers are shorter, their patience exploding now at the slightest disruption? We are shouted at more often; I feel there is less tolerance and sorting out disciplinary issues has become a dominating issue taking up large chunks of lesson time. I enter each classroom on tenterhooks, desperate to gauge the atmosphere, the attitude of the teacher. Is the lesson going to pass without event, or more often than not, will there be yet another outburst of impatience, a crisis of comportment? Is it just me being too sensitive, my volatile intestines too susceptible to emotional disturbance? Everyone else in my year group seems to be coping.

Harold Wilson's October 1974 general election win continued dealing with a country in crisis troubled by recession and high inflation. His unpopular proposed cuts in education spending and the emergence of politicians now arguing that teachers should be more accountable highlighted a growing disenchantment with the current education situation. The Labour government's attempt to complete the education reform had now begun to face mounting opposition from industrialists and the media. The initial sympathetic encouragement for the comprehensive education system by the tabloids had completely reversed.
On the 18th of January 1975 the Daily Mail reported that **'*parents throughout the country are becoming increasingly frustrated by the lack of discipline and the low standards of state schools'*.** Just one month later the Daily Mirror would publish that **'*literacy in Britain is marching backwards'*.** According to a report by the National Youth Employment Council many employers felt that young people were now **'*more questioning'*, '*less likely to respect authority'*** and more likely to **'*resent guidance about their appearance.'***
Employers were complaining that schools were failing to prepare pupils for entry into the world of work. They painted a picture of unaccountable teachers teaching an increasingly irrelevant curriculum to bored teenagers who were poorly motivated, illiterate and innumerate. It would still be another whole year before the Times Education Supplement published the damning article by Sir Arnold Weinstock entitled '*I blame the teachers'*.

No wonder then that some of the staff at my school were already becoming dispirited, dragged down by the current rumblings in the media. There certainly did seem to be a constant flow of changing teachers. Quite a few left between my first and second year, I counted five of the elderly grammar school teachers were no longer around...maybe it was genuinely their time to retire! but interestingly, even some newer faces disappeared during the Christmas holiday after only appearing at the school for one term. Recently qualified fresh-faced and excited teachers continually arrive. I cringe when I see their vulnerability. Good luck, I silently mouth to them. You're going to be thrown to the lions! The headmaster and his stoic 'Heads of School Years' remain for the time being. Maybe they hope that their experience and former strict discipline ethics will steady the rocking boat.

I just wish the teaching staff would stop treating us all as an entirety. So, some of them are disappointed and frustrated with the first comprehensive mixed ability intakes? Why can't they recognise that actually, there are some pupils in their classes who are desperate to learn but denied the opportunity! Why is it always the actions of the degenerate youth incorporated in our experimental classrooms that tarnish the experience, the reputation for the rest of us?
Is it really so awful to try and teach us? Some of the country's media makes it seem that way.
It's not my fault though. I didn't want to be part of this Labour Government educational reform programme just as much as maybe some grammar schoolteachers didn't want to teach mixed ability classes, but apparently, we are all in this together. The teachers are being unfairly lambasted for bad results and those of us trapped in this educational reform experiment as silent pupils could perhaps tell a thing or two, but we are never asked.

Since the beginning of this term, Tuesday lunchtimes for me are now the designated hour for my piano lesson. Recently I've changed to a different, more advanced teacher who lives nearby. After a rushed lunch of tomato soup, cheese on Cream Crackers, I set off for the short walk through my housing estate, past the preserved Norman Motte, over the little bridge crossing the stream, my thin leather briefcase of piano music tucked under my arm. Mrs Williams lives in a cul-de-sac on an adjacent, more modern estate. Sitting at her grand piano, I quickly lose myself in my playing. Have I practised enough during the past week. As always, her living-room scents fill my nostrils; spicy pot-pourri, furniture polish and peppermint. Sitting beside me on the long piano stool whenever Mrs Williams turned towards me, I would be engulfed in a cloud of icy mint emanating from her breath. She certainly like sucking on her Polos. What a sheltered life I had led! One Tuesday at the end of February, walking up the garden path to Mrs William's front door, I came face to face with Philip, the pupil before me, as he left the house.
"Good luck in there," he grinned at me, "She's even squiffier than usual!" I must have looked puzzled. He gave me a *'what planet do you come from'* stare.
"Yes, you know, squiffy, drunk, plastered. Don't tell me you didn't realise? Our Mrs Williams simply loves her gin and tonic!" Philip did a tilting drinking glass mime in front of his mouth and chuckled.
 No, I hadn't realised at all. I was far too naive to interpret her regular sorties from the living room into the kitchen as not genuine.... "Just popping into the kitchen dearie, to check on something on the stove, play it through again" or "I'll just nip out and see what my husband Bernard is up to.... carry on working with that left hand phrase". During last week's lesson it had been... "Goodness, is that the cat scratching at the back door, let me go and let him in".
Enjoying my horrified expression, Philip filled me in. He told me to lean back on the piano stool as she disappeared through into the kitchen and I would catch a glimpse of her hand reaching out for the tall, filled glass, poised ready on the edge of the work top. One bit of information I won't be passing on to my mother.
Mrs William's need for the surreptitious swig and then the refills would often prolong my lesson and delay my return to school for the first lesson of the afternoon. It would depend on which particular piece we worked on together for the last minutes of the piano lesson. If it was a slow one, an adagio, I was doomed and resigned myself to being back late. If it was a fast piece of music and the, by now somewhat merry, teacher wasn't paying too much attention, I could speed up a little to the tempo

of presto rather than allegro and race towards the final bars, get the piano lid down, music back in the leather case and be away in time for the school bell. Every time the piano lesson overran, I would invariably have to run back to school to be in time for the start of the first afternoon lesson.

It simply never occurred to me to tell anyone about my piano lessons taking place off the school premises during lunchtime break or the fact that I might be back late. My music life and 2B life were such separated existences. No possibility of the two ever merging. There never seemed to be an opportunity to bring it up. What on earth would I have said? Who would have been interested? It was obvious that most of the teaching staff were far too busy dealing with other problems happening around them. Piano lessons out of the school during the lunch hour. Whatever next! *'We can't be making exceptions for that. No one else in your comprehensive intake is asking for such special treatment!'*
The first few times I arrived back late, the bell having already sounded, the corridors empty, I hid myself away in one of the girl's toilet blocks. I definitely didn't have the confidence to knock on my classroom door, walk in and explain why I was late for the lesson. I sat alone in the cubicle, door locked, until I heard the bell marking the change to the second period of the afternoon. I hadn't enjoyed it, feeling lonely and bewildered, my heart thumping at every door creak, echoing footstep or voice outside in the corridor. I was lucky. No one came in.
The fourth time it happened I wasn't quite so successful with my choice of hiding place. I rushed into the toilets, shut the door quickly behind me and came face to face with four other girls. Two from the 'Village Girl' group and two of their friends, I supposed, from the year below, the first year. They probably all came in on the same school bus.
"Wotcha! What the fuck are you doing here in our bogs?" asks one of the first formers ungainly hoiking herself up to sit on the edge of one of the sinks. What insolence but it wasn't too intimidating. I ignore the question for the moment, move further into the strong disinfectant-smelling space as though I have as much right to be in there, skiving a lesson, as they do! The other first former carries on her swinging, monkey-style, from the metal door frame of a cubicle. For the moment they are all giggling and don't seem too threatening. I hope I can handle this okay. My shop-lifting success last term at least means that the 'Village Girl' group have left me alone.
They look at me expectantly,
"Dunno, just didn't fancy going to me lesson". I shrug my shoulders dismissively, trying desperately to imitate their body language and speech. Instinctively I withhold the real reason, but it's okay, they have accepted my reply. Absurdly I am meant to be sitting in the exact same classroom as two of these girls right now. Somehow, we don't mention it to each other!
"Well, you're a fuckin' secret bitch then ain't you, skivin' lessons an' all like us". I think that's code for I will survive unscathed for the next fifty minutes. They include me in their conversations, it's almost as though we are suddenly friends, fellow conspirators. One of them takes out her make up bag and they face the big mirror, reapplying mascara, eye shadow and lipstick. I watch and feign interest, complimenting them on their over-painted faces. They want to look in my make up bag, see what I've got, do I nick the stuff from Woollies like they do? Make up bag, that's a joke! The bell mercifully sounds, and I rush to the door to escape.
"See ya then", they shout after me as though it had been a regular jolly girls' get-together, but It wasn't an experience I wanted to repeat, so the next time I walked away from Mrs William's porch knowing I would be late back to school for the start of the afternoon lessons I took a detour turning right into the wood and found a fallen tree trunk to sit on.
That tree trunk became my refuge, my hiding place and I spent an awful lot of my next three school years sitting there.

Chapter Twenty

Every morning at eight forty-five, I leave the house for the short walk up to the end of the road, turn left into tree-lined avenue and there is the school facing me, just two hundred metres away. So close in proximity, so far removed from any connection with my home life. I've done this exact same walk for approximately 330 mornings since the 4th of September 1973! Walking from one environment towards the other, the two can never converge. The abyss between home life and school life is now impassable.

I feel like I have split into two personalities. The thirteen-year-old who heads off to the school each day and the same girl who walks back to her home atmosphere each evening. One person trying to fit into vastly incompatible worlds. Classrooms where I have nothing in common with the pupils surrounding me and a home with parents who have no comprehension of modern 1970s life, but really, does the building I'm in make any difference? I've realised I am just the same character wherever I am. A confused and introverted person who says nothing but watches everything. Inwardly distressed and angry but outwardly showing only obedience and compliance. An isolated non-being at both home and school. Do I even have a personality?

The atmosphere and behaviour codes inside my house were definitely more 1950's then even the more recent 1960's. Embracing the current world of the 1970s was unthinkable. My father was unapproachable and emotionally restrained. The only thing we had in common to talk about was working on the clues of The Times crossword every day. My mother was the obedient stay-at-home housewife. She lived in the world of classical music, magazines such as the People's Friend, Woman's Realm and the detective stories of Agatha Christie. Absolutely no opportunities to broach more contemporary, challenging social issues with her. I had never really thought about how she filled her day. Shopping I suppose, cooking, sewing. Every evening at five o'clock she would change into a smarter frock, smear a bit of lipstick across her lips and open the garage door in preparation for her husband's return from work. The evening meal would be ready at precisely half past five and served up on the table as soon as he arrived. I never got to see the last few minutes of Blue Peter. The meals were excruciatingly solemn and formal. Chatting or discussions were not encouraged.

On the evening of my very first day at the school back in 1973 my mother had prompted my father to ask me how my day had passed. Where on earth did I begin? Not that I could ever tell the truth. "Very well, thank you." I replied of course. That was all they wanted to hear. My father then attempted a witty remark asking if the school was now using barbed wire in the corridors to keep the grammar school and comprehensive pupils separate. Catherine laughed, I didn't. It just proved to me how little my parents were prepared to open their eyes to what was actually going on in the schools and how futile it would for me to bother to try and explain. How trapped I was going to become between the incompatibilities of home life and school life.

My parents had such predictable middle-class opinions. These were expected to be unquestioned and accepted however blinkered and prejudiced I was now beginning to realise they were. By the end of my first secondary school year, I was already struggling with the differences, the disconnection, the conflicts between my two, now very separate lives, of home and school. How was I going to manage with being exposed to, and involved in, all the new antagonistic opinions, unfair situations, clashing social attitudes at school and carry on saying nothing at home?

Rarely a Blue Peter programme would appear on television without my mother making some comment about Lesley Judd joining the team of presenters in 1972. *'She was just a dancer for goodness sake!'* or *'What on earth were the BBC thinking of employing someone so unrefined.'* Nothing Lesley Judd could do would ever be good enough for my mother. She wasn't a *'patch on Valerie Singleton'*. The new presenter's hair was a *'mess, her hippy outfits dreadful'* and *'she didn't speak as well as Valerie Singleton......'*

With such bigoted, narrow-minded comments ringing in my ears twice a week what chance was there, what possible opening for me to tell the truth about my days at school. If my mother thought that Lesley Judd was lowering the standards, a bad influence on today's youngsters, then I soon realised that I might as well keep silent about what was going on daily around me, the foul language, the sexual innuendos, the bad behaviour, the negative attitude to learning.
Anyway, I secretly liked Lesley Judd! Just another opinion I kept to myself.

The teachers were noticing my increasing ill-humoured demeanour. My reports now contained comments such as:

English: *Her written work has been of a consistently high standard throughout the year. She tends to remain somewhat aloof from class discussion; a pity, because she could obviously contribute a great deal.*
Ah, the word aloof was going to reappear so many times in various teacher's appraisals of me for the next few years. Detached and sullen or simply 'switching off' to get me through each unbearable day?
The end of term reports showed a continuous vertical line of **A** against every subject for *Grade* achieved but my father was horrified to note a decline in the marks for *Effort*, now mostly **2** or **3**. Art was the only subject in which I was continually awarded an **A 1**. This teacher was obviously the only one still pleased with my effort (but then drawing and painting didn't involve much class interaction!):
Art: *Very promising indeed. Many fifth-year pupils would be pleased to be able to draw as well.'*

The French teacher made a more cryptic comment:

French: She *maintains a good standard. More participation in oral work would be helpful to the class.*
'Helpful to the class'! Whatever did that mean? Was the French teacher subtly trying to hint that, although I had merited an **A**, the highest possible mark for knowledge of the language, my decision not to participate as much as I could was holding back the standard and motivation of the <u>whole class</u>? Of course she was! It was the same French teacher as my first year, Verity's mother. Whilst refusing to recognise me in class (I still practised string trios and quartets with her violinist daughter for goodness sake!) she was well aware of my academic ability, my potential and was therefore disappointed that I didn't help out more in the classroom.
Why should I? Why should I offer anything to the teachers who force me to sit ignored in rowdy, distressing, frustrating lessons? Did the French teacher, and all the others, expect me to put aside my hurt feelings of non-appreciation, my confusion about non-recognition and be prepared to contribute unquestioningly?
I'm not mature enough yet for that. My petulance and indignation continue to cloud my reasoning and ruin my prospective.

Chapter Twenty-One

It has been announced, letters have gone home, that we are all going on a trip. The entire second year is being offered time away from the school. We are going to spend a few days at a castle in Northumberland.
The reaction to this news amongst 2B has been mixed. Are we really ready to spend time thrown together, twenty-four hours of each day; it's considerably more than the usual seven strained and

awkward hours of each normal school day? How will we cope separated from our established home environments, our background social groups?

The boys are already excited. They can't wait to *'have a bloody good time away from this shitty school'*. I wonder if 'No Bag Boy' will be able to find a rucksack or carrier bag to use for his belongings! The 'Village Girl' group are undecided. One minute looking forward to the trip, the next minute derisory.

"Where the hell is this Northumberland anyway?". "Hope this castle isn't fuckin' haunted" and "Anyone got a tranny to take?" A couple of the girls, 'Blonde Hair' girl being one, are petrified at the prospect. This will be taking them a long way, in every sense, out of their comfort zone.

I'm ambivalent about the news. It seems such a strange idea (until I realised the real reason) to transport us in two separate groups of roughly a hundred pupils at a time all the way up to within thirty miles of the Scottish Border. A logistic nightmare with hiring enough coaches, finding available staff to accompany us. Then losing two whole days of the trip to travelling there and back....

Although maybe not such a bad thing...what havoc could we cause if we are all confined in travelling coaches! Surely there were similar opportunities with available accommodation much nearer to our town.

Staying in a fortified castellated castle sounded ominously like it could be the only option possible for unruly comprehensive pupils. Would anyone appreciate the National Heritage Grade One listed building originating from the thirteenth century? I don't think I was particularly looking forward to the trip. I almost wished I had a music exam scheduled which would give me a veritable reason for not being able to go. Unfortunately, I didn't.

Form 2B was timetabled to go during the first trip, the second week of June. Sadly the *'dream form'* was scheduled for the second trip the week after, so I wouldn't even be getting the opportunity to have a week back together with my friends. Did I know any of the girls in the other two forms we would be going with? I didn't think so, I anticipated I would be doing a lot of lonely standing around by myself, ostracised as always. Same daily routine for me, just taking place in a more northerly location!

I'm confused about the nature of this trip. Was it an educational trip for history and geography projects although nothing appeared to correlate with our current historical period of study about Joan of Arc and Northumberland was hardly compatible with the rain forests of the Amazon. If it wasn't for any relevant educational topics, then this foray up North could only be for us to work on improving our social mobility skills. That would be interesting! It was whilst commenting to Catherine that I would be away from the house for some of her O levels exams that it dawned on me what the real reason for our trip might be. Of course! We were being <u>physically</u> removed from the school during exam weeks. My sister confirmed this. Her fifth form year had been discreetly informed that *'everything possible was being done to keep the atmosphere in the school as calm and quiet as possible so they could concentrate on their O level examinations'*.

As the Northumberland castle trip approached something wonderful happened. Mary returned to my side and wanted to become my *'best friend'*. She chose to sit next to me. In lessons we saved the neighbouring tables for each other. We giggled together over trivial things. I realised that there had been a falling out between her and Julie. I'm sure all the other girls in form 2B knew the exact details of what had happened, but I didn't. I was in awe at the ease Mary showed in simply sidling back towards me for the replacement friendship, gliding effortlessly between the various social groups. Deep down I knew I was being used as a temporary support, but I didn't resent it, I was just so grateful to have a friend! I garnered minimal details; the rift was caused by Julie and Mary fancying the same boy in 2W. Mary smiled contentedly but didn't bother to reveal too much to me. My thoughts were still a long way away from boys. How on earth could girls my age already be thinking about *'all that nonsense'* (my mother's words)?

I watched the classroom rituals with curiosity and the beginnings of jealousy. If a girl expressed an interest in a boy, it would be up to her group of friends to approach the desired person and ask him if he *'wanted to go out with'* their named friend. They then reported back his decision. All very third-party. It was easy to guess the verdict. Girls either shrieked in delight and feigned coy surprise, faces flushed pink, or they ran in tears to hide away in the bogs, surrounded by commiserating friends. Their lives ruined *'for ever'*.

Jason Smith of 2W had been approached by the 'Village Girl' group. Who did he want to go out with?

He snubbed Julie and picked Mary. Julie was distraught, Mary triumphant but, with the threat of being bashed up, wisely decided to change friends. To me it all seemed such a bewildering and unnecessary complication to everyday school life.

Mary suggested we hide during the morning breaks for the first few days. I went along with it of course, like the weak accomplice I was. I showed her the gap between the terrapins. I took her into the music instrument cupboard where I stored my cello. We sniggered together. It was fun. I was doing something with a companion. I didn't think to ask her how she managed in the lunchtime breaks when I had music rehearsals or walked out of school.

How much Mary had changed from her meek, timid self of the first year. I wondered if I had changed. Probably not at all.

The acrimonious atmosphere of the unrequited love predicament soon resolved itself. By the start of the very next week Julie had already secured herself another boyfriend and the fact that he was in the THIRD FORM trumped any trivial, immature 2B relationships. Even the 'Village Girl' group were impressed, standing huddled together on the other side of the form room, arms folded tightly across chests, listening to all the details from Julie as she revelled in her elevated, promiscuous status. Mary and I paled into insignificance. At least all these tangled and, incomprehensible to me, rites of passage meant that Mary remained my friend for the time being…. although I have spotted her smiling at Julie and when I came out of a German lesson, they were walking together ahead of me in the corridor back to the form room. Had they both been in the same lesson? Were they talking to each other again?

One more week before the trip up to the top of England. One more week of lessons to get through. A dreaded double cookery lesson. Who wants to spend two hours in a stuffy cookery classroom on a shimmering, searing early June afternoon? The sun glaring through the big, metal-framed windows, bouncing off the white worktops, glinting off the glass-fronted oven doors. Who can be bothered to make a perfect Quiche Lorraine? I'm feeling out-of-sorts, disgruntled with a thumping headache. Double cookery is irritating enough, doubly annoying is that it falls on the same day as orchestra lunchtime rehearsal. I somehow must struggle towards the school building wrestling with my full-size cello, my music case, my satchel and the carrier bag containing all the food items required for that day's cookery lesson recipe. None of the other girls from 2B have to cope with all of this, none of the other girls grapple with bringing in a musical instrument. Some of them who come in on buses don't even make the effort to bring in the ingredients needed for the cookery lesson anyway. Why do I bother?

The pastry has been made, rolled into circles and partly cooked in the fluted tins. The golden cases wait cooling, lined up on the worktop next to the ovens. At our individual work benches we work on the filling, whisking the eggs, chopping the bacon, thinly slicing the onion. Everyone's head is down, concentrating on the contents in their mixing bowls. Mrs Pugh, the elderly cookery teacher walks around, watching us all with her hooded hawk-like eyes. I've noticed she doesn't like to put her head down too much. We might then notice the white roots that run like a zip through her dyed coppery hair.

A commotion arises when Michelle drops an egg on the floor. Mrs Pugh bustles over, her high heels briskly clicking on the floor like a metronome clattering through my aching head.

"Oh, my goodness, what a silly girl you are! This will hold everyone up." She flutters her hands in anguish at her throat.

"Everyone, carry on. Michelle, you put your bowl down and set about cleaning up this mess on the floor. I'll give you another egg for now and you'll pay me back next week." Michelle keeps her head down in mock submission, but she is looking sideways at the rest of us, smirking. Next week we won't be here, we will be off on our trip. There will be no cookery lesson, the egg payment will be forgotten.

I am instructed to walk across to the ovens and turn down the dials to reduce the heat during this delay. I carry the bowl with my egg mixture and the fork I had been using to froth up the yellow mixture. I regulate the heat as requested and pour my mixture into my quiche base. The fork still in my hand becomes a vicious tool. All of a sudden the heat, the hormones, the hideous pointlessness of this lesson overtakes me. I stab randomly at the bases of other pastry cases waiting on the worktop. Six or seven are now punctured through to their metal base.

I hear Mrs Pugh click-clacking towards me. I immediately regain control of my rage and busy myself with making a show of using the fork to crimp the edges of my pastry. Had Mrs Pugh spotted my startling, uncharacteristic vandalism? She stares for long time at the fork in my hand and then with her chin held high, head up, she leans exaggeratedly over the pastry cases to examine them. Fortunately, the fork's tines had been too thin to reveal too much damage. Only I knew there were holes in some of the wretched Quiche Lorraine pastry cases.

Mrs Pugh claps her hands. It's time for us to gather around the ovens, the cooking has finished. Each quiche will be ceremoniously removed from the heat, studied and commented on. Who has made the most perfect savoury dish during this lesson? Six girls are somewhat disappointed with their finished product. It appears that most of the egg and milk liquid has seeped through their pastry, (through holes?) and disappeared underneath, burnt black. Just charred shrivelled bacon and onion pieces sit in the empty, very crusty cases.

The eyes of the suspicious teacher remain fixed on me for the final minutes of the lesson. I flee the room with nothing further said but I suspect I might not be getting quite such a good mark on the forthcoming end of term report:

Cookery   Summer 1975

Grade **A**   Effort **2**
A very good examination result.
She can do good work, but her attitude is not always co-operative.

Chapter Twenty-Two

It's a bright, blue-skied Monday morning. We are waiting to board the coaches and set off for the trip to Northumberland. The classes are to be divided between the coaches. Mary and I stand together in a queue for a coach containing all of 2B and some of 2G, Mrs McGregor's form. 2W is waiting to climb up into another vehicle. Mary looks longingly towards the back of the bus, but I persuade her to sit with me in the second row of seats just behind the front one already reserved by teachers who have placed their bags there.

Experience has taught me, after many primary school outings, that sitting unobtrusively and silent in the seat behind loose-tongued, relaxed staff is often rewarded by overhearing snippets of information; unknown details of teachers' mysterious married lives, future events being planned by the school and, most importantly, which pupils are giving cause for concern…. now, that last category could probably take up the whole of this long and hot journey ahead of us!

The engine rumbles into life. "Righto!" Mr Bradshaw shouts down the coach, standing at the front with his back to the windscreen, facing us, "Off we go!" I wonder whether, knowing his past career, he was in fact tempted to roar *'Tally Ho!'* or *'Chocks away!'*. Setting off on some dastardly, and difficult mission!

It was quite exciting, after all, to be setting off on this trip, Mary sitting beside me. The radio crackles on, 10cc are assuring me that *'they are not in love, it's just because….'*

There is the first toilet stop just before Leicester, we eat our packed lunches far too early and the atmosphere in the coach becomes stuffy and stale. Mary munches on an apple and then falls asleep, her head lolling onto my shoulder, her acidic musty breath rhythmically brushes my cheek. It's not very pleasant but I don't mind, I have a friend.

At a second toilet stop just after Leeds a commotion breaks out between some of the boys of 2G. Big Pete of Morris dancing fame has inexplicably stuck his discarded chewing gum into the hair of James. Boredom or mischievousness, who knows. Big Pete remains silent. Mrs McGregor attempts to calm the situation in her usual unruffled manner.

"Aye, well what silly boys ye are!" Her admonishment is sufficient to deflect any further retaliation. Our return onto the coach is delayed whilst she slowly opens her handbag and after a deliberately prolonged rummage around, removes a small flowery case which she unzips and pulls apart to reveal a manicure set. We stand around, watching fascinated as she extracts a pair of delicate pearl-encrusted nail scissors and commences to snip away at matted sticky strands of James's blonde hair. "We'll have no more of that sort of silly nonsense, thank ye. Now everyone back on the coach. Won't be long noo."

Seven hours, three hundred miles since our morning departure, the coaches slow down to drive through the grey-stoned, arched portal and then trundle over the cobbled courtyard. In front of us is the impressive castellated gothic building, rectangular around a central courtyard, towers at each end plus the later dominant addition of a three-storey square pele tower. We stagger off the coach in the early evening sunshine, disorientated and tetchy. Forbidding grey turrets tower upwards, gargoyles leer down on us. Beyond the crumbled low grey-stone walls, green fields slope away as far as the eye can see, a river shimmering far away at the bottom of the incline.

Even the cockiest of the second formers are stunned into silence. This is beyond their supposedly world-wisely ken. I think, for once, we are all as one in our sentiments; *'What the hell are we doing here!'*

Hands being clapped startle us from our confused torpor, we obediently search out our suitcases, holdalls, rucksacks, our sleeping bags and follow the form teachers into the formidable building. We trudge along the narrow corridors, whispering to each other, up a stone circular staircase, along another narrow passageway. Everywhere dark, dank and musty. Up another three steps.

"Right, stop here." A voice is shouting out at the front of our line. It's hard to see who in the gloom. "This is the upper second floor with the dormitories. 2B girls, you are all in this one."

Mary and I follow Julie and Linda through the doorway into a bright airy room filled with wooden bunk beds. The evening sun is throwing low slanted rays through the large stone-framed, pointed-arch gothic windows. The 'Village Girl' group push past us all to get in first and choose the best beds. They only want the bottom bunks nearest to the door.

"Ain't sleeping up on top of these crappy beds, looks like they've all got woodworm anyhow." This gets a laugh from us all and relaxes the nervous atmosphere. "We've gotta be by the bloody door, girls, cos we're gonna be sneaking out every night to meet the boys."

Mary wants a bottom bunk by the window, so, woodworm or not, I happily take the top and we throw our bags onto our chosen beds. Plump Michelle climbs up the rickety ladder onto the top bunk alongside mine and heaves her body up over onto the mattress. The whole frame creaks and wobbles.

"Bloody hell, Mitch!" shrieks the more lithe Lorraine from underneath. It all seems very precarious and ancient. I don't like to suggest that maybe they should swop around.

I can't imagine what it will be like sleeping in this same room with all the other girls from 2B. Now I'm worried that my frilly, nylon Ladybird-labelled nightie is going to appear too babyish. Will they laugh at my children's strawberry flavour toothpaste because I dislike the taste of mint. I decide I won't even bother to clean my teeth. How will we get dressed in the morning. Will the 'Village Girl' group look around to see who has started to wear a bra? It's all going to be very nerve-racking.
Mrs McGregor does the tour of the girl's dormitories to see that we are all settling in. She gives a brisk hug to 'Blonde Hair' girl who has been snivelling with home sickness and doesn't want to sleep in the bunk bed above Linda. I notice that Julie has positioned herself over in a corner with Tracy. We descend the stairway and all congregate in the main hall for the introductory talk.

The castle was used as a POW camp from 1945 to 1948 and then as an isolated and stark boy's preparatory boarding school. (I doubt much has been changed or updated since then, certainly not the thirty-year old wooden wobbling bed frames!). A perfect place to keep us all confined for the next four days. Mr Bradshaw informs us that any entering a dormitory of the opposite sex is forbidden. There is to be *'no mingling'* whatever that could mean. I don't dare look at anyone's face. I think quite a few of the second form pupils standing around me have got their own agenda for this trip. One that involves a considerable amount of the prohibited *'mingling'*.
The evening meal is lettuce, tomato, a slice of ham and a bag of crisps, followed by a yoghurt and a Kitkat. There are still several hours of warmth and light left. I get involved in a game of rounders on the vast sloping lawns, having fun and laughing with three girls from 2G who I knew from the previous year's lunchtime Scottish Dancing Club. We had bonded during those first-year rehearsals preparing for the Summer Show, but I haven't had any lessons with any of them or spoken to them during the whole of this second year. I had forgotten they were from form 2G, so I needn't have worried about not knowing any other girls during this castle trip. I realise that my *'new best friend'* Mary isn't around, so as soon as I get run out and the game is coming to an end anyway, I head back up towards the castle buildings. Mary and Jason Smith are sitting together on a low wall kissing, oblivious to my presence. I'm annoyed but carry on walking past.
Mary was never brave enough to sneak out with the 'Village Girl' group after dark and the supposed curfew, but she spent an awful lot of time in a reverie, staring at Jason sitting in a window opposite across the courtyard. Once confined to our dormitories, they waved, grinned, continually mouthing *I love you* to each other. During the night I would stir awake and see her shadow crouched at the window blocking out the moonlight from the arched frame.
It all got rather annoying; Mary obsessed with Jason. I couldn't understand all this being in love. It seemed so time-consuming and possessive. I was, of course, jealous that Jason was occupying the time I thought I would be spending with Mary. I was inwardly crabby and out of sorts. I had been misled by such fickle and transparent false allegiance, how I wished I could understand all this conflict of teenage emotions, the selfishness, the uncertainty. Was Mary still my friend?
If the 2G girls would accept me as part of their group, I joined in activities with them, otherwise I hung around by myself. For me, the trip had lost a bit of its sparkle. As if in sympathy the weather deteriorated and a *'haar'* drifted in bringing fine drizzle.
We spent an unseasonably damp and chilly June day visiting the Roman fort of Vindolanda. Mr Bradshaw wanted us to march a little along Hadrian's wall. Why were we doing Roman history? It meant little to most of the teenagers around me. It all seemed a bit bleak and pointless apart from the comical moment when a guide picked cocky 'No Bag Boy' to sit on the top of a circular pile of rocks. 'No Bag Boy' positively glowed with the attention and the guide, obviously enjoying this perfectly timed, well scripted moment, then commented wryly that the rocks used to be the Roman's toilet. How we all laughed! Even 'No Bag Boy', whose face split into the widest grin.

The third day was the visit towards the west of the county. An hour and a half tedious drive incarcerated in our coaches to Keswick and then on even further to Derwentwater where we were scheduled to eat our pack lunches sitting at the water's edge, never mind the intermittent light drizzle and grey sky. However, our meal stop there was quickly terminated when some boys started throwing pebbles at a suit of mallards bobbing up and down on the surface just a few metres out from the rocks where we perched eating our cheese sandwiches and crisps.

How I loved collective nouns. Pencilled into my notebooks at home were lists of any new ones I came across. A murder of crows, a murmuration of starlings or a conspiracy of ravens. Always useful for answering crossword clues and quiz questions. I'd spotted a wren flitting in the branches of a gnarled bent tree behind me as I ate. I wonder what the collective noun for wrens is?.....

…but no time to lose myself in thought now, as, yet again, the unacceptable behaviour of just a small unruly minority has ruined the calm, the attempt at equilibrium for everyone else. By annoyed and embarrassed teachers, we are unceremoniously and hurriedly hustled back up into the confinement of our coaches. Next is the short drive south to Kendal where we are instructed to use our spending money buying the ubiquitous Mint cake to take back as presents to our parents.

Judging by the pervading peppermint smell and the continual rustle of tin foil wrapping on the coach on the way back in the late afternoon, I suspect that not many parents will be receiving the souvenir. I feel more and more queasy surrounded by the odour of mint which I detest.

After too many hours of the day sitting cooped up in the coach, I am so thankful to stagger down the steps once we arrive back and breathe in the fresh Northumberland air uncontaminated by the stench of adolescent sweat, foul breath, farts and mint. At least the sun has reappeared, and the evening is going to be mellow and warm.

Bewildered by our unnatural confinement during the long day (did any of the government anticipated, innovative social mobilising take place?), once released from the coach, everyone from 2B quickly regroups back into their safer, smaller, familiar groups. 'No Bag Boy' and his gang of followers race off to start a game of football. Julie and the 'Village Girl' group disappear behind some outbuildings probably for an elicit smoke. Linda and Tracy link arms and skip away singing, no doubt, the latest Bay City Roller pop song. Mary rushes off to find Jason. I see them, holding hands, walking towards the woods. 'Briefcase Boy' has found a friend in 2G. Similar greasy hair and lank fringe covering spotty foreheads. They stand together awkwardly but companionably.

The coach with 2G girls must have arrived back earlier. I can't spot my former Scottish country dancing friends anywhere. They must have vanished off up already to their dormitory. I find myself standing forlornly in the courtyard with only 'Blonde Hair' girl. For some reason she has been abandoned by Lorraine and Michelle. I suspect there has been a shift of friendship there too. It's so exhausting trying to keep up with the undercurrent bitchiness and shallow alliances. Three more years ahead of me. I doubt I will ever understand how fickle these friendships are. One day enemies, next day best mates. I'm thinking of something to say to 'Blonde Hair' girl like… *'shall we walk up to the dormitory* together?', but am mercifully interrupted by Mrs McGregor walking towards us, briskly clapping her hands.

"Right gals, There's an hour before evening meal. Anyone with a swimming costume, run along now and change and I'll take you doon to the river for a swim."

I'd love to go swimming and without a thought for 'Blonde Hair' girl turn away from her and run back through the ornate stone door frame, along the dark, dank, green-stained corridor towards the upwards staircase. Three minutes later, Mrs McGregor is still standing waiting in the courtyard when I return. Black swimming costume on under my T-shirt and slacks, towel rolled up, tucked under my arm and hurray! hurray! my 2G dancing club friends are there too. We run, laughing together, down the green-sloped field towards the river flowing at the bottom of the incline.

At some point in the history of this POW castle or boy's preparatory school, someone had dammed the River South Tyne as it meandered through the grounds. A manmade stone wall trapped the water into a pool before trickling away again off on its course through Northumberland. A murky pool deep enough to swim in. I was having fun splashing around with the other girls until I swam underwater through the dark, cloudy depths and managed to crash headfirst into the unseen stone wall of the damn; result, one badly grazed nose. However, my injury was nothing compared to the damage inflicted on each other by the two boys fighting during our final evening at the castle.

Two boys on this *'educational trip'*, one from 2W, the other from 2G, each with their own very specific behavioural problems had been goaded into fighting each other. The whispers of the imminent skirmish rippled around the evening dining hall. The teachers were unaware. As soon as the meal was finished, dirty plates stacked together on the metal trolleys, chairs turned upside-down on the tables, murmurings started that everyone was to secretly gather behind the East Wing tower to watch the fight.

Mrs McGregor was suggesting that, for this last evening, we could play hide and seek around the grounds or we could have a singsong around a campfire. The sort of activity I loved doing during Girl Guide camp evenings. I wonder how many of the other girls around me know all the words for Ging Gang Goolie, Heyla, heyla, sheyla! Probably none.

Unsurprisingly, there isn't much interest in Mrs McGregor's infantile ideas. In fact, just a lot of derisory quiet muttering. She eventually gets the message and standing up to smooth down her kilt, sets off to the private staff- only room with the other teachers turning back with an ineffectual admonishment.

"Aye well, lads and lassies, sort yersels out then."

The fight begins. I watch in utter horror, what on earth has possessed these two boys of my age to harbour such uncontrollable, vicious feelings? How can they be so violent, so physical, so destructive? My primary school years had been protected, my housing estate sheltered and blinkered from other, cruder social cultures, I can't believe what I am seeing at all! For the umpteenth time since beginning my secondary education my eyes are yet again opened to incomprehensible degenerate behaviour. Before 1973 in my town these two boys, and other adolescents with similar behavioural problems and special educational needs would have been placed in schools offering them the specific handling and controlled environment they required. I would not have come into contact with them. Now we are all expected to sit in the same classrooms. At least in the school daytime there are teachers present to control outbursts of rage. It's scary that I am standing here now, surrounded by unknown comportment or attitudes, an unwilling bystander. *'Fight, fight, fight'*, the menacing low, tribal rhythmic chant pulsates around me. A punch is thrown but misses. Hair is pulled, clothes torn. Both boys land together on the grass and writhe around. A face is jerked upwards, blood appears from a nose, a cheek is badly scratched. The mostly exhilarated second form spectators edge forward, I've had enough though and push back through the crowd to hurry towards the main stone archway. Mr. Bradshaw rushes past me alerted to the commotion.

As we clamber up the steps of the coach the next morning for the long drive back south, the atmosphere is somewhat subdued. As well as the fight, whilst waiting in the breakfast queue, I had overheard a whispered staff conversation concerning some girls caught in a boy's bedroom during the night. Mr Bradshaw is in a BAD mood. His face white, a blue vein pulsing just under his left eye. As designated Head of Second Year, he must do the whole trip again next week with the remaining forms. I just want to get home. Had our five days away been considered a success I wondered. A hundred mixed ability 12- and 13-year-olds from an experimental intake thrown together in such close proximity. Not just for school hours but whole days and nights.

Had we triumphantly transitioned into the government desired homogeneous and socially adaptable typical comprehensive pupils?

Mary appears at my side, *'can she sit next to me?'* Of course! But we don't talk much, slumped together on the scratchy, blue and green-patterned seat, both of us wearily lost in our own thoughts. I'm feeling nauseous as the word *imbroglio* spins round and around in my head like a phenakistoscope in its continuous loop.

The coach takes for ever to wend its way southwards.

Third Year

Chapter Twenty-three

Tuesday 2nd September 1975. I begin my third year. Some very big changes to my school days were about to happen. I was to find this out later that first day of term as we once again sat up in the *'treehouse'* of our same first-floor form room waiting to write down the new timetable on the inside cover of our blue rough books.
I have managed to get the same table in my favourite place in the corner. Windows on either side behind me. After a week of disappointing grey dampness, the typical end of August bank-holiday weather, today is, of course, tantalisingly sunny with azure blue sky and wispy white clouds. A poignant early autumn morning teasing me as I make my return to the beginning of a new school year.
Looking around, everyone has turned up except for the 'Rocking Boy'. His name is not called out from the class register; I imagine he has gone off to a school more suitable for his behavioural problems. I notice discreetly that there have been some physical changes over the six-week summer holiday. A couple of the boys appear to have downy hair above their upper lip.
"Bum fluff, bum fluff", chant the giggling 'Village Girl' group attempting to regain their dominance of the classroom after the summer holidays and probably hoping to begin a new nickname for the red-faced, furious Kevin.
It goes without saying that I haven't met up *'as friends'* with any of the others sitting here in this classroom for the last month and a half.
'Mooching' (one of my mother's derisory words for meeting up with friends and doing something mildly insalubrious and intellectually degrading) around the town, was not encouraged. It had been another lonely school holiday. My activities having been determined by my mother. There had been the county orchestral summer school to attend the first week of the summer holidays and of course, the individual daily music practice to be done. 1000-piece jigsaws to be completed on the dining room table listening to classical music LPs. The jigsaws, chosen by my mother, were invariably unstimulating scenes of thatched cottages with hollyhock, foxglove and rose-filled gardens. I pretended I enjoyed completing them with her, sitting together at the mahogany dining-room table. She probably cherished the closeness but her pedantic sorting out of the pieces by colour and shape annoyed me and in silent teenage provocation I completed the puzzles as quickly as possible to get the wretched pieces back into the box. We drifted further apart.
There had been the weekly visits to the town library and, of course, the strained, restrictive and, now for me, acutely embarrassing two-week family holiday to the Bed and Breakfast in Devon. Sitting bored on various beaches every day, whether sun or cloud, I'm pretty sure no one else's mother carried a small blue Primus stove onto the beach, so that a kettle could be boiled for the essential cups of tea at the lunchtime picnic. I'd overheard Julie telling Mary she was going to

Tenerife and then she had giggled, admitting that she didn't really know where it was! My music friend Jane was excited to be flying with her family to Canada for a three-week holiday.

My eyes were opened wide, my senses tuned in to all the differences of lifestyle.

Of course, I'm not going to talk to anyone in this classroom now about my holiday activities. I'm sure they've all had a far more exiting and stimulating six- week break from the school. I bet my fellow form mates have been meeting up, having fun together, listening to pop music, dancing, drinking shandy, going out with someone, holding hands, kissing, maybe even going *'all the way'*. The kind of activities I hear them all talking about as I pathetically hover on the edge of their friendship circles.

Unusually, I had done something out of the ordinary and very different during the first two weeks of August this year. I had gone by myself to France (approved by my parents as an educational visit) to stay with the formidable Madame Roussin and her hen-pecked husband, the *mari soumis* Hubert. This Madame Roussin had been part of the school's French department pupil exchange programme several years before in the late sixties which my eldest sister had been involved in. Rosemary, too, had stayed with Monsieur and Madame Roussin. For some reason which I never fathomed my mother and Mme Roussin had continued to keep in touch, exchanged a few letters over the years and between them had obviously arranged my summer holiday trip.

I'd had repeatedly excellent grades in school reports for French lessons, always performing well in end of term exams. My *'effort'* in the classroom had been less remarkable! Never bothering to put up my hand or speak out loud. Maybe this trip was an attempt to improve my oral contributions during weekly lessons!

I flew as an unaccompanied child with British Airways into Charles de Gaulle Airport near Paris. The sweet and quiet Hubert was waiting to pick me up. He didn't speak any English, so it was an immediate crash course for my rudimentary linguistic skills as we attempted awkward conversation together driving through Paris streets in their noisy Citroen. The two weeks were spent between their stunning modern apartment on the Boulevard de Magenta in the 10e arrondissement of Paris and their *maison secondaire* in Compiègne, a town in the French department of l'Oise, some two and a half hours drive northeast of the capital.

The trip had had some highlights, walking under the Eiffel Tower of course and, in Compiègne, visiting the railway carriage of 1918 Armistice signing fame. But, apart from these two organised trips, I'd felt quite isolated and lonely in the company of the childless elderly French couple. Whilst out in the *campagne* there had been nothing much to do other than help with the weeding in the small vegetable patch and take a lot of solitary rides on an ancient, unforgiving bicycle along empty straight roads, passing endless fields of vivid yellow sunflowers.

However, I was looking forward to telling the French teacher about my summer trip to France. I didn't know yet that my French teacher for this forthcoming year would be Miss Roseau herself!

Julie has seated herself amidst the 'Village Girl' group at the tables on the opposite side of the room. Her bouncy perm is gone, she now has an upward flicked fringe and shoulder length hair finely sculptured in waves on either side of her face. It looks natural but I wonder if the suspect rigidness of the outward curl took a bit of work with a hair dryer and some spray. A couple of the other girls have similar styles. It must be the fashion. I notice that Julie is wearing red lipstick as well as long thin dangling earrings. I presume some school rules are being deliberately flaunted.

My hair is the same, no change of style. I'm wearing the unchanged hand-me-down grey cardigan and grey skirt from the first year. However, I did achieve one small victory in terms of being fashionable. At the usual dreaded *'buying new shoes'* ordeal before the beginning of term, I'd persuaded my mother to let me have tan lace-up shoes with the smallest of wedges. There really wasn't much other choice, thank goodness!

'Blonde Hair' girl now has a feather cut, the fine layers just reaching her shoulders. No more plaits to flick or fiddle.

'No Bag Boy' looks very different with his black baby curls shorn close to his head in a threatening military Number One. With no fringe as cover, his forehead is a raging red mess of pimples.
Mary arrived late, there had been a problem with the bus driver not knowing how many new pupils he was supposed to pick up. An argument with a parent had delayed the journey towards the town. She entered the classroom, flustered and pink-faced, panicking eyes darting around, searching a place, an empty chair.
I had wondered where she would choose to sit this term, next to me or next to Julie. Mary's friendship with me had lasted just the few weeks after the castle visit, until the end of the term, a superficial school hours acquaintance, but I haven't seen her since that last day, 18th July. It hadn't occurred to either of us to arrange to get together during the school summer holidays. It always felt that our perfunctory alliance existed only between 9 am and 4 pm, Monday to Friday during term time. Would she still want to be friends with me now? I'm sure the falling out with Julie would be forgotten. Maybe they even met up during the summer holidays and *mooched* together around the town?

There were, of course, empty chairs either side of me and nothing free beside Julie, so the decision was made. Mary slipped quickly into the chair on my left. We smiled shyly at each other,
"Wotcha!"
"Wotcha!"
Mr Bradshaw is strutting around the room,
"Righto 3B", he chuckles, "third form already, heh! Slight difference to the timetable this year, go ahead and fill in the lessons when everyone is together and then I will come around and tell you separately which classrooms and which teachers you have been assigned to for the other lessons".
This is all very confusing. What is going on?
Oddly, he approaches me first and I see my name on the top sheet of paper clasped in his broad hand. He leans down over my table, his leathery- skinned face tanned brown, no doubt from a lot of summer outdoor activity. I notice he is wearing new silver- framed bi-focal glasses, each lens divided horizontally into two. His pupils appear to wobble and distort, changing size as he moves his head up and down. It makes me feel slightly queasy.
"Hello, did you have a good holiday?"
"Yes, thank you Sir". Was there any other reply?
"Jolly good then, now copy this into your timetable. These are your new classrooms and teachers. Things are going to be a bit different this year. I think you'll find everything to your satisfaction".
'Briefcase Boy's' name is on the next sheet and Mr Bradshaw eases himself slowly to standing position, hand clutching his spine, I hear a faint click of protesting bone, and he walks away towards the front of the room. For this third year in our form room, 'Briefcase Boy' has yet again chosen to sit by himself at a table just underneath the tall roller blackboard.
I scrutinise the paper he has left on my table. English lessons I am now supposedly with the O level teacher, producer of Alice in Wonderland, Mrs Matthias, she of the swirling skirts and multi-coloured floral neck scarves, in classroom 3. For French I am now to go to classroom 10 with Miss Roseau as my teacher. That pleases me. I do like Miss Roseau, the '*old school*', no-nonsense teacher with her brogues, her brown heavy twinsets, her thick tortoiseshell glasses, even if some others find her too intimidating.
Apparently for my maths lessons, I am now with teacher Mr Evans in classroom 5.
History will continue with Mrs Jacobi in my favourite classroom, geography will be with a new teacher in a different classroom...
This year we are even going to do the separate science subjects of Biology, Chemistry and Physics.
Next to me, Mary receives her new lesson timetable from Mr Bradshaw, and we concentrate on filling in our lessons. I've finished, I look across at her table. She hasn't written Mrs Matthias as her English teacher; she is not going to classroom 3. She isn't going to classroom 5 for her maths lessons. For French she doesn't have Miss Roseau.
Something very strange is happening.

Of course! The *'setting'* has taken placed.

For this third year of our comprehensive schooling, we are apparently no longer going to be a mixed ability form for most of the academic subjects. Yet will still be the same motley 3B for the remaining subjects of art, music, religious studies and sport.

That's going to be interesting! How will this strange mix-matched form group cope with the unannounced segregation? Are established friendships formed over the last two years now going to be severed? I thought I might have just found a friend in Mary now I am instructed that I won't be in the same classroom as her for many lessons at all. We are all going to be splintered apart, assigned unquestioningly to different sets for some lessons and then expected to reunite back together for others. I wonder if that can possibly work. I wonder too, childishly, if Mary will be in Julie's classes, drift away from me and no longer be my friend.

I just know I am going to experience unvoiced fury at the school for throwing this at me without saying anything. Simply the next stage for us uncomplaining and acquiescent guinea pigs to cope with in this comprehensive education experiment. Haven't I just spent two years trying to fit in with everyone else in this classroom? Trying desperately to pretend I had things in common with them. Dumbing down my work to appear on the same academic level.

Have those last two years just been a complete waste of time?

Behind the scenes there must have been so much constant secret assessment and evaluation of achievement levels on every piece of work we completed or handed in. All those conspiratorial decisions being made about our future exam potential. Because really, isn't that what secondary education is all about, whether grammar or comprehensive based, or confusingly stuck somewhere in between, it all just amounts to which exams we will be entered for during our fifth year? The deceit and pointlessness, the boredom of the last two years is hard for me to cope with. Should I have done more to deliberately mess up my work, disguised my abilities, maybe, then, I could have remained in classes with Mary!

Chapter Twenty-Four

Setting versus Streaming

Setting and the more heinous **streaming** were the antithesis of the proposed comprehensive system of education, but the large intakes of mixed ability pupils would inevitably still need to be divided into smaller, more suitable aptitude groups once the preparation for public examinations began. The abolishment of the eleven-plus selection exam simply delayed this process, the assessment of each pupil's academic potential, until typically the third year of secondary education or sometimes later. The deferment of the 'setting by ability' procedure by a couple of years responded to opinion that this would offer a fairer opportunity for the late developers.

Streaming: During the 1950s and 1960s most primary schools in England felt obliged to operate the rigid system of streaming children which had been promoted by the now discredited advice of British educational psychologist, Sir Cyril Burt. The concept of streaming being that pupils were divided into classes based on some measure of intelligence and/or attainment and always remained in those classes for all lessons. Therefore, pupils were grouped into classes for all lessons, regardless of the subject being taught.

Traditionally the streams were named 'A', 'B', 'C' etc. It was confirmed that children from the middle classes tended to be allocated to A streams, those from manual working-class homes would be found in C. Transfers between the streams were minimal (only about two per cent) so that the great majority of children remained in their original stream throughout their school life.

The result was that streaming became a self-fulfilling prophecy.

The teaching in the top junior classes became dominated by the requirements of the eleven plus exam. Children in the A stream were intensively coached to pass the test. The brighter streams, under better teachers, were encouraged to proceed more rapidly.

Children placed in the lower streams were more likely to be taught at a slower pace. These streams were destined for the Secondary Moderns. Children were experiencing the negative effects of such early and possible incorrect determining of their future as young as six or seven years old. Educationalists recorded a mechanical, distorted form of education isolating children from their peer groups.

As Dr James Douglas, the eminent social researcher, stated in 1964,
'Streaming by ability reinforces the process of social selection'.

As early as the 1950's doubts were emerging about the use of streaming in primary schools although a survey by Brian Jackson, a British educationalist and co-founder of the Advisory Centre for Education, published in 1964 found that 96% of the sampled schools still streamed their children. The Plowden Report of 1967: *Children and Their Primary Schools* made many recommendations for change including the abolishment of the use of streaming for the under-11s. During my primary school years, I had certainly profited from her child-orientated, more relaxed teaching theories. Even into the 1970s, Lady Plowden continued her campaign for educational reform. She wrote, *'It is not the fault of the children that they fail to profit from their education. It is their family background and history, the environment in which the family lives.'*

<u>Setting:</u> Setting was considered a kinder, more subtle organisational device for grouping together children of similar ability. In the comprehensive school system, pupils were to be initially allocated to mixed ability classes and remain in these for most of their lessons, but for the third year (or sometimes later) would then be divided into ability-based groups for certain subjects (typically English, maths, sciences and modern languages).

The class groups being based on aptitude in <u>each</u> subject.

An individual pupil might therefore be in the *'top set'* for English but be assigned to a lower, less academically demanding set for maths.

The allocation of the pupils for each set would invariably involve a considerable amount of testing and work assessment as well as deliberation on potential.

The whole purpose and undisguisable necessity of setting was for the individual schools to begin the preparation of the thirteen/fourteen- year-old pupils for public examination requirements. The schools needed to decide which pupils would be suitable for which public examinations and thus directed towards a particular mandatory curriculum.

A particular problem began to be recognised in the new comprehensive schools. Had enough attention been paid, in the planning of many schools' curriculum, to the effect on the previously mixed- ability pupils being suddenly allocated to their new third year 'setted' classes? How would the pupils cope with the changes in work expectation from being in equal groups to now being expected to work in ability selected groups?

Would the third- year pupils be able to respond to the unsettling change of pace and style of study? During the middle 1970's it was (unsurprisingly) observed that the setting of pupils sometimes revealed deficiencies in what had been learnt in the first secondary years. I certainly felt I had completely wasted my time during my first and second year. The emphasis had been on teaching the whole class as an equal unit and no consideration given to individual abilities.

Also discussed at this experimental third year academic setting was whether the transition to the demands of work for the looming fifth-year examinations after a slow-paced, informal first two years would, for some pupils, be a disturbing experience which often intensified the problems of the reluctant learner, though the more willing, of course *'usually seemed to recover'.*

If the reorganised comprehensive schools continued to pursue the curriculums of the two established parallel public examinations: the GCE O level and the CSE (which was introduced in 1965), pupils from third year onwards would forever be subjected to being placed in different teaching groups according to their ability. The pressure would remain to divide students between 'academic' sets and 'lesser-academic' sets. The undeniably different expectations, different coursework, different pace of study dictated the inevitable fact that O-level potential pupils needed to be placed in contrasting teaching classes to the CSE pupils. The GCE O level had always unquestionably been accepted as catering for the top 20% of the ability range. The CSE had been created for the pupils who would not have passed an O level in a particular subject, offering qualifications to a wider ability range of fifth form leavers in more vocational subjects.

What had been lacking in the late 1960's and early 1970's and throughout the first years of my experimental secondary education was a national debate about the kind of education a comprehensive school would be expected to provide.

However much the process of 'setting' was still considered the only answer in those first years of educational reform, it was surely irrevocable that this would cause tension and discord amongst the year groups. The ideal of equal education, opportunity for all, informal and relaxed learning, suddenly shattered as pupils who had shared two years of identical education were then ultimately and inevitably segregated by ability.

A *'top set'* would emerge for every single examination subject. Quite often this class became vilified and derided by pupils in lower sets and I would certainly struggle with this, trying to fit back into being a member of original form 3B.

It seemed ridiculously obvious to me, had the Government Educational Advisors on the *'reorganisation to comprehensive education for all'* not picked up on the fact that when pupils experienced a change to ability setting in the third year, after two years of acquiescent mixed ability classes, this might produce a loss of motivation in those designated to the lower ability sets? Had they not foreseen that the present inapproachable social rift would remain omnipresent and uncontrollable, maybe even amplified, after the first two years of shared lessons, between those now selected to be in the top academic sets and those placed in the lower ability sets?

I would certainly notice a deterioration in the behaviour of certain clusters of pupils in lower sets. It was, after all, only natural they would become stigmatised, it was like the reappearance of that wretched **C stream**! Back in the bottom sets for most academic subjects, why should they be bothered to try? It would be just as much fun to be as disruptive and abusive as possible!

And after the third year 'setting' what would become of the much- heralded social mobility experiment? How on earth could the tentative, fragile friendships formed during the first two years of mixed ability classes survive this delayed selection by academic ability? They didn't. How quickly it all disintegrated painfully and predictably back into safe, similar social classification and recognised compatible ability groups. I had tried to become friends with Mary, but it was doomed from the outset and destined to fail once the third -year setting took place. How could I be friends with someone who now I would only share so few hours of lessons with each week? Some school days I wouldn't even have any lessons with her at all. We would have nothing in common.

As I filled in my new timetable, I should have been ecstatic that I was now going to be in all the 'top set' O level classes surrounded by like-minded pupils eager to learn but, strangely I wasn't. Instead, I was blinded by indignation and immature ill-humour as to how the school had already treated me. I had barely been able to make any friends during the first two years of mixed ability 2B whole class teaching. Failing miserably the social mobility test. Now, further separated from my original form group, was there any possible chance of me making new friends, being comfortable, in the now selected 'sets'? Top academic- ability pupils suddenly converging in one classroom from all the previously, very segregated, seven different forms. I'm already worried that friendships might already have been forged and I will be left struggling.

For the academic late developer, the relaxed first two years would have been the ideal atmosphere for gaining self-confidence and exploring previously unthought of exam possibilities, but for me it had just been a confusing and self-destructive haze of boredom and irritation.

Chapter Twenty-Five

So, all my worrying about trying to understand those intricate rituals of friendship groups taking place in my form during the last weeks of our second- year summer term had been in vain. It no longer mattered if Mary was my best friend or would choose to go back with Julie, whether 'Blonde Hair' girl would get back in the threesome with Lorraine and Michelle, or if Tracy was still a member of the 'Village Girl' group?
No, it was all now evidently insignificant because I see from my new timetable that I am hardly going to be spending any lesson time with any of these other girls from 3B. Not a <u>SINGLE</u> girl from this room would now be in the same classroom as me for English language, English literature, History, Geography, French, German, Maths, Biology, Physics or Chemistry. Very unsettling and infuriating. What had been the point of me being in form 3B in the first place? Trying desperately to connect with the other girls in the form when it was destined for me to be separated from them all. I feel like I'm being ostracized yet again. I wish I could understand what is expected of me.

Obviously, all the heralded and innovative experimentation into mixed ability teaching finished brusquely and unceremoniously once the third year of my secondary education was about to begin and, it would seem, that the aspirations of improving our social mobility skills also ground to an immediate halt as soon as the prospect of public exams, especially getting good O level results, loomed on the horizon.
Somewhat abruptly and covertly, with little consideration for the individuals involved, setting has taken place. I finished the summer term of my second year as part of a mixed ability class. Six weeks later, I start the autumn term of my third year being expected to accept vast changes in the organisation of lessons involving new academic and social structuring. As always, an unwilling guinea pig in these early experimental education reorganisation years.

No more time for the puerile tactics of equal opportunities, the delicate sympathetic approach or whole class informal teaching methods. That obviously has all come to an abrupt finish. There was now the much more pressing matter of an examination board curriculum to get started!

It is only the first day of the new term, my third year, but already I feel tricked and indignant. It would have been courteous to have been informed that we were being continually assessed, graded, discussed. I wonder if our parents had been informed that the beginning of the third year would involve us all being allocated to suitable academic level sets. We were no longer the mixed ability experimental intake. I doubt mine had been aware, probably not understanding what had been going on before, or why there was a need for this sudden 'setting'. I'm sure in their blinkered way they still felt that everything was carrying on as normal within the school. I would be sitting O levels as my sisters had done before me.
Nothing would have been discussed with me anyway!

If I had known of all the stealthy testing of our ability, would I have been maverick enough to continue to fluff deliberately my handed-in work, mess up my answers? I'd certainly been doing that quite often in the last two years during class work just so that I appeared at the same academic level as everyone else in my form. I hadn't been mature enough though, to realise that the individual testing, the submitted homework, the constant assessments had shown the teaching staff my true potential, which they had covertly known, anyway, since the very first day I started my secondary education.

Comments on my last end of term report made me suspect the teachers were already frustrated by the fact that I was deliberately underachieving and always petulantly uncommunicative.

If I had been summoned to the office of the Lower School Head to explain the intentional *'ruining of my prospects'*, would I have been brave enough to use the opportunity to express my feelings, my pent-up frustration, my unhappiness...

Of course not, who am I kidding? I don't have the perversity or courage to rebel (not yet!). I continue to be the same submissive, obedient fourteen-year-old girl who keeps her emotions, her opinions, her turmoil locked away deep inside.

I'm snapped out of my red haze by Mary leaning towards me. She is peering at the timetable still sitting on my table.

She isn't sharing my despondency, but tapping her finger on the lessons that we will still share in this third year: art, sport, music, and religious studies. That's not many hours each week. How strange it will be, being separated so much, disconnected, setting off to different classrooms, maybe only meeting up with each other in a classroom once a day and some days not at all.

How strange it is going to be too, or probably impossible, to try to reconnect with form 3B when we are now all so splintered, so dispersed. Was I ever actually connected to Mary and the other girls? I'd like to think I did try!

First lesson in the afternoon is maths. Off I trudge by myself to classroom 5. Three boys have begun a queue at the closed door, lining up along the wall. I don't know any of them. I stand behind the third, leaning back against the pale-green painted, scuffed walls, trying to appear nonchalant. I recognise one of two girls approaching. It's Christine, the girl who did the Christmas reading at the nine lessons and carols service during our first year.

I spot another familiar face walking towards the queue. It's Margaret from my primary school class, although I haven't spoken to her since we started at this school two years ago. Four more boys I don't know arrive making a lot of noise, shouting and laughing. One of them has an odd-sounding deep voice.

Big Pete and his 'sticky-haired' friend, James join the end of the queue followed by two more girls I don't know. From an opposite direction, Gillian arrives. She was in the same year at primary school but in the other class. Julie's class.

My heart does a little gambol, I spot Sally and Katherine walking together along the corridor. This isn't going to be too bad after all then. I will have some familiar faces in the classroom! Is it too much to hope that Jane and Helen aren't too far behind them and will arrive in a few seconds as well?

Too late, I won't get a chance to meet up with them in the corridor if they are indeed on their way, a tall, dark-haired man dressed in a beige chequered suit opens the door and invites us in. The queue slides along the wall and fans out into the bright, airy room. I do a quick glance around. The tables are in a formal arrangement, all separated, two chairs at each, all facing the front blackboard. I quickly establish myself at a table half-way down on the right-hand side of the classroom and choose the inside chair tucked up against the wall. A pretty, brown-haired girl stops and asks me if the chair next to me is taken. *Of course, it isn't!*

"Oh well, I'll just sit here for today then if that's alright? Hi, I'm Paula. I'm in 3R, what's your name, which form are you in?"

I stutter my name and hastily busy myself, head down, pretending to do something in my satchel. I was hoping I might be able to start using a tote bag this year, be like everyone else but, yet again, I have been idiotically left way behind by shifting fashion patterns. Today I have already noticed that the accessory trend has changed. The cool girls now have cloth, patterned Hippy bags slung over their shoulders. Paula throws her blue and white tasselled bag onto the table. I'm impressed by, and jealous of her confidence, her easy-going manner.

I watch "Briefcase Boy' enter the classroom and make the difficult narrow trajectory between the tables to find an empty chair. He lumbers past our table and, although his greasy fringe threatens to soon cover his eyes, his eyes sneak sideways towards us, and he smiles.

Was he smiling at me? We're now in the same maths top set, does he finally want to be friends with me? Paula quickly quashes my fantasy,

"Oh, that's just a mate of mine, we went to the same primary school, come in on the same bus every day."

She gazes around the room. "No one else in here I know though, what about you?"

"Oh, just a couple of girls from my primary school......and…oh some boys as well". What an utter fool I am making of myself! Paula won't want to sit next to me again that's for sure. But no sign of Jane or Helen and Mr Evans is shutting the classroom door and turning back towards us. He welcomes us to his class. He talks fast, his body twitching in jerky movements. I am fascinated by his whole animated self. He expects us to work hard and at a fast rate. If we are to stay in this class and succeed at O level, there is *'a lot of work to catch up on over the next year'*. I'm intrigued, what does he mean?

There was apparently now a reluctant realisation that the course work of the first two years had been at too slow a pace, with limited demands, and sometimes prolonged a style of working more appropriate to younger children. Ah! All that colouring in and decorating of my margins!

It seemed that problems still had to be resolved during this third year. HMI inspectors were recommending that the work covered, and the tempo should be *'more carefully planned during Years 1 and 2 and further monitored to ensure a smoother transition during Year 3 when pupils are selected to embark on whatever examination courses are deemed appropriate for them.'*

It was noted that some teachers, while admitting that the level of attainment of potential O level examination candidates arriving in the third year had been limited, then argued that this did not matter unduly as they *'always caught up'*.

This theory of the brightest pupils needing to *'catch up'* was open to many arguments:

Why had the pupils been put into the position of needing to catch up in the first place? The catching up would then involve three years of intense lessons covering narrow exam-orientated work (the absolute inverse of our previous two easy school years) and, interestingly, would the pupils have achieved better grades, been receptive to wider and more liberal learning, if it had not been necessary for them to make up for the lost ground?

Criticism was mounting for the curriculum, pace of work and expectations of the subject material taught during the first two years of comprehensive reorganisation. No wonder I had been so bored and frustrated!

So, Maths Mr Evans expects us to *'catch up'*. He is vibrant, intense and accustomed to quick-thinking, responsive students. I'm loving this. I feel mentally stimulated and excited. I've never had this expectancy, this impetus to work, this motivation since arriving at this school. Sadly, it wasn't going to last long though! There would soon be the difference of opinion between Mr Evans and myself on resolving equations and the working through of other algebraic problems. As in all my other third year subject classes, maths would soon see a downward spiral in my overall effort, attitude and attendance.

First, though, we are each to have a hardback textbook. He walks around the classroom handing out the heavy books. My <u>first</u> textbook to take home after two years at the school. I can't wait to look through it later in my bedroom! What other maths secrets have so far eluded me, what else can I discover?

Mr Evans is strict; he expects our complete attention when he talks. The atmosphere in the room is nervous but crackling with intellectual anticipation. None of us sitting here have yet experienced at this school a lesson of such intense formal teaching.

He informs us we are all to cover our textbooks to protect them and fill in the necessary details on the designated glued -in form on the first page. Our name, form, school year and condition of book. I find that my maths textbook has the name of one of my sister's friends three lines above. I fill in the required details but hesitate to grade the condition of the book. It would seem that previous owners of this textbook had varying standards of assessment. The first pupil had noted **1** of course, new book. The following year the next pupil had decided on **3**, perhaps it was a bit ripped and grubby. The third owner had reverted to **2**, some repairs had maybe taken place over the summer holidays. I look across at Paula,

"Just stick in a **2** or **3**," she helpfully suggests, "It's not really important. You don't want to be accused of damaging the book."

My first textbook. I'll be treating it with the greatest respect!

"Right class, turn to chapter 5", Mr Evan's authoritative but quiet voice has our complete attention. No need for him to shout, there is none of the perpetual, disrespectful muttering going on around me in this room today.

"We'll start with the chapter on statistics, handling data. Quickly everyone, find the page. Does everyone understand the principle of Venn diagrams?"

A rhetorical question, he turns his back on us and makes exaggerated chalk circles on the blackboard. No time to talk further to Paula. Questions swirl around the room; correct answers are greeted with enthusiasm. Homework is set, page numbers noted down in our rough books and the lesson is finished.

Next lesson is German. That's good because I can meet up with Jane and Helen and ask them what is happening with maths. Why didn't they appear in my classroom?

I spot 'Briefcase Boy' striding off ahead. I feel like I should make the effort to catch up with him, being in the same maths set surely gives us something in common to talk about now. However, at the end of the corridor he heads towards the staircase and leaps up, two at a time. The opposite direction of my next classroom. Of course, he doesn't do German. He chose the harder option of Chinese for his second language.

Chapter Twenty-Six

"Jane, Jane, wait for me!". I've spotted my friend ahead of me in the dim corridor. I catch up with her as we turn together into the doorway of the German classroom. Fraulein Farblos (Miss Mousy) stands in front of the blackboard welcoming everyone back into her room for this, the first lesson of the new term.

We throw our bags onto a table for two along the side wall. I look enviously at Jane's blue denim hippy shoulder bag. Am I the only one still walking around with a ridiculously worn and scratched beige satchel? The wretched item must be at least ten years old now. It was Rosemary's school bag. Maybe I could broach the subject of having a different bag with my mother. My only worry is that if I start trying to describe the brightly coloured cloth item to her, she will immediately suggest she *'runs one up'* on her Singer sewing machine using odd scraps of leftover material. I suspect the finished product might be even more embarrassing to sling over my shoulder than the current satchel.

We shuffle about getting our chairs into position and I suddenly remember Helen,
"Hang on, shouldn't we keep a place for Helen? I can throw my satchel onto the chair in front...."
"No, she's not doing German anymore. Didn't you know? Her mum spoke with the teachers."
How strange and no, of course I didn't know. I hadn't spoken to anyone from school during the entire six- week summer holiday. I pause to glance around the classroom and realise that there have been some changes. Two new faces against the five who are no longer here in the room. I wonder why Helen is no longer studying German. Was she finding it too hard? Did her mum not want her to take a second language?
All these changes taking place between my second and third school year, I knew nothing about. Imagine how I am going to feel about that! Even more irritated and ill-tempered towards the teaching staff and the school. My parents, obviously, never discussed with me the appropriateness of each of my lessons, the possibility of changing courses. It goes without saying I am always expected to keep my head down and unquestionably work hard towards the goal of passing as many O level exams as possible.
I was aware that there had been a 'Second Year Parents Evening' back in June of the last term. I read about it in the May 1975 school bulletin. Always wary now to scan quickly through the stapled, typed sheets before I hand them to my mother. I don't want to get caught out again and find something I have written printed without my permission.
The object of this parent's evening was *'to provide an opportunity for the school to describe the course for the coming year and for parents to meet informally to discuss matters of general concern with form teachers, heads of departments and others.'*
...... *'and others'* had intrigued me. Who else could there be? Surely not the headmaster himself!

On receiving an invitation for the parents' evening, my mother had typically dismissed it,
'Oh, we don't want to be bothered to come in and listen to all that unnecessary claptrap. Nothing they can tell us we don't know already. Besides, your father will be far too busy......'
It seemed that Helen's mum, and quite a few parents, by the look of the changed faces in the classrooms, had used the opportunity of that parent's evening to make the school aware of their children's particular needs, their individual wishes and find the coursework more suitable for their abilities.

I'm itching to ask Jane about the maths lessons. Why hadn't she arrived in the same classroom as me in the last period, but Fraulein Farblos wants to get her German lesson started. We are to work in pairs (thank goodness I'm sitting next to Jane) and we are to have conversations about what we did during the summer holidays. Write down some sentences.
This is a difficult task. The tabletop is empty in front of us, without the help of dictionaries our vocabulary is too restricted. I could attempt to fabricate a travel story and mention the word *ZUG* (pronouncing it correctly this time, of course!) but we don't yet have sufficient knowledge of sentence structure. During last year's German lessons, we had laboriously grasped basic but very isolated vocabulary. The days of the week, means of transport, pets, colours, numbers, parts of our body, but our incompetence in verb conjugation is leaving us floundering. I think the only two verbs we had used during past lessons had been Haben and Sein. Ich habe einen Hund........ Ich habe eine Katze...Ich bin 13 Jahre alt.....
Both Jane and I are frustrated by our inability to create correct German sentences. Without the prompt of a textbook, a table of verb conjugation, example phrases or even a xeroxed worksheet it seems an impossible task and I am immediately annoyed with Fraulein Farblos for her expectation. It was an enormous daunting leap forward from second year lessons. Should I have spent the summer holidays teaching myself German sentence structure?

There was obviously so much more to learn. Was the whole class behind? Perhaps we were just expected to somehow *'catch up'* to an acceptable third year linguistic standard. How often I was going to hear those two words in the next few days!

Jane pushes her blue rough book away from in front of her, only a few words are scribbled down, "God, this is impossible. I can't write a single sentence; I don't know what the words are". I share Jane's despondency. I certainly don't want to feel so defeated especially after how much I had enjoyed the maths lesson.

I shrug my shoulders, "Well, if she asks us, we'll just say we couldn't do it, okay? But listen, tell me, where were you in maths. Did you have to go somewhere else?"

The Verwirrtheit and Vereitelung of the German lesson going on around us are completely forgotten as I listen open-mouthed to Jane's explanation of her absence in my math's classroom.

For maths lessons, Jane has been placed in the set below the 'top set'. Maths set n° 2. She was not going to be in my maths class.

The top set in each subject was unquestioningly the O level class and then it seemed that the next set down *(Set N° 2)* would serve as a possible double entry class, either O level or CSE. Pupils could be selected for either exam according to how well they responded and coped with the coursework. Keeping the option open for either exam was used as an incentive (because the O level exam was still the more prodigious result) as well as the, somewhat futile, hope of avoiding discrimination between pupils. Grade 1 at CSE was supposed to be the equivalent of an O level pass but the CSE, unfortunately, never quite achieved comparable esteem amongst employers or the public.

For the next few weeks, all of us in the third year would be obsessed by the question *'which class are you in?'* We weren't stupid, we could see what had happened. Mixed ability, all supposedly equal, for two years, then suddenly the division of us all between academic and lesser-academic classes, O level classes or CSE classes. The inevitable return of the 'selection by ability' stigma.

There was also a simmering, underlying discontentment with some pupils who were placed in the sets just below the top one. It could be that they would, in fact, try for and pass an O level in the fifth form, but for the intervening years there would be some very derisive, hurtful comments thrown about, especially when someone could be in your class for one subject and then not for another. No one could have anticipated the social effects of this. Different classroom alliances now had to be created for each separate subject. Friendships developed over the last two mixed ability years became superficial and shallow.

Two parallel examination choices continuing within one experimental comprehensive school year. One with significant kudos, reputation and influence relating to grammar school education and one with implications towards a previous secondary modern orientation. Two very different curricula. Pupils who had been treated equally for the previous two years now pretending it didn't really matter which *'set'* they had been allocated to. A single curriculum would be needed to correct all this detrimental diversity. The merging of the two exams would be proposed by Labour Education Minister, Shirley Williams from 1979 but the arrival of the combined **GCSE** was still a long way off! It wouldn't be until 1988 that the first results of this new public examination were published.

Even twenty years after the education reorganisation, experts were still discussing the failings of the curriculum during those first experimental years,
In 1991 Brian Simon, an English educationalist and historian noted,

'Comprehensivisation had been undertaken in a half-hearted manner with no overall planning, no official thought, enquiry or study made as to what should comprise an appropriate common curriculum for the new comprehensive schools.'

I hoped Jane would continue to be my friend for the next year. She was telling me about being in a different set for maths although we would remain together in the top set for history. We compared our timetables. She wasn't going to be in my English class, but she would be in my top set French class. So, some lessons I would have with her, some I wouldn't. I was excited by the fact that I would now be in some of the same classes as her. Would it be possible to maintain our friendship through this unsettling third -year upheaval and division? At least we still shared our music. Hopefully I could meet up with her for lunchtime rehearsals and would still see her at Saturday morning music school. How did she know about all this setting? Was she happy being in the classes she had been assigned to?

"My Mum and Dad came into the parent's evening, chatted with loads of teachers". Of course! Her Mum's a teacher at another school. They would be very aware of all the new educational trends, "I've chatted everything through with Mum. I'm fine with the classes I'm in. I'm going to go at a slower pace in maths and English and the three science subjects, understand everything, then I'll probably take the O level anyway".

That wasn't Jane talking. That was her mum's opinion coming out of her mouth but I'm okay with that for the moment. My most overriding sensation is jealousy which I must not show.
Jealous that Jane can chat with her parents about her school life. Jealous that her parents had gone to the parent's evening to discuss what they thought would be best for their daughter.
Just jealous.

The 'end of lesson' bell shatters the atmosphere in the room. Phew! I think that Jane and I had completely switched off from that German lesson and my mind is certainly buzzing with all this information from Jane about the newly selected classes. So much is going on. So much I don't know about.

The last lesson for this afternoon scheduled on my timetable is biology. I really don't have the confidence or desire to walk into yet another classroom with yet another twenty-nine ability-selected pupils. Jane won't be heading to the same classroom. She is in a different biology set. I'll have to walk there by myself.

I'm sure 'Briefcase Boy' will be there, arriving from his Chinese lesson in the opposite direction. Christine, Paula, Sally, Katherine will arrive together in their little groups from their various classrooms in other parts of the school. Probably 'Big Pete' and his friend James. The usual group of four boys, maybe Margaret and Gillian too. It's all getting so predictable. The same pupils appearing in every class, just not any other girls from 3B.

I've had enough, disorientated and deceived by being part of this strange education reform experiment. I walk out of the school and head towards the wood where I know my log is waiting for me. I'll just sit on that by myself for the next hour until I know the school day has officially finished and it will be the correct time for me to walk back into my house, listen to the classical music resonating through the ground floor rooms, reply to my mother's staccato enquiry and pretend that the day has gone *'really well, thank you'.*

Chapter Twenty -Seven

Wednesday morning, 3rd September 1975. It's 9 o'clock. The first lesson written in my timetable for today is music. The new music block is finished so we are instructed to walk over to the modern hexagonal building situated in front of the sports hall immediately after registration.
Gathering back together in our form room that second morning of term was a strange sensation. Apart from 'Briefcase Boy', I hadn't been with any other members of 3B for the lessons the previous afternoon. On arriving in the room for morning registration I wasn't included in any of the ongoing

conversations. Only a few had looked up when I entered the classroom, and one of those had been Mr Bradshaw! No one smiled at me, no one waved or greeted me. Mary was perched on Julie's table, heads huddled together, laughing, not a glance in my direction as I enter and sit down in front of my lonely corner table.

I want to catch Mary when she is by herself, if that is ever going to be possible, and ask if she is still doing her clarinet lessons but I'm sensitive enough to realise that she definitely won't want to be caught talking about that *'sort of thing'* with me if overheard by Julie and the 'Village Girl' group. I am still envious of how Mary can drift between friendship groups. She does it so successfully, effortlessly slipping into whichever character mode is required. Brazen, daring, confrontational when amongst the Village Girls. Giggly and secretive with Julie and yet serious and quiet when with me. Which, I wonder to myself, is the real Mary though?

I suspect that Julie and Mary might have been in the same classes yesterday afternoon. Had they sat together for a maths lesson? What did they study when I was in German? Where had they been when I was supposed to be in my top set biology lesson. So much for me to discreetly find out if I am ever going to get my head around just exactly how this year is going to unfold. Were the two of them now, in fact, laughing over something funny that they had experienced together yesterday afternoon? Something I wasn't part of it and now never can be, since the third form setting has divided us all.

Register taken, bodies begin to push and jostle their way through the door frame. I follow. My feelings are mixed about this forthcoming music lesson. I am really looking forward to seeing the new music building. What a relief it will be for me to be able to dump my cello there in the mornings. No need to enter the main school building, now all I will need to do is veer right at the entrance and follow the service road, past the dustbins at the back of the kitchens, the bike sheds and slip quickly into the new building.

But, as I trail behind the rest of my form, I am already beginning to feel the usual anxiety, stomach churning and bowels cramping. How I hate these form music lessons. Am I going to manage to survive the next exasperating hour? The last two years of class music lessons have been painful and dispiriting. The young Miss Gilbert had been completely unable to control the first -year class, the majority of who simply treated the lessons as an opportunity for disrespect, rude behaviour and insolence. Thank goodness she had never mentioned again to me about bringing my music theory workbook into the class. I made sure I always sat well- hidden, tucked away in a dusty, dim corner of the garret-like old music room, shading in the segments drawn into my rough book as the minutes ticked agonizingly slowly by. Anyway, Miss Gilbert had left the school after the first year of comprehensive intake. An undynamic flute-playing Miss Smith replaced her.

The O level music teacher, Mr Digby, is standing, waiting for us at the double door entrance of the new music block, his untamed black wavy hair sticking up as if having recently experienced an electrical shock, reminding me of the faded manic-eyed picture of Hector Berlioz which used to hang on the wall in the old music classroom. I wonder if that poster has travelled over to the new building! Mr Digby is wearing his seemingly immutable faded beige corduroy jacket with the brown leather, oval elbow patches.

"Ah, there you all are, 3B is it?", he enquires. "Come along in".

So, he is going to be our music teacher this year. That's good news, I think. He teaches me theory of music at the Saturday morning music school, he conducts various orchestras I play in, he trusts me enough to let me be his concert page-turner. He is completely devoted to grammar school music teaching, an excellent keyboard player and an expert on Baroque music.

But will Mr Digby be able to impart his enthusiasm to uncooperative 3B? Will he be able to control the challenging behavioural issues of some members of this form. The queasiness in the pit of my stomach has not diminished.

As we file past Mr Digby, he catches my eye and gives a small nod. At least I have been recognised as I walk into the classroom, but I doubt my musical prowess will be acknowledged during the lesson as he tackles the very mixed ability 3B.

Wow! I am bowled over by the new main classroom. Large enough to fit a small orchestra inside, high ceiling criss-crossed with wooden beams. I am already looking forward to the first lunchtime rehearsal so I can hear how good the acoustics will be. Ceiling to floor windows fill the space with sunlight. This is going to be a wonderful room to play music in, whether orchestra, choir or a smaller string quartet. And, joy of joys, the floor is carpeted. No more need for us cellists to worry about our end pins slipping and sliding!

Shiny laminated, blue -topped tables scattered around the bright expanse seem lost in all the space.

Mr Digby instructs us to sit two at a table and hands out small blue exercise books filled with faint inked staves. These will be our music exercise books for when *'we write music'*. I can't help but wonder to myself if that might just be a little bit of an overenthusiastic and impossible expectation for some members of this class.

I have ended up at a table with 'Blonde Hair' girl as Lorraine and Michelle rushed to sit together and left her stranded, standing awkwardly, next to me. We smile briefly at each other. I throw a sideward glance at Mary sitting next to Julie. She hasn't touched the little blue book placed in front of her and is making no visible sign that she can read music or understand its notation. She is in a deep conversation with Julie, paying no attention to the rest of the room. What can they be talking about?

'Briefcase Boy' is sitting next to Kevin, but they are not talking to each other. Separate tables for two people make established friendship groups of three very awkward.

Mr Digby informs us that we are going to do some *'composing'*. He pauses in his explanation, hopefully waiting for a sign of approval, impressed excitement. There is none. 'No Bag Boy' is picking his nose. Tracy is passing around chewing gum. A familiar, but still frightening, sense of dread floods icily through my body. The change of environment, a different male teacher has momentarily subdued the troublemakers, but I fear it won't last long.

Mr Digby strides out of the room in search of some chime bars. He's not sure *'which cupboard they have been tidied away in'*. As soon as the door swings shut behind him, noises erupt, laughter explodes. A boy's croaky voice calls out,

"He thinks I'm gonna write music? What a fuckin' joke. "

"Hey", yells out Julie, "Maybe you'll be famous then, we'll see you on the telly!"

"Yeah, you'll see me on Top of the Pops alright, standing next to Gary bloody Glitter!"

'No Bag Boy' is egging on John who runs up to the open-lidded grand piano and starts thumping hard on some bass note keys,

"Listen everyone. I'm playing Jaws" It wasn't the right notes at all for the Jaws theme. He should have been repeating low E and F. I was furious he was banging so hard on the keyboard, probably damaging the ivory and the wire. *'Stop it'* I wanted to shout at him. Of course, I didn't. Thankfully Mr Digby bursts back through the swing doors, a cardboard box between his hands.

"You boy, get back into your seat this minute". The threat of a whole class detention silences the room. I swallow back down the acidic bile which has risen into my throat knowing I will just have to sit uncomplaining through what remains of this lesson. I think longingly of my log waiting for me in the woods! I should be there now. I'll definitely be there next music lesson. I couldn't bear to endure another hour like this. Poor Mr Digby, whatever is going on inside his head?

Three chime bars are placed on each table with a round rubber- ended stick. The room immediately rings out with discordant metallic chimes.

"Put down your sticks" yells Mr Digby irately, "No one plays until I give permission to start". I should have forewarned him. Don't hand out the sticks yet!

The object of the lesson is to compose a short repetitive melody. Mr Digby will come around to each table and show which notes we have on our chime bars and, if we are able, how to write the corresponding notes on the stave printed on the first page of our music exercise book. Really?

Hasn't learning some basics of theory of music been somewhat neglected during our first two years? I fear Mr Digby's expectations of the third -year class in front of him are somewhat naïve and misinformed. He wants 3B to write musical notation? What happened to learning about value of notes, key signatures, time signatures, pitch, bar lines or even just learning how to draw a treble clef? The familiar suffocating haze of disillusionment and exasperation enfolds me.

I hand the stick to 'Blonde Hair' girl who is disproportionally delighted that I have handed over all control of the lesson to her. I don't respond to her quizzical look as she becomes absorbed with her percussive banging. I simply zip up my pencil case and place it, along with the unused blue music book, back into my satchel. Trying desperately to block out the confining, encompassing cacophony, I gaze out of the window. Two crows bob up and down in comic syncopation on a branch in an adjacent, orange-leafed beech tree.

Despite the high ceiling, the vast space around me, the metallic discordant jarring din clangs through my head. At best, the Anvil chorus from Verdi's Il Trovatore, at worst a headache -inducing, penetrating work by Xenakis.

Mr Digby gets no further than leaning over the first couple of tables. The bell goes indicating the end of the lesson. I make sure I am first out of the room.

The next morning, I successfully arrive at the new music building without anyone spotting me walking in with my cello case. The door is already unlocked so I decide to have a good look around. First, I locate the large storage area for the musical instruments and lodge my cello between two of the designated wooden cylinder pegs which have been thoughtfully knocked in at regular intervals along the wall to keep the cellos upright. On the shelf above I spot violin cases, a tambourine and cardboard boxes full of those annoying chime bars.

To the left of the entrance door is the Head of Music's office, the main big classroom, then a door leading into a second much smaller, darker classroom. Opposite are the two practice rooms, both with upright pianos. Practice room n°1 big enough for a string quartet. Smaller, more intimate, practice room n°2 would become my favourite space. Just enough room to pull the piano away from the wall and sit on the floor behind. Hidden from everyone and everything. Both practice rooms had high-mounted oblong windows. No possibility of anyone peering in from outside. Perfect for future refuge.

I'm just leaving the building to head back to my form room for morning registration when I come face to face with Mr Digby,

"Ah, there you are!", his standard, trademark greeting for everyone, "Have you found the instrument storage? Jolly good, we're all very pleased with this new building. By the way, I wanted to catch you, a couple of points…. Would you be willing to get together into another string quartet this term? Get some Haydn and Mozart in your repertoire. We'll start with the Haydn quartet Op.2 No. 4. I'll sort out getting the music to you."

That means we are going to be asked to play in a forthcoming concert.

The fact that he asks me when I am by myself isn't lost on me, just something I have now come to accept, even though it is distressing and confusing for me to cope with. Yesterday, I was sitting in his classroom, a member of form 3B having a music lesson. Yesterday, I was a 'not to be recognised' or 'singled out for any reason' pupil in a mixed ability class. Today, I am apparently an individual acknowledged for my music ability, appreciated for who I really am, someone capable of discussing and understanding classical music. I appreciate the discretion of Mr Digby but, oh my goodness, this is so hard for me to deal with. Tossed between comprehensive education ideals and lingering grammar school ethos.

"Also," he continues, "I'm thinking of doing the Ralph Vaughan Williams 'Fantasia on a Christmas Carol' with the senior choir in December for the Christmas concert. Would you be willing to do the opening cello solo?"

I nod enthusiastically.

Of course I would be willing to do the cello solo! Rehearsing and performing with the senior choir; my idea of heaven encapsulated in working with, and being accepted by, musicians from the upper school years.

I can't wipe the stupid grin off my face and have to stop myself from skipping back across the concreted playground area, pass the terrapins, through the scuffed double doors and up the staircase to my form room.

Chapter Twenty -Eight

That very same week in early September 1975 of my lessons now being 'setted' in preparation for commencing the O -level curriculum, the columnist Lynda Lee Potter reported in the Daily Mail that the *'O Level grading system had mysteriously altered'*.

Her article published in the newspaper of 10th September drew attention to the government's changed policy.

Up until July 1975 O level candidates had been awarded only a *pass* or *fail* classification. The grades achieved for every exam attempted were given to the pupils on a flimsy slip of paper, but certificates were then only awarded for the actual O levels passed. The examination board used by my school currently offered the numeric classifications of **1** to **9** for exam results. **1,2,3,4,5** and **6** were passes, whilst **7,8** and **9** were failure grades.

Now, in the new government policy, there were apparently going to be just five grades for O level results: **A** to **E**.

A, **B** and **C** were to be the equivalents of the old 1 to 6 grades, a pass of varying success but a **certificate** would now also be awarded to those who received grades **D** and **E,** which were equivalent of the old failing grades 7,8 and 9. There would be no further mention of a pass or fail at O level standard. <u>Regardless of the grade achieved all pupils would be awarded certification of their O level examination attempts.</u>

As Miss Lee-Potter complained in her article,

'The government have now abolished the words 'pass' and 'fail' because they think it's wrong to tell children they have failed.'

Notification of the public examination grading changes had been sent home in the summer end -of - term school bulletin, June 1975, before the commencement of my third year. I had just arrived back to finish the last weeks of term after that bizarre visit to the castle in Northumberland. I wonder how many parents bothered to read it and then ultimately struggled to understand the somewhat ambiguous phrasing. The sentence for new grade D is a good example of weaselling. This is the exact wording from the bulletin and what parents would have read:

<u>G.C.E. 'O' LEVEL GRADES</u> *The Secretary of State for Education has decided that the same system of grading shall apply to all G.C.E. Examination Boards in and after this year's summer examinations. This is what the changes mean:*

Grade	Description	Old Grades
A	Grade A indicates the standard of attainment to be expected of the ablest candidates in the age group for which the examination is designed.	1 and 2
B	Grade B indicates attainment which, though not of the highest quality, is substantially above the minimum	3 and 4

C	standard required for Grade C. The lower boundary of Grade C is equivalent to the minimum performance formerly required for an O Level pass.	5 and 6
D	Grade D indicates performance not far below that required for Grade C.	7 and part of 8
E	Grade E indicates the lower level of attainment judged by the board to be of sufficient standard to be recorded on a GCE certificate.	7 and part of 8
Unclassified	Candidates in this category are those whose level of attainment is below the minimum judged by the board to be of sufficient standard to be recorded on a G.C.E. certificate.	Remainder of 8 and the whole of 9

Complicated reading! No wonder my parents made no comment on this to me.
Surely even those parents with a less critical and cynical viewpoint could realise that had been a certain amount of fudging of standards required, some sort of devaluation of the actual examinations. For example, the details of the grading changes state that the lower boundary of new Grade C is equivalent to the minimum performance formerly required for an O -level pass. What does it mean if you achieve a new grade D on your certificate and your performance was 'not far below' that required for Grade C? You haven't in fact *'passed'* the O -level examination but would have failed in the previous year's grading system. Good news though (so as not to discourage any pupil who was entered for a GCE O level) you very nearly achieved a pass and for your effort have been awarded a certificate to state you have a Grade D!
What on earth would the country's employers make of these new certificates? Would they have any indication of the actual academic standards of the youth, the school leavers, now entering their businesses, factories, companies?

My O level exams were still two years away when these public exam grading changes were introduced in 1975, although I did sit, and pass with a grade A, an O level English language exam one year early, during my fourth year. The sudden change of grading would have been more significant, though, for the two school years above me who would be preparing for their O levels before I did. I wonder how they fared, presumably they were relatively unbothered, and their exam certificates appeared full of **A**, **B** and **C** passes. After all, they were still the 'eleven plus selected' pupils focusing on the O level curriculum.

The secondary schools in different counties around England who had made the change to comprehensive education before mine, during the last years of the 1960's and first years of the 1970's would now be seeing their fifth-year comprehensive pupils sitting public examinations. The results, the success rates or the deterioration, the disappointment, the academic achievement trends would be, without doubt, publicised and thoroughly scrutinized.
Would any connection be made between the analysis of these first public examination results of the new non-selective education experiment and the Government's decision in 1975 to suddenly simplify and facilitate the grading system? No longer the decisive *pass* or *fail*.
Could this new blurred and ambivalent grading system have anything at all to do with a covert attempt to distract from a noticed downturn in academic standards. Were parents being subtly prepared for a change in education expectations, an apparent devaluation of public examination marking, so that the annual results, covering the first experimental years, would not show up just how disappointing the comprehensive education concept had initially been?

Published in the Daily Telegraph in October 1975, a report noted *'a gradual decline in the percentage of comprehensive school pupils succeeding in GCE examinations.'*

This information printed on the school bulletin of June 1975 relating to the Secretary of State for Education and Science's decision to change the O-level examination grading system would be important reading for the parents of the 60 or so pupils in my intake who were deemed by the headmaster, (this sentence would appear in a later school bulletin), to be the *'pupils who would have been selected for grammar school education in former years and this group may be seen as the normal G.C.E. Ordinary level group'*.
Any parent reading about the new grading system must surely have been aware it was only ever going to be applicable for the twenty to twenty-five per cent of my school year who were judged to be in the top academic attainment ability. Those of us who had obviously and clandestinely been recognised (and counted) from the very first day of our arrival at the school as potential candidates destined for that particular course.

Did all this mention of O- level preparation presented in the school bulletin cause uneasiness and frustration to other parents I wonder? The ex -grammar school's obsession with obtaining O-level passes overshadowing the inescapable fact that the school now consisted of a majority of mixed ability comprehensive pupils. If only sixty of us in the experimental intake of 210 pupils going on to sit the fifth- year public exams in two years' time had been earmarked as the *'normal G.C.E. Ordinary level group'*, an approximate 30% of the entire year, then what were the expectations and the thoughts of the parents of the remaining 70% adolescents? There was still the opportunity for the late academic developers, placed in the one or two ability sets below the top set to aim for either an O level A -C pass or a CSE grade 1 but, after five years at the school, half of my entire school year were unable to pass either an O level or a CSE grade 1.

The CSE examination was designed to cater for roughly 60% of the ability range. There were five pass grades **1** to **5** with a CSE grade **1** pass accepted as *'at least an O level **C** grade'*. This was explained on the back of the current CSE certificates at that time: *'Grade 1 in CSE describes a standard such that the candidate might reasonably have secured a pass of ordinary level of the GCE examination had he followed a course leading to that examination.'*

In the summer of **1978**, my experimental mixed ability intake sat our fifth-year public examinations.

The results were printed in the school bulletin and the local newspapers. It was crucial for everyone to know how the first comprehensive year intake had fared.
Unfortunately, I never got to see the results from the other two comprehensive schools in the town. I had drifted too far away from my music friends who had attended the red- uniformed primary school and subsequently disappeared off to one of the other secondary schools in the town. It would have been interesting to compare. My intake had started at the existing grammar school with O level selected pupils in the years above us being taught by teachers accustomed to O level standards of attainment in the classroom.
The other two schools had been previous secondary moderns converted into comprehensive schools now accepting pupils of all academic abilities.

The Examination Results article in that school bulletin of Autumn 1978 heralding the achievements of us in the fifth year was full of statistics. After our five years of being subjected to experimental education reform, we were simply reduced to percentages, facts, figures and academic ability data.

The achievement of O level passes (A-C) including the CSE grade 1 equivalent still, unproportionally considering the vast academic range of all the pupils in my school year, being the most important and sought-after piece of information apparently still required by everyone.

The article in the **1978 school bulletin** read as follows:

Examination Results

The fifth-year results were those of the first comprehensive year group. About 60 of the total of 205 pupils would have been selected for grammar school education in former years and this group may be been seen as the normal G.C.E. Ordinary level group. The examination is designed for the top 25% of the ability group. C.S.E. is designed to cater for the top 60% of the ability range.

This year, of 205 pupils of <u>all abilities</u> in the fifth year:

189 achieved at least one certificate at GCE or CSE level.
102 achieved at least one pass (A-C) at GCE O level, CSE grade 1
51   achieved 5 or more passes at GCE O level
19   achieved 8 or more passes at GCE O level

Just what did all the parents make of these printed examination results of the first comprehensive year?
O levels, O levels, O levels! Their attainment dominated the public examination results table. Despite five years of comprehensive education reform, the ex-grammar school still not yet able to detract from their pre-eminence. The parents bombarded with the successful facts and figures. Half of the entire years' pupils had achieved at least <u>one</u> pass at O level or equivalent and 51 of their first-ever comprehensive intake managed to pass 5 or more. Does that correlate with the 60 initially recognised pupils as being in the *'normal O level group'!* A sentence I still find distasteful, given the climate of the radical education environment we were expected to fit in to. No praise or admiration ever given as to how we coped within the experimental mixed ability chaos.
19 pupils achieved 8 or more passes at O level: what a triumph for the school! What an acknowledgement for the dedicated and persistent O level grammar schoolteachers who had remained on the teaching staff!

The parents of the 100 or so pupils who hadn't achieved anything *'O level standard related'*, what was their opinion of this 1978 public examination result publication?
So little space given to the achievements of the pupils who had followed the CSE curriculum. What about their successes? Over 50 of them (a quarter of my school year intake) gained at least 4 or 5 CSE certificates with grades **2** to **5**. No mention of their personal academic accomplishment. Were they and their parents pleased and satisfied with the outcome of the five years of secondary education? Would these certificates, these grades, help them move into further education or employment?
A brief nod in the published statistic (*189 pupils….*) to the six pupils who managed <u>one</u> certificate at CSE grade **5**, but no mention of the 16 pupils, who, unfortunately, after five years of secondary education, couldn't manage to pass any exam at all.

How many parents were taken in by the enthusiastic announcement that:
'189 pupils achieved at least one certificate at GCE or CSE level'.

Taking in to account the 1976 Government decision to change the public exam grading system, this sentence doesn't seem quite so exhilarating! Certificates were now being awarded for any attempt at sitting an exam whether it was a *pass* or *fail*! Of those 189 pupils, some would have achieved an O level grade of **A** to **C**, a *pass*. Some, however, would have received certificates recording grades of **D** and **E**, a *fail,* and a hundred or so pupils had been awarded certificates, not for an O level pass, but for their CSE results of grades **2** to **5**.

So *'achieving a certificate'* being a somewhat embellished, self-congratulatory phrase not entirely reflecting the true level of academic attainment, and which could easily be misinterpreted by parents, statisticians and government advisors.

Chapter Twenty -Nine

Fridays are the days when I don't have any lessons back together with 3B. What exactly is the point of me still being in this form? At 8.55am I walk into the first-floor room and seat myself at my usual table in the corner where the windows meet at right angles waiting for the day's registration. I don't speak to anyone, pretending that I don't really mind. I have my satchel to rummage through and the windows to stare out of. Anyway, it is only for five minutes and then we all get up again to leave, heading off to our various assigned classrooms.

Mary is seated on the other side of the room, her chair wedged into a small gap between Julie's and Linda's table. She perches precariously, it's not really an assigned seating space, her legs sideways. It doesn't look very comfortable! I'm sure her change of place has been noticed by everyone else in the room but no one says anything. She seems to have so much to talk about now with the girls opposite. This morning their heads are bent low together, faces hidden by identical, stiffly- flicked fringes.

The chatter on Friday mornings is always about the previous evenings Top of the Pops. I don't watch it, of course, as it is county youth orchestra rehearsal night, but I do like to keep my ears open and pitifully try and catch the gist of the conversations. You never know, I just might have to discuss the pop songs with someone! I tune into the end of a discussion about Showaddywaddy and then learn that Rod Stewart is at number One with 'Sailing'.

Mr Bradshaw snaps shut the thin orange coloured register,

"Right, off you go you lot, if I don't see you again, have a good weekend. Don't do anything too wild."   He chuckles at his own joke. No one responds with laughter.

I head towards the door, hoping to be one of the first out through the doorframe and therefore avoid standing in the bottleneck as we all try to pass through the narrow entrance. The 'Village Girl' group push into the melee behind me. They are sniggering and whispering,

"Look at her with her babyish skirt and satchel! Thinks she's so brainy going off to her bloody top class with all those other fuckin' smart-arses. I can't stand any of 'em...."

It's so unfair! What have I done to make them resent me so much? I bet they are still together in lessons, laughing, having fun, talking about me. Does even Mary detest me now because we are hardly ever together in the same classroom? Why has the school put me in this position? I am SO furious with the teaching staff, the headmaster, everyone.

It's started already, the rumblings of discontentment, the implication of *'them and us.'* The resentment of being treated as equals for the first two years and then abruptly segregated and categorized according to ability. It's not my fault, I want to scream at them. I didn't want to be part of this education experiment. I didn't know that I would be sent to lessons completely separated from all the other girls in 3B. My intestines clench ominously and now I will have to stop off at a toilet on the way.

I fly down the stairs, stumbling on the last two and jog along the corridor to the swing doors. Thank goodness my sister is now in the sixth form over in its own separate building and hardly ever walks around these main school buildings. It would have been just my luck for her to have passed me this morning, stopped me and demanded to know why I was so red-faced and running along the corridor, which is punishable by a detention.
I've got to get to room 3. It's double English for me.

The classroom door is already open and after my hysterical Olympian dash I'm the first to arrive. I see Mrs Matthias standing beside her desk, flicking pages in a paper-back. I give a quick rap on the door frame and without looking up, lost in her book, she waves me in. I walk to the back of the room to choose a table safely tucked away in the furthest corner. I don't want anyone to have to walk past me and notice my flushed cheeks and moist eyes.
I take the chair off the top of the table where they have all been left poised after the previous evening's floor sweeping. Obviously, Mrs Matthias does not deign to walk around her teaching room each morning and replace the chairs, two under each table, facing the front.
The classroom is bright, airy, white walls, pale yellow paint on the door frames and the dado. The act of swishing my metal chair through the air disturbs motes of minute dust and I watch them float aimlessly above me trapped in the morning sunlight shafts. Piles of identically spined paperback books fill the shelves on the back wall behind me. Thirty orange and white Penguin editions of 'The Great Gatsby' in one stack. A crooked untidy heap of thin brown copies of Romeo and Juliet lies next to four tattered dark blue Oxford Concise dictionaries. I smell paper, the mustiness of old books. It reminds me of the town library and calms me.
Laughing girls' voices herald the arrival of others along the corridor before they appear at the open door. Christine and Paula stride confidently into the room and sit together at one of the front tables. Margaret walks in, followed by Sally and Katherine, the 'inseparable pair'. Big Pete and James, then the group of four self-assured loud boys.
A curly-haired girl hesitates at the door and looks shyly into the room before entering.
"Come in, come in", invites Mrs Matthias, which draws our attention to the timid figure, increasing her anxiety. I'm surprised, it's Judith from my primary school. Judith who was one of the girls who sat the common entrance exam for the girl's school in the town. The exam I wasn't allowed to take. I'd seen her now and then over the last two years, occasionally in the corridor as our form groups slithered past each other, but never spoken to her.
I give a little wave which she spots, and the relief visibly lights up her pale face into a smile. She quickly weaves between the front tables and claims the place next to me by dropping her bag onto the tabletop and collapses into the chair.
I can't help noticing, enviously, that she too has a brightly coloured hippy bag, the beads on the tassels making a delightful tinkling F sharp note as they hit the surface.
"Hi, you", she does a small self-deprecatory shrug and giggle, "God knows what I am doing in this class! I was relieved to see you though."
So, Judith has been selected to be in the top set for English but hadn't appeared in my class for maths.
Judith had been placed in maths set N° 2 and like Jane she would be studying maths at a 'slower' pace and then be advised whether to try for a O level or a CSE examination pass. Judith would also appear in my French class too but none of the other third year subjects.

This setting by ability for each subject is so complicated but, I think for us in these first years of the comprehensive education experiment, even more unsettling and disorientating. Maybe it is simply just me who is struggling to cope. Why can't I seem to find friends in any classroom I sit in?
Mary from my original form was a *'sort of'* friend but now I rarely have any lessons with her. Jane and I share our musical instrument playing but she is only going to be in the same classroom as me for six hours of each week. French, German and history lessons. I will have four hours of lesson every

week with Judith, but will she always want to sit next to me? Sally and Katherine had cemented their friendship over the past two years, being in the same 'dream form'. Neither Helen from primary school nor violin-playing Verity, who I spend extra curricula hours rehearsing with, have yet appeared in any of my third- year classes. I've noticed that Paula has chosen to sit next to Christine. Our brief encounter in the maths lesson probably already forgotten. Margaret has pointedly used her yellow hessian hippy bag to reserve the space next to her for someone not yet in the room.

Had the decision to disperse us between different ability classes at the beginning of our third year after the two- year trial of mixed ability teaching been sufficiently researched? We were the first year of this, so there was obviously no documentation or data as to what effect this pre-planned segregation might have on us, the teenagers involved?
With my ever cynical and questioning mind, I couldn't help thinking that the inevitable selection for academic potential, supposedly so criticized and reviled, had still taken place, simply just delayed by two years? By keeping us together in mixed ability classes for the first two years did it not make the third-year segregation by ability then crueller to accept? Surely some of the intelligent pupils in my year around me were beginning to realise this. Were they? I had no friends to ask, no one with whom to share my thoughts. It was so much to keep to myself, carry silently around, poisoning my perspective.
How much were these new comprehensive schools being used as excuses for social experiment and how much for genuine education reform? Obviously, the social experiment had to be curtailed once we were still inevitably going to be selected by academic ability in order to meet public examination requirements.

I look surreptitiously at Judith who is sorting through her pencil case and then further around at the others in the room.
I haven't been to a science lesson yet or had a geography class. Who will turn up in those lessons? Who will I know in the classrooms, will anyone save a place for me? Disappointingly, so far this week, none of my first-year Scottish dancing club acquaintances have appeared in any of my classes. There will now be no further opportunity for me to associate with any of them.
All this fragmentation, this dissipation is bewildering and for me, infuriating. The friendships and attachments created throughout all the seven forms over the last two years have suddenly been splintered. It's going to be tricky to understand and react to the modus operandi of each new separate subject grouping, have adequate social skills to cope with the shifting allegiances.
More importantly for us thirteen-year-old/fourteen-year-old girls, who will sit with whom in each of the classrooms!

I was destined to become a lonely figure walking by myself around the school buildings, arriving solitarily for each lesson, worried sick with a churning stomach that since the last gathering of any top set class group, fickle friendships and seating partners had altered.
Would I walk into an English lesson and find Judith sitting at a table with someone else (yes often!) Would music friend Jane choose another girl, a friend from the 'dream form', to work together with on a history project (it did happen many times). Would 3B girls accept me back and talk to me during art or sport? (very rarely). Would they ignore and snub me? (most definitely). Any self-confidence or happiness was fast eroding.

Not many spaces left now at the separated two-person tables. What must surely be the last two figures appear at the open door. It's 'Briefcase Boy' (he's taken his time getting here. Ah no, I forgot, I ran!). Wait a minute, he's walking in with Gillian, and they are talking together. She's smiling up at him. How do they know each other? Maybe they do Chinese class together? I feel a dart of jealously.

I want to be able to talk to him too. They move apart and Gillian heads towards Margaret who has saved her a place.

Once the two of them are settled into their chairs, Mrs Matthias decides to look up from her paperback and does a slow gaze sweeping around the room. Her eyes exaggeratedly half-shut. Her blue-framed glasses atop her head.

"Are we *all* here now?" I'm impressed by her dramatic presence. Her wonderful contralto voice with just the right amount of inferred indignation. It makes me think of Lady Bracknell in Oscar Wilde's The Importance of being Earnest! No wonder she produces the school plays! She has our utter attention. As if in a dimmed auditorium, we wait, hushed, for her next theatrical phrase.

"Well, I'm sure you realise this is going to be the O level English set. We've got a lot of work to do, there's quite a bit of catching up to do…"

There's that phrase again. We've got to *'catch up'* for everything we have apparently not achieved during the first two years. It's hardly our fault that we were expected to work at such a slow, infantile pace.

In 1976, an HM Inspectors report was to note that the *'average achievement of the 'top set' in comprehensive schools was still lower than the equivalent class in some selection schools.'*

I wonder how our third- year teachers felt? Were they depressed, worried about the possibility of getting the class to the required standard or were they excited by the challenge ahead of them? Despite the ritenuto of the first two years, did we in fact have the inherent intelligence to *'get on with it'*, to perform as expected and earn the school the expected commendable number of public examination passes.

On a positive note, it was later agreed by educational reformists that setting at year three found that the exam results of the ablest pupils improved following the reassessment.

Mrs Matthias slowly fixes her glasses back down on her nose and does another dramatic slow eye-sweep of us all in the room. Without her glasses, had she not been able to see us before? Or maybe her glasses were in fact just a plain glass prop, and she thrived on the theatrical effect! Anyway, it worked, she still has our complete engrossed attention.

"Welcome everyone to my English class. We will be moving swiftly along with both English language and English literature. We need to start working hard ASAP, that's as soon as possible for those who didn't know that acronym. Look up the word acronym at home". She does a deep, nicotine-induced chesty chuckle.

"I would have expected you to all to have, at least, studied some texts by now…." she trails off mid-sentence with an affected sigh and dramatic shaking of her head,

"Sadly, that didn't happen….", I glance sideways at Judith who responds to my raised eyebrows with a comical grimace.

"So, I'm sure you all understand", a quick single handclap and jangle of bracelets, "I expect you all to move quickly on with reading the books I will be handing out. We will spend quite a bit of time on grammar. I need to find out how much you know. There will be a lot of creative writing and, also, we need to start analysing poems and get working on some Shakespeare."

My heart is singing. I'm loving this. It's fast, demanding, recognizing our intelligence. Today, she informs us, we are going to look at the subjunctive. This is SO good. We are back to using the proper grammar terms and even exploring further. She explains what the subjunctive clause is. Which expressions it can be used after. What form of the infinitive follows….

Why have I been colouring in the margins of my books, shading in five-minute clock segments in frustrated boredom for the last two years when stimulating and intellectually vibrant lessons such as this could have been offered to some of us since our very first day at this school?

Mrs Matthias tells us to get out our rough books. We are to write down the beginning of the sentence she reads out and then we are to finish it:

It is important that you…….

The teacher insists that……..

I demand that……

Judith and I quietly giggle as we look at each other's work. I attempt to write as complicated a sentence as I can. Something I wouldn't have dared do for the last two years. We pass around the class reading out our work. No one guffaws derisively, no distracting paper aeroplanes come gliding past, no metal chair legs are purposely scaped back and forward. The atmosphere is respectful and electric. Everyone listens, we laugh out loud at the funniest phrases. The others in this class are so clever. I think I will have to work hard to keep up. I am excited.

Mrs Matthias's yellow-stained forefinger with its heavy Bordeaux- red painted nail arrives last at 'Briefcase Boy'. He reads out his witty and immaculately correct sentence,
"The teacher insists that the boy arrive in her classroom at the required time without any unnecessary display of subordination."

Mrs Matthias lets out an unguarded cackle of appreciation and delight. We all laugh too. 'Briefcase Boy' raises his eyes, looks around at us all enjoying the moment, the praise, and grins. He will definitely become her favourite pupil!

Oh my goodness, my stomach does an odd unfamiliar flutter. I think I might be falling in love if that is how it feels when you admire someone for their confidence, their resilience, their intelligence? I just don't know anything at all about this 'getting a boyfriend' thing.

I know 'Briefcase Boy' has a spotty face and lank greasy hair, he stoops because he doesn't yet have the confidence for his new height and he struggles to coordinate his lengthening but still gangly limbs, but then I'm not pretty or fashionable, or even noticeable, really. How can I make it work that we walk together to a classroom? We are the only two members of original 1B who have been diverted into top set classes, yet at the moment it seems that if he spies me from under his fringe, he purposefully dashes off in a different direction. Am I really that unappealing? Lucky, lucky Paula who gets to travel with him on the same bus every day.

Mrs Matthias motions with her hands to calm us all down and orders us to write down our homework to be done for the next lesson. We are to write sentences using the past subjunctive beginning with If……

'If I were rich……'
'If I had arrived earlier……'

The end of lesson bell clangs around the room but we remain seated. Another hour to go.

Mrs Matthias walks between the tables placing a paperback collection of poetry on each. As expected from respectful and interested pupils, we sit in silence as she manoeuvres her multi-layered billowing skirts through the gaps. Such anticipation and patience unparalleled with previous incidents ingrained in my memory in the 1B form room, when work material placed on tables met with complete refusal to engage, insolence and even destruction.

"Right class, turn to page 27, quickly now, we need to move on. Find the Blake poem 'Tyger, Tyger'. For the next hour we study the poem. We look for, and find, with a bit of help, examples of '*alliteration*', Mrs Matthias asks us to look at word association. Sally puts her hand up and says she has spotted '*loads of words to do with the body',* Blake uses the words hand, heart, shoulder, feet. Mrs Matthias praises Sally with an encouraging, "Well done'".

I'm not confident enough to put up my hand.

'Briefcase Boy' is swaying, effervescent with excitement, he thrusts his arm up. He has found a lot of words associated with a blacksmith, he has spotted the word anvil, furnace, hammer, chain….

I am in awe. Oh, 'Briefcase Boy' we need to get together, only to talk of course. Please, please notice me….

I can tell Mrs Matthias is enjoying the class, I am too, it's quick, quirky, so vibrant and vivacious, sparking off in every direction. Like -minded pupils are working together, throwing ideas. The pupils in this class are so clever, so confident.

I wish I had been with all these *top set* pupils since day one at this school. How different my attitude, my feelings, my confidence would be!

The bell clangs. I don't want this lesson to end.
I sense that Mrs Matthias feels the same. She seems startled that the bell has broken up the spell of the class. Was she surprised that some of us in this first 'unknown comprehensive intake' would be capable of such an eclectic lesson?

Chapter Thirty

So, this year we are doing the three separate science subjects: biology, chemistry and physics. Each of the classes has been setted by ability of course and I'm pretty sure I will look around the different science labs and see the same twenty-five or so top set 'core' pupils who now appear in all my classes and as always it will be just 'Briefcase Boy' and myself from form 3B.
I amble slowly alone towards the physics lab, my mind in a quandary. Do I arrive one of the first in the room, get myself established at one of the wooden benches and wait expectantly for the other girl friendship groups to arrive in their twos and threes, maybe they will choose to sit alongside me, or do I arrive as one of the last, slip unobtrusively into the room and just perch on any stool where there is a space. I seriously doubt anyone will look up as I come through the doorway and call out for me to join them.
I choose the latter, to arrive as one of the last in the classroom, and to delay my arrival, make a quick detour, slipping out through the double doors on my right, leading onto the tarmacked area facing the old gym building and the terrapins. This will add a few more minutes if I do a vague solitary circuit of the playground before returning inside. A squally shower of fleeting rain causes me to briefly pause in the shelter of the porched area, much to the annoyance of a group of tall, grey - blazered boys who need to push past me as they rush to get back into the building. Damp material, chip-fat, spearmint chewing gum odours briefly engulf me. Once they have disappeared raucously into the dim corridor and the doors have shut, abruptly cutting off any noise from inside, I search through my satchel in the pretence of finding something. A few more seconds tick by.

The door of the physics lab is still open, I sidle in, but the movement catches the eye of the teacher. "Are you the last? Hurry up then and shut the door behind you." He turns his back on me to continue writing on the blackboard.
Five parallel thick wooden benches face the board. High stools placed haphazardly along each. Low chatter hums around the laboratory. I recognise the faces of course. 'Briefcase Boy' and his friend from 3G sit at the front gazing up at the blackboard. Alongside them are Paula and Christine. Sally and Katherine are along the bench behind next to Gillian and Margaret. The group of four boys are on the third bench. James and Big Pete are laughing together sat at the bench at the back of the room. I walk towards the fourth bench, there is an empty stool at the end, so I quickly perch myself on it. The two boys on my left stare at me incredulously as I settle myself and then they turn to each other, eyes wide in an astonished smirk. I don't recognise them and certainly haven't come across them before during the last two years. They must be particularly interested in the science subjects because I didn't notice them in my English or history lessons. They might have been in maths, I don't remember, and I'm certainly not going to look at them again now anyway. I keep my eyes straight ahead looking at the blackboard.
The physics teacher has our attention as the lesson begins. He seems young, I think he must be a new teacher, with crinkly ginger hair and heavy, black-framed glasses. We are going to study friction.

He asks us to open our exercise books, write the date and the title, then copy his sentence off the board,
> *Friction is the force that opposes motion between any two surfaces that are in contact.*

We are then to copy down the formula $f = \mu N$

The atmosphere in the room is attentive and concentrated. This is something new and academically stimulating, we are being treated and respected at a level worthy of our intelligence.

Mr Ginger-Hair gives us a basic introduction to friction. He slides various things along his top table, a pen, two different textbooks, a tennis ball, a toy car. After launching each object, he dashes to the far end to catch it. He doesn't arrive in time for the ball or the toy car, the ball bounces on the floor and off towards the first wooden bench. The car drops off the edge and hits the ground with a metallic chink. We laugh at his antics.

Mr Ginger-Hair seems pleased to have won us over so easily. He has our complete attention. He grins at us.

"I think you are beginning to understand friction! Of course, class, we won't be working with the formula today. We'll come round to that maybe next week. Today we'll just start off with some experiments to give you a basic understanding of how frictional force is exerted. I'll bring around the equipment you will be needing. Make a note of what happens, what conclusions you come to in your rough book and then write it up in your exercise books for homework."

Mr Ginger-Hair passes between the benches placing down different items, carpet tiles, strips of lino, plastic trays, small planks of wood, toy cars.

"Give the car a small push and let it slide over each surface. Record what you observe. I think I've put out enough for you to work in twos. Sort yourself out with a partner" ……

I should have seen that coming.

The now familiar grey mist of annoyed disappointment immediately encircles me, and I slump on my stool lowering my head. The boys next to me begin to have fun with their little red Matchbox car. I commence a complicated doodle in my rough book. After fifteen or so minutes, the teacher has arrived at our fourth bench. He immediately senses there is a problem,

"Everything alright here?" He stares at me through his thick lens, "Ah I see, you don't have a partner to work with. Hey, you two boys, are you letting this girl here have a go?" They shrug, which saves them having to reply in the negative.

"Well, just share your results with her so she can jot them down". Fat chance of that.

Mr Ginger-Hair gazes at me again.

"Well, anyway, have you got any questions about our experiment today?" Is this his attempt at including me back into the lesson. I can't believe he would be feeling sorry for me.

I stare down, hot-faced, at my exercise book lying open on the bench.

"Just one question Sir, what is this μ?" He takes off his glasses to wipe a greasy lens,

"Ah, that is the Greek letter M, but as I have already said, we won't be using that formula today".

He has lost interest in me and turns to talk to the pupils on the bench behind.

The Greek letter M? I never knew mu was written like that. Why had no one ever told me and whatever is it doing in this physics formula? I knew most of the Greek letters. They were used quite frequently in the Times crossword puzzle:

The clue *Greek character in dark apparel (5)* had been too easy, but I had been pleased to beat my father in working out the anagram: *pinoles (7)*.

I am now puzzled and a little bit annoyed that, yet again, I have stumbled across something I didn't know. How have I got to Third Year in this school without knowing how the Greek alphabet is written? The basics of friction, toy cars and the two boys next to me completely forgotten. I am determined now to get to the town library next Saturday afternoon, find the encyclopaedia A-L and copy down all the Greek letters.

The physics lesson continues around me, but I have switched off.
Friction is so obvious anyway. Things move slower over a rough surface and quicker over a smooth surface. Everyone can surely see that. Who wants to study it further? I don't need to copy the boys' stupid notes. I haven't enjoyed the lesson. I fold my arms petulantly across my chest and hunch over the bench. The white-chalked formula for friction taunts me from the blackboard, but no longer intrigues me. Strangely, for someone who used to love codes, puzzles and notations, there is now little enthusiasm left.
I spend the last minutes of the lesson staring out of the window, across the courtyard, watching the heads of the pupils sat in the classrooms opposite. I wonder if they are enjoying their lessons.

A little something inside of me was slowly beginning to recede. My desire to learn, my thirst for knowledge was being suffocated by my loneliness, my isolation from the school life around me and my inability to fit in.
Sadly, I was not going to succeed in physics. As was typical of my performance in all subjects at the school in this, the third year, I started full of enthusiasm being incorporated in the top set classes but then, so quickly, so inevitably, became swathed in that dark poisonous cloud of embitterment and unhappiness.

My third -year reports for physics acutely captured this deterioration:
They began with:

Autumn term 1975:   *'Her work is always of a high standard'*

And ended with:

Summer term 1976:   *'She offers little in a subject which does not motivate her'.*

Chapter Thirty -One

Monday 8th September 1975. My new third year timetable shows me I have double French for the first two hours of this Monday morning. I haven't had a top set French lesson yet and I am looking forward to it. I am excited about having Miss Roseau as my teacher. Will she at least recognise me I wonder? For once, I intend to try and sit at the front of the class and put my hand up as much as possible. That will certainly be a first for me since my arrival at this school!
I do hope Miss Roseau will want to hear about my recent two -week stay in France. I'm sure she will know of Mme Roussin with whom I stayed. However, instinct tells me to make my sojourn chez les Roussins sound as successful as possible. Miss Roseau won't want to hear how isolated and awkward I sometimes felt. Besides, I don't think I have such words as bored, cut-off or eccentric, yet in my vocabulary. As always, I will give one version of events to an adult, feeding them what I believe they want to hear, and keeping the real events and my sentiments to myself. I seem to be doing an awful lot of that these days. Is that what being a teenager is all about?
During my two week stay chez Mme Roussin she insisted that I kept a little *cahier* with me at all times and made sure I wrote down every new word I heard. Whilst we were at their *maison secondaire* in the countryside I picked up a lot of French names for all the birds I spotted. *Les petits moineaux*: the sparrows. The silent circling buzzards: *les buses*. The diving swallows: *les hirondelles* and I even saw my first ever hoopoe: *une huppe*.

Under Mme Roussin's critical eye I faithfully noted down the French words for the crops I cycled past on her rusty, upright *bicyclette*, endless fields of *les tournesols* and *le mais*. I filled page after page with French words for the flowers in their garden and the vegetables in their little potager. I very quickly learnt the word for the much-hated shutters, *les volets*, which I didn't realise had to be pulled together tight shut every night. How was I to know that it was *obligatoire* for my bedroom to be plunged into absolute darkness, airless and stuffy, as soon as the sun began to set.

The days spent at their Paris apartment were much less intense for me as Mme Roussin and her *mari soumis*, Hubert were far more involved in their city lives and seemed to forget me for hours at a time. I was, however, sent off to the boulangerie every morning and early evening to buy *une baguette* for the meal. I was instructed to ask for one *bien cuite*. The colour of the crust and the texture of the doughy bread within would be scrutinized on my return.

When Mme Roussin did remember I was in the Paris flat she kindly included me in her visits to the local market and took me along when meeting up with other elderly friends in the café at the corner of Rue Magenta. How could these ladies make one tiny cup of coffee last so long? Interminable hours of boredom, my head aching with the confusion of trying and failing to follow the rapid muttered conversations of *les vieilles dames*.

All these experiences, the new vocabulary I have stored away in my brain. I hope I can use some of it in this year's lessons.

Would I dare to try and explain though, how utterly astonished I was when during our first evening at their country house in Compiegne, Mme. Roussin calmly filled a pipe with tobacco and started puffing on it! I think that's probably a memory, I will not share with anyone else!

I'm wondering who will turn up in this French class. Presumably it will just be the same twenty-five or so pupils who now turn up for every lesson I have been assigned to. I'm sure 'Briefcase Boy' will arrive in the classroom... although, of course, he won't have walked there with me and I'm sure that none of the others from 3B will be there. The last two years of shared French lessons have opened my eyes to the fact that not many of the other twenty-eight pupils in my original form seemed interested in learning a second language.

I do realise how lucky I had been with my particular primary school having such a forward-looking headmaster who embraced the arts, music and even French. One of the outside classrooms tucked away near the playground, next to the swimming pool, was designated the 'French classroom' and decorated with all possible things Gallic. Pictures of the Eiffel Tower, Paris streets, bereted men in striped jumpers, market scenes. A frieze of numbers written in French ran around the walls, bright posters showing the colours, the days of the week, the months of the year. An enormous tricolour even hung above us strapped to the rafters. A Mme. Morden came in twice a week to teach us, she was vibrant, excitable, enthusiastic and how we responded! We sang French songs, shouted out the numbers, the days of the weeks, catchy rhymes, we played endless board games and listened to simple conversations on the bulky and unreliable reel to reel tape recorder.

But for the past two years the French lessons with my form had been, as expected, unstimulating and frustrating. Unfortunately for me it had just been continual repetition of the basic vocabulary I had already had the opportunity to learn at primary school. A lot of colouring- in of food items drawn on xeroxed worksheets, always the appearance of that ubiquitous *baguette*! A little bit of pretend shopping with chanting *je voudrais acheter un(e)* ….

In keeping with the comprehensive ideal of equal education opportunities for all, my school were obliged to offer French lessons to the entire mixed ability intake. Pupils who arrived from primary schools never having had a French lesson would then be given the opportunity of learning a second language. Maybe those who had already had an introduction to the French language would inspire, encourage and 'pull up' those who hadn't had the chance. I'm sure this did happen for some pupils during those first two years, but had the teaching staff foreseen the constant irritating interruptions and disruptive behaviour from class members in the lower academic ability range who were intimidated in these foreign language class environments and would never be interested in learning another language? Inevitably too many delays caused by frustrated and uncooperative pupils would hold back the more able.

Not much chance for getting to grips with the essential groundwork of grammar, verb conjugation and correct sentence structure.

Back in August, during my two -week stay in France, Mme Roussin had accomplished the most wonderfully disparaging exhalation of air through her pursed lips when I had to admit to her that I had not yet fully studied the *avoir* or *etre* verbs. I didn't know my regular verbs from my irregular verbs and *quelle horreur!* I didn't even a recognise a reflexive verb.

I got the distinct impression that she was horrified with my lack of knowledge of her beloved language.

Now I just can't wait to get into a French lesson with Miss Roseau surrounded by other third year pupils who are genuinely interested in continuing to learn another language. I need to study all the things that Mme. Roussin derided me for not knowing.

But wait, oh no! Mr Bradshaw slaps together the pages of the thin orange register book and tells us the start of the morning's lessons have been delayed. We are all to walk immediately to the sports hall for a very important assembly.

Whatever is going on?

I walk by myself through the corridors, out through the heavy swing doors, across the courtyard, pass the terrapins towards the sports hall. A heaving grey mass surges in the same direction.

Teachers stand huddled at the doors of the massive, grey-bricked building ushering us all in. This is unusual, all the classes from the entire five years are getting together for an assembly.

I do a quick calculation in my head, there will be around 900 of us altogether in the sports hall. We aren't even expected to take off our normal shoes, usually the rule is plimsolls or trainers only. The floor will be ruined. It must be something very serious.

We surge through the double swing doors into the sports hall and are immediately instructed to sit on the floor. Low conversation hums around, soles squeak on the floor surface. The headmaster is standing, arms folded, waiting.

"Good morning to you all. I expect you are wondering what this is all about?" Heads nod, faces turn sideways to look at friends.

"Well, I'm sure you've all heard about the dreadful incident in London last Friday evening".

An IRA bomb had exploded in the lobby of the Hilton Hotel. Two people died and over sixty had been injured. I'd seen the headlines on the Times newspapers over the weekend and watched with detached interest the BBC News broadcasts. It seemed very removed from our everyday life though. These 'Mainland Attacks' had been happening for several years, inevitably causing shock and horror for the days afterwards and then receding into old headlines.

I had only been vaguely aware of the first atrocity in the winter of my first year at secondary school February 1974. The M62 bombing.

I hadn't bothered to read through completely the Times newspaper reportage of this latest bombing in the London hotel. I presumed the IRA were threatening to continue their bombing campaign, cause more deaths and injuries, increase the 'climate of fear'.

My mother's only comment on seeing the newspaper headlines had been along the lines of *'what dreadful people they were but what could you expect........'* A discussion was not expected, my opinion not encouraged.

I tune back into the headmaster's voice, *'we are to be always on our utmost vigilant, no bags are to be left anywhere. If we see a suspicious parcel or box in a corridor or doorway, we are to report it straight away to a member of staff....'*

His concern seems somewhat excessive. I doubt anyone of us share his dramatic anxiety as we filter out of the sports hall, laughing, chatting, relieved it wasn't anything more serious concerning our narrow, selfish lives. I could even imagine the cogs whirring in certain pupils' minds. Reporting an abandoned carrier bag – the school being evacuated - not a bad way to avoid lessons for several hours!

The IRA did strike again just a month later in October with a bomb left outside Green Park Underground station. One dead, twenty injured. Yet again in London and not really impacting our lives. However, when two IRA volunteers shot dead Ross McWhirter later in November, now, that did really make me think and react to the horrors and destruction of terrorism. How dare they murder someone who I watched on television in the weekly BBC Record Breakers programme.

I walk back towards the main school building suddenly realising I am behind 'No Bag Boy'. I slow my pace to avoid arriving alongside him, his hands are, as usual, stuffed deep into his pockets making the bottom hem of his blazer curl up. His grey trousers are scruffy and too short showing different coloured socks and a lace trailing from one of his trainers. I had been lost in my own thoughts about hoaxes but shadowing 'No Bag Boy' causes me to chuckle suddenly, my amused reasoning shifting to the hilarious fact that here was one person in front of me who could never, ever be accused of being the owner of a strategically placed, abandoned bag! As if he had been aware of my presence, reading my mind about hoaxes and misplaced packages, he suddenly turns around and grins at me. Without realising it, I smile back at him, our eyes lock for a second or two. Oh no! Did I just respond to his gaze? He turns back, walks away and discreetly disappears into a gap between two terrapins and I've got double French to get too.

I arrive at the open door leading into classroom 10. Miss Roseau has her back to the room writing on the blackboard so I am disappointed that she will not recognise me as I enter her room. Stupid, stupid me, anyway, for thinking I was someone different or special who she might want to acknowledge.

I always dread walking into a classroom by myself, so pause for a moment in the doorway to see if there is anyone else approaching the room. If I recognised anyone arriving, I could then fiddle with something in my satchel and time my entry to walk through the door with them. Everyone already in the classroom would notice my entrance and think I have walked to this lesson with a friend! The corridor is annoyingly and uncharacteristically empty. Okay, here I go then, head down and in.

I sidle into the empty front table up against the windows overlooking the bike sheds, the caretaker's bungalow and the side road with the dustbins outside the kitchens, leading up to the new music block and the sports hall.

Using the excuse of hooking my satchel on the back of my chair I turn to look behind me.

Cold dismay floods through my body. I can't believe what I am seeing, my throat tightens with silly, childish emotion. Jane and Judith are already sitting together at a table at the back of the room, leaning forward and laughing with Sally and Katherine who are established at the table in front of them. They must have arrived here before me, probably all walking together to the classroom as friends. My shoulders give an involuntarily shudder. I tell myself not to be so ridiculous, so immature for *'goodness sake'*. But it has already tainted any pleasure for me at being in my first top set French class.

Over on the other side of the room I spot the usual partnership of Big Pete and James and behind them, two more faces from my primary school; pineapple chunk sharer, my bulldog chaser Paul and next to him the bespectacled Martin. Their heads together discussing something, probably Saturday afternoon's football team results.

I see Christine and Paula together at another table. The group of four boys, one with the already bass voice, have established themselves on adjacent tables. No one is looking towards me sat up at the front.

Margaret and Gillian come bursting into the classroom laughing, then immediately put their hands over their mouths in exaggerated *'Oops, must be quiet now'* gestures. 'Briefcase Boy' lumbers in behind these two girls. Had he walked to the classroom with them?

I realise that quite a few of us already sitting in this room were from my primary school. I can even count six from the 'dream form'. That confirms my awareness of how lucky we were to have had such an excellent early introduction to the French language but also fuels my perpetual fury that despite all attempts at successful dissipation of ability on our arrival in the first year, some form groups were bound to harbour clusters of similar equal intelligence and social background. Why, oh why hadn't I been put in one of those forms!

I suddenly spot Emma from my primary school, my Morris dancing club partner, standing hesitantly at the classroom door. She sees me and runs quickly towards the chair next to mine. I smile at her, and she sits down. Emma, who I have had nothing to do with during the entire second year at this school but who apparently has sufficient language skills to be assigned to this French O level class. She has not appeared in any other of my third- year classes. After this lesson I won't meet her again until the next timetabled French class and, if she arrives there before me, she might even choose to sit next to someone else anyway!

Miss Roseau turns towards all of us now installed in her classroom.
"Bonjour" she says, we reply with hesitant bonjours and giggling which she ignores. "You are now my potential O level class, and we need to move along quickly. I'm expecting good things from you but there is a lot to catch up".
There it is again. The phrase 'catch up'. I'm sure Mme. Roussin would whole- heartedly agree with that!
Miss Roseau hands around heavy hardback textbooks which we are to cover of course. My first French textbook. I am certainly looking forward to studying that. I flick through the tables of verb conjugation at the back. Goodness me, I never knew there were so many different tenses and all those changed endings to learn!

I can't worry about that now though as Miss Roseau instructs us to copy off the blackboard. We are going to look at some regular verbs ending with -er. We recite aloud together : *je donne, tu donnes, il donne, nous donnons, vous donnez, ils donnent.* Then we have to recite individually, standing up one by one. This is quite scary, but I manage a passable attempt. Miss Roseau nods approval at me. Others stutter and stumble over the syllables. Miss Roseau is harsh with her criticism. Now I know why she is feared as a teacher but realise the advantage of sitting at one of the tables at the front of the room. As we stand facing the blackboard reciting aloud, no one else in the room behind can see reddened faces, stammering lips or panicked expressions.
The bell sounds for the end of the first lesson, we remain seated and silent.
During the second hour we practise writing and then enunciating prepositions. The lesson is exhilarating but exhausting. Not a worksheet in sight to be coloured. I haven't contemplated once drawing my usual boredom circle and shading the segments every five minutes. My attention has been utterly focussed on the subject material. What a drastic difference between these third -year lessons and the two previous years.
Miss Roseau claps her hands to get our attention,
"Jolly good class. Five minutes of the lesson left. Open your textbooks to page four. For homework, I want you and the person sitting next to you to practise the printed conversation. It's between two people at a railway station. Next lesson, you will come up to the front here with your partner and act out the scenario by heart".
Emma and I look at each other in horror. It sounds horridly daunting, but more importantly, how I am going to see Emma before the next lesson and get together with her to rehearse the dialogue? The next French lesson is on Wednesday. Too soon.
"What about this lunchtime?" Emma suggests,

"No, sorry, I've got a quartet rehearsal in the music block".
"A *what*? Oh, never mind. Well, then, what about tomorrow lunchtime?",
"Can't do that either, I have a piano lesson". I sense Emma's annoyance. I am the one at fault here. In despair, we decide to meet up during morning break the next day. I wonder if Emma will turn up. It won't be enough time to prepare the discourse properly anyway and I already feel like I have let her down. I wonder if she will even want to sit next to me on Wednesday.

Nobody walks out of the classroom with me when I leave.

Chapter Thirty -Two

Art is the next lesson for me. The first lesson on this Monday afternoon. This will be back with my form 3B members. I head off, walking quickly by myself, towards the ugly grey terrapin, there aren't many people still circulating and I'm worried I am a little bit late.
I've come from the music block where I have just spent a wonderful forty minutes rehearsing a Haydn string quartet with three other girls. The first violin and the viola player were even fifth-form pupils preparing for O- level music this year. It was exhilarating for me to be included in doing something musical with them. I tried to achieve every nuance, Alexandra, the first violin player demanded from me. She thought I was too loud in a particular phrase...had I been a half-beat late in the fugal motif? She looked sympathetically at me when I messed up a tricky semiquaver passage. She smiled at me in mutual music appreciation when I instinctively let my bow pressure diminish in a dramatic diminuendo, my low E flat minim fading, drawing attention back to the two violins as they entered, fortissimo with the new modulated theme.
My cheeks flush with her praise, treated as an equal in her grammar school music world. I want to be like Alexandra so much. Be in the fifth form with her, be accepted as one of her friends. I want her to notice me. Out of school hours I watch her confident, vibrant personality during the Saturday morning music school and during the youth orchestra Thursday evening rehearsals. She is always surrounded by like-minded music friends, sometimes her group even burst into song together in the middle of the hall achieving exquisite vocal harmonies or they gather around the grand piano after orchestra rehearsals playing impromptu jazz duets. I gaze from a corner with envy.
However, at least I have had her attention during our string quartet rehearsal. Maybe now there will be more ways I can contrive to be involved in school music activities with her.
I just wish we had finished our playing a bit earlier. We were so absorbed in our work, the start of afternoon- lesson bell had sounded discordantly through our music. Next time we must keep an eye on our watches and finish before the bell sounds. It takes me another few minutes to pack away my cello, wriggle it into its soft case and stack it in the music instrument cupboard. Alexandra and Suzanne, the skinny, freckle-faced viola player leave together, carrying their black-cased string instruments with them to their next lesson, no need for them to hide their instruments, their musical ability.
The second violin player in the quartet had been my friend Jane. There hadn't been much chance of chatting, the rehearsal had been serious and intense. Now we are released from the consuming atmosphere, she clips her violin case shut and laughs,
"I'm staying here anyway. I've got music with my form now. Couldn't have worked better! I'll get in the classroom first and grab a good table."
As I pass through the door, Mr Digby is standing, hands flapping around, ushering 3F, the dream form, into the bigger of the two music classrooms. I'm intent on not looking at them as I exit the

music block, they brush past me, chatting, giggling as they stream in. I need to get to the art terrapin.

Mr Digby is clicking his fingers behind me, trying to get my attention.

"Ah, there you are, I've just been talking with your cello teacher. I understand you are taking the next grade in December. Good, good, get the piano accompaniments to me as soon as you can, and we'll get together for some practices. The Saint Saens swan won't cause you any problems, but I presume you are doing the Beethoven variations? Right well, I'll need to run through that a couple of times with you. Some devilish syncopated passages for us both in that one" …

Mr Digby has the habit of never waiting for his questions to be answered.

'Yes sir' is all I can manage when he has finished but he has already turned away walking into the classroom. Now I really must get to my lesson.

I quicken my pace, turn it into a jog, my heavy satchel bumping against my right hip, my left-hand fingers curled as if around an imaginary cello neck tapping against my thumb tip, trying to sort out the fingering for that semiquaver run I'd messed up.

Thank goodness the art room door is still open. I can hear heavy footfalls, a chair being scrapped along the floor, echoing voices from the prefabricated room. I climb the two steps and enter.

The art teacher turns to look at me,

"Are you the last? Hurry up then, shut the door and sit down".

The sitting down part is what I dread the most. A quick glance around the terrapin shows me that all my form is already here. The 'Village Girl' group along with Julie, Mary and Linda are huddled around two tables pulled together at the back, heads down, faces hidden by long fringes and supposedly tousled but stiffly sprayed hairstyles. A colourful magazine is open on a table surface. Thank goodness they are not looking at me.

'No Bag Boy' and his faithful followers sit awkwardly squashed around a table next to the rusted metal window frames looking out over the playing fields. The boy's bodies seem too big for the space, or maybe it is just because these terrapins are more compact and confined, the ceilings lower, the windowpanes smaller than the main building classrooms.

I never really look at the boys from this form (apart from watching 'Briefcase Boy' walking in and out of my other lessons of course) but glancing across at the group now, yes, I suppose their bodies are changing. They are getting taller, their shoulders broader, more muscular. 'No Bag Boy' has the eruption of angry spots on his forehead, Kevin's blazer sleeves no longer reach his wrists.

For a second time that day, as if knowing I am studying him again, 'No Bag Boy' swivels his head and looks directly at me, a defiant challenging stare. He turns to nudge John; they smirk together and then 'No Bag Boy' does the crude sexual gesture of hand in opposite elbow crook towards me. Everyone at his table laughs. Some deeper chuckles these days amidst unbroken higher pitched giggling.

My face reddens. Quick, I must sit down somewhere. There are two spaces left in the room. One is next to 'Briefcase Boy' who is slumped against a grey wall. The other on a table with Lorraine, Michelle and 'Blonde Hair' girl. This could be the perfect opportunity…. Can I do it? Can I do it? No…. I can't. I can't walk over there; I don't have the confidence. I tilt my head enquiringly towards Michelle.

An *'oh, alright then'* is begrudgingly exhaled in my direction as she leans over the table to lift off her bag from the remaining unoccupied plastic chair. The weight of her plump body pressing against the table causes it to judder and rock on its thin metal legs.

"Bloody hell, Mitch, sit the fuck down", squeals Lorraine. The three girls laugh.

"Thanks" I mutter, my eyes downwards, occupied with opening my satchel.

Today's lesson is going to involve creating a pattern using tessellation. We are to fill a sheet of paper using the same repeated geometric shape with no overlapping and *'NO GAPS,'* emphasises the art teacher.

'Pick a suitable polygon and off you go'. The art teacher assures us he will walk around and see *'how we are getting on'*.

Lorraine bends low over the table and whispers across to me,

"What the bloody 'ell is a polygon?" Instinctively I keep my answer relatively simple. I draw some shapes to show the three girls at my table what they could possibly attempt.

I get absorbed in my design, my wretched late arrival in the terrapin forgotten. Nothing could interest me more than having to adhere to the discipline of patterns.

A rustle of material, a shifting of air movement and a distinct whiff of tobacco alert me to the fact that the teacher has arrived at our table.

He leans down to look at my effort. "Hm. Not too bad. Watch this corner here" His yellow- stained, gnarled forefinger taps on my paper. He places a large open book on our table,

"Let me show you girls this". We look at a brightly coloured illustration of a Roman mosaic floor. It's beautiful, vivid orange and blue tiles in intricate patterns. All four of us 'ooh' and 'ah' in genuine awe. The art teacher revels in our appreciation,

"Of course, the word tessellate connects with the word tessera which is the word given to the small tiles used in these mosaic patterns" ...

Now, that's interesting. I didn't know that, and I'll store it away for further use. My brain starts whirring around with how the word could be used in a crossword puzzle. It has two anagrams: reseats and teasers. I wonder if it relates to a similar word which I have heard during choir rehearsals at my music school, *'Tessitura'*. This, our choirmaster explained, was the word used to depict the range within which most notes of a vocal part fall, being derived from the Italian word for texture.

"That's lovely Sir, but mine ain't looking nothing like that" pleads Michelle and we all laugh. A moment of *'just being girls together'* shared and makes me feel good for a few seconds. The flimsy metal table rocks again as Michelle begins to vigorously rub out her pencilled attempt. Tiny pink shards of rubber fly off into the air around us. I sense that most of 3B are enjoying this lesson which makes me feel at ease. After only a week of third year 'setting' I'm beginning to dread coming back into these few lessons with my original form members, but if I can just get into the room and sit down somewhere maybe it won't be too bad?

Who was I trying to kid? This is the best it would get!

But for now, the art teacher, Mr Irvin has achieved a good atmosphere. This one hour- long art lesson has passed without confrontation or aggression, no obvious division of academic ability. I look around and survey the poky space, most heads are down, a low buzz of reverberating chatter, some laughing.

But 'No Bag Boy' and the others hunched around his table are not actually doing anything other than staring out of the window, transfixed by fourth form girls running around the sport field's intermittent, white-painted circuit. An abundance of bouncing breasts and wobbling thighs keeping them lustfully distracted.

The end- of -lesson bell can be heard jangling outside the terrapin. Now we must all disperse again.

That evening my father was uncharacteristically late back to the house. I even got to watch the last five minutes of Blue Peter. My Mother was struggling with the change of routine, flustered in the kitchen with perfecting the timing of her cheese soufflé being ready and placed on the table, coordinating with his arrival. She informed me he had called in at the car dealer garage to order his new Vauxhall Cavalier.

The delayed meal passed, as always, in awkward silence, punctuated only by my mother asking my father what colour he had chosen for the car. There will be a new license plate number to learn with a P at the end.

No discussion about my day at school. I don't bother to tell them about the assembly concerning bomb threats. There had, obviously, been no discussion at the meal table about any recent terrorist events. No point in saying anything about the top set French lesson, an art lesson back with my original form, a good string quartet rehearsal. No point.

The meal finishes. I escape up to my bedroom with the excuse of homework and cello practice. I've got that French conversation to learn because I don't want to disappoint Emma and I want Miss Roseau to like me. I've got to finish my tessellation pattern for Art, I've got to sort out the fingering on that semiquaver passage in the Haydn quartet and I've got piano practise to do for my lesson tomorrow lunchtime.

Chapter Thirty -Three

The autumn term continues. Crisp October ends, grey November starts. My least favourite month of the year. At least I have the end -of -term Christmas music concert to look forward too. Rehearsals have started. The choir is preparing seasonal songs and carols. I am composing a complicated song to enter into the traditional carol writing competition. As well as the junior orchestra preparations, I have started attending one or two rehearsals with the senior Orchestra and choir (years 4-6) working on the opening cello solo for their planned performance of Vaughan Williams' Fantasia on Christmas Carols. My sister watches me over the top of her music stand sat amongst the first violins.

Our string quartet still meets for one lunchtime a week to practise. We now have both a Mozart and a Haydn in our repertoire. I've mastered the tricky semiquaver passages. Alexandra smiles at me, I hope, in genuine appreciation of my accomplishment. Then, something wonderful happened. She turned to me one lunchtime in mid- October just as the bell clanged, heralding the start of afternoon lessons (we were late finishing again!) and suggested that *"maybe we could now walk to the weekly evening youth orchestra rehearsals together"*. I was ecstatic. She lived on the same housing estate as me so *"why didn't I wait for her at the end of her road?"*.

The usually dark and cold detested walk now became a pleasure. The aching of my upper arm muscles protesting at the heavy weight of the cello didn't seem quite so unbearable! Alexandra and I talked as we walked, we laughed, we discussed music. It's almost as if I have a friend. Now I have her attention during both our string quartet lunchtimes and our weekly evening walk. How precious these allotted times are. On the rare times we pass each other in the school corridors, her class going in one direction, mine in the other, no acknowledgement could ever be made. She is fifth - form grammar school, I am third-year comprehensive intake.

I head slowly towards the chemistry lab. Same corridor as the physics classroom. Same layout, parallel solid wooden rectangular blocks, same high stools. The only difference being gas taps fitted into the surfaces of the scarred, stained tops and the chemistry lab is so much brighter, full of colour, and yes, there is a periodic table taped to the wall. I have fun trying to memorise it every week. So far, if I turn away, I can recite the elements by heart up to number 19: K for potassium. It gives me a challenge during less motivated moments and I realise that I already know quite a few as chemical symbols are often used in the puzzles I try to complete at home.

A cryptic clue in the Times Crossword, back in the summer holidays had been: 'Look! New silver about, together with...' (5)

My father had, annoyingly, cracked it straightaway, I struggled for most of the morning and then, when I realised that *lo* was a synonym for *look!* and *ag* was the chemical symbol for silver, and the letter *n* represented new, I got the answer too.

It's a dark, dismal, windy afternoon. Bare sodden branches are being rhythmically thrown against the windowpanes, sounding like the swish of a brush stick sliding across the skin of a drum. The fluorescent lights assault my eyes as I walk into the bright chemistry lab from the dim corridor. I'll probably get a headache, the dragging ache across my lower abdomen reminds me as well that my period is due. I do hope it doesn't arrive overnight. A nightmare for most of us girls and always so unfair. Tomorrow, I have double sport.

There had been no 'mother to daughter' discussion about the onset of my monthlies. My mother had simply appeared in my bedroom one morning during the previous summer holiday, thrown a mauve packet of bulky Nikini sanitary towels on my bed and said, "There you are, I'm sure you know what these are for." An excruciating moment of intimacy thankfully terminated by her brusque exit from my room. Good Heavens! This sort of thing was simply never discussed. Never mind that 1975 was about to finish, the atmosphere in my house continued in repressive Victorian style.

My mother did turn briefly back towards my bedroom once she was out on the safe, neutral landing and call out to me,

"Oh, by the way, I forgot to tell you, your cello teacher telephoned earlier whilst you were at the library. She will pop by and drop off that Mendelssohn sonata she wants you to start looking at."

Phew! Well, that's alright then, now we are back on safe conversation topics! I wait for my mother to descend the stairs and then rip open the plastic packet and study the thick sanitary towels. It looks like they have an adhesive strip along them, so I presume you just stick them into the gusset of your pants. I had already discovered the weird crackling plastic belts being secretly dried in the airing cupboard, hidden underneath other items. Presumably these were what my sisters currently used for their 'inconvenient days'.

After the first couple of months of this third year, a settled seating plan has become established for chemistry lessons. It's all the usual members of the 'core top set' of course. The two boys who ignored me in the physics lessons reappeared in chemistry. I've found out they come from 3W, obviously budding scientists, but I make sure I go nowhere near them again!

Sally, Katherine, Christine and Paula usually all sit together along one of the wooden blocks. They accept me if I perch on an empty stool at the end of their row, but they are now established *'Science Experiment Partners'* and I am just the odd- one- out, the to-be-tolerated, non-involved observer. They arrive at the classroom in their friendship groups, I arrive by myself. They work together at the experiments, animatedly and enthusiastically, writing down their results. I watch listlessly from the periphery. I make notes if I can be bothered, but mostly I gaze out of the window.

My enthusiasm and participation in chemistry lessons is sadly going in the same downward spiral as in the physics lessons. How can this be happening? I used to love doing chemistry experiments at home with my Merit Chemistry set. All those little glass tubes filled with exotic, exciting specimens: iron filings, a piece of cobalt, slivers of copper oxide, the test tubes slotted professionally into the red plastic holder, the book of intriguing experiments.

The very first chemistry lesson of this third year I had childishly and naively approached the dumpy, white wiry-haired teacher and told her that I had already made soap. How clever was I? She wasn't impressed.

"Very good my dear, but we don't do that yet, that's O level curriculum. Go and sit down somewhere, there's a good girl". Deflation, disappointment but mostly annoyance.

The very same teacher now waits for our attention in her classroom on this dreary November afternoon. Today we are apparently going to carry on with our investigations into understanding the Ph scale. Is a liquid acidic or alkaline? We are to stick our litmus paper strips into various test tubes and record the results. If the litmus paper turns red then the liquid has a Ph less than 5, if the strip turns blue then it is greater than 8.

I can think of nothing more unstimulating or boring. Simply do the experiment, record the result. Homework, of course, will be writing up the experiment in our chemistry exercise books, drawing the equipment used. There seems to be no scope for independent thinking, no suggestion of researching further. Why are we doing this experiment? Will it have any relevance on other things in our life? If it does, then Miss White Wiry hair should be telling us now, keeping up our interest, instilling a desire to think ahead.

I presume the grammar school classes above us probably did these litmus paper experiments in their first or second years. Eager, top ability pupils focused on preparing for the public exams ahead. Compared to us I'm sure they would be well ahead in chemistry studies by now in their third year, probably doing far more advanced, thought-provoking experiments.

Had any of us even realised we were studying science during those first two experimental years of integrated subject material, the mishmash of blurred lessons, the banal worksheets. I presume the education reform principle had been to introduce us gently to *'general scientific studies'*. No mention of the preparation for the actual disciplines required for the three very different subjects of biology, physics and chemistry. We obviously weren't deemed ready to cope with such specification. After those years of dumbed down science lessons, I wonder if it makes us less tolerant, less able to concentrate on accepting the three separate subjects and unable to 'knuckle down' in each field of study?

I'm certainly questioning the pace and level expected from us. After the introductory whole class teaching methods, two years of endless meandering discussions, informal learning, immature and irrelevant subject material, this third year 'setted' science class now demands zero debate and one hundred percent unquestioned recording of experiments. Will just one year of separate science study be enough to guide us towards fourth year public examination choices?

Yet again, we guinea pigs will be expected to adapt, cope and cooperate.

Doesn't anyone else share my cynicism and annoyance at the inadequacies and failures of our comprehensive science curriculum for the last two years? It surely just can't be me who feels so enraged and betrayed at the assumption that the colouring in of a butterfly on a worksheet would adequately prepare us all for future biology lessons or that sitting around in a semi-circle thinking of words describing water movement would prepare us for hydrodynamics or Bernoulli's principle!

I'm waiting to hear the usual phrase 'catch up'. With all due respect, this particular chemistry teacher hasn't uttered it yet!

How are the rest of this third-year top set class coping with their chemistry lesson. Are they enjoying it, getting something more out of the lesson than I am? I look briefly backwards at the two 3W *'science boys.'* I have to smile. No! At this very moment they are spraying each other with pipettes full of water, far more fun! Well, it's good to know that it is not just me who is uninspired. Seated further along my wooden bench, it seems that even Sally and Katherine have found the lesson too boring, too easy. They have switched off from anything to do with litmus paper and are now talking about pop music. I lean in to listen. Sally has recently bought the new single released by the pop group Queen entitled Bohemian Rhapsody.

"Oh my god, it's awesome". Sally is ecstatic in its praise, "Six minutes long, so really good value for money too". She laughs. "Let's listen to it together at my house". I overhear Sally invite Katherine to walk home with her. They live on my housing estate, identical houses to mine, just one road apart from each other across the green. Three years ago, when we were all still primary school friends and walked together to and from school, I would have been invited too, but the first two secondary years of separation, assigned to different form classes means that I am now excluded from their friendship. I am not included in the invitation and the other two girls along the bench, Christine and Paula, have buses to catch to take them back to their homes.

It doesn't matter anyway. I don't mind that much. I have never heard of this Queen pop group or their song Bohemian Rhapsody. I won't be stealing coins from my mother's purse to buy it.

I haven't been able to play my Abba single much, the one that I bought using the stolen fifty pence piece.

It's been annoying to realise how rarely my mother leaves the house. She doesn't seem to have many friends, never 'pops' into neighbouring houses for a cup of tea or meets up with other mums for social events. Shopping trips for food and walking into the town must take place when I am at school. Once, on a rare occasion she announced she was going to visit Mrs Parker, the cleaning lady, and take her an apple crumble she had made from the windfalls in our garden. "Did I want to go with her?"
No, I wouldn't accompany her this time, thank you, I had *music practice* to do.
As soon as I watched her disappear, crossing the road over into the other housing estate I rushed to put my Abba single on the HMV stereogram. I played it over and over, the opening saxophone ascending motif was a new exotic sound to my ears. I was too naïve, of course, to realise that it had probably been recreated in a music studio on a synthesizer, not a woodwind instrument in sight.

My mother knew I had played a record when she was out. She knew I had been listening to unacceptable pop music. I had made the stupid mistake of not returning the record speed switch back to 33rpm after clicking it to 44rpm to listen to my single. My mother only ever played her beloved long-playing classical music records on her stereogram. I denied it of course although in my mother's eyes I was the only possible culprit. I did try suggesting that maybe Mrs Parker had knocked the switch whilst dusting. The implausibility of this proposal completely deserved the disparaging look returned by my mother. The subject was closed. Silence followed.
I had disappointed my mother yet again and my protective shell simply hardened. Layer upon layer of lies bouncing off the carapace I had created to survive the painful chasm between school life and home life.

Chapter Thirty- Four

Well, thank goodness my period hasn't arrived yet although the throbbing pimple, swelling alarmingly on the side of my nose, reminds me that my time of the month is surely due at any moment. I've got double sport after the lunchbreak, back together with form 3B.
I've just come out of junior choir practise. I'm loving the Christmas carols we are learning for the end-of-term concert. Calypso Carol has the most wonderful lilting syncopated vocal line across the 4/4-time signature. We are singing it in E flat major. Some of us third year members standing along the back row are going to be given percussion instruments; maracas and tambourines, to accentuate the Caribbean rhythm. The sort of modern Christmas music I know my mother detests, but she will be there in the front row of the audience of course, a fixed smile on her face, enduring our swaying rendition.
It was annoying that the last minutes of the rehearsal were marred by younger members of the choir, years 1 and 2, losing concentration, messing around and chatting to each other. I shared the desperation and barely controlled annoyance of the young music teacher, Miss Smith.
I stand and sing in the junior choir alongside former primary school friends Jane, Sally, Katherine and Helen. No other girls from my form 3B are in the choir so once we are released from our practise in the hall, I walk slowly by myself, as always, towards the sport building. My choir friends from 3F have an art lesson next.
Ahead of me I spot the line of the 'Village Girl' group walking along with Julie. Identical haircuts bouncing on their shoulders, identical grey zipper cardigans, white blouses with large, pointed

collars. Grey skirts of similar length, the new 'midi' look, reaching below their knees, dark tights and black shoes. I'm still wearing my sister's handed down worn, grey skirt that doesn't reach my knees, long white socks and the lace up tan shoes with the smallest of wedge. Persuading my mother to get me the wedge shoes at the start of the term had been a hollow victory. I quickly realised the fashion had changed yet again and, as ever, I was left behind. Most of the girls are now wearing similar heavy-looking, black, much higher-platformed footwear.

There has obviously been an upper school netball practice during the lunchtime break. I enter the changing rooms just behind the other 3B girls. A warm fug tinged with perspiration and shampoo engulfs us, condensation from the recent hot showers drips down the walls. We change, with backs turned, into our Aertex white shirts and blue shorts. My shirt feels tight across my chest and digs into my armpits. The thought of having to broach my mother about having a larger sport shirt fills me with dread. I wonder if my sister's discarded one is still around the house somewhere. Lucky her, now she is in the sixth form she doesn't have to do sport lessons.

The curly-haired, sprightly sports teacher pushes open the changing room door. She is nicknamed Sue Barker, partly because she resembles the rising tennis player, but mostly because she is, herself, obsessed with the sport. As a whole class punishment last summer, us girls of (then) 2B even had to do a written homework project on 'The rules of tennis'. Very annoying.

'Miss Barker' is scarily unpredictable, one minute we are being lashed by her acerbic sarcasm, humiliated on a freezing hockey field. The next minute, if there is an international tennis tournament going on, or if it is Wimbledon fortnight, we are allowed to all sit around the big television screen watching a match as if we are girls together, sharing a jolly sleepover.

Her appearance in the changing room prompts a collective intake of breath. What will her mood be today?

"Right girls, listen to me. We will be doing cross country today. We'll run together to King George Park and then twice around keeping on the path. I'll be watching everyone, so absolutely NO messing about. Off we go now, get behind me". She claps her hands. Once she has disappeared back through the changing room swing door most of us release our breath in disgruntled moans.

I loathe cross country running. I SO don't need this today.

Lorraine, Tracy and the 'Village Girl' group are already off and away, following 'Miss Barker'. How they can enjoy such a tortuous sport activity is completely beyond my comprehension! Maybe their tall bodies, long legs, a sense of release to be out of the classroom inspires them. I resort to an awkward fast walk/slow canter at the tail end of the girls as we trickle out of the sports hall, down the side entrance, past the bike sheds, the dustbins, out on to the pavement heading southwest towards the nearby park. Mary is jogging slowly with Julie; they seem quite inspired and keep a coordinated rhythm going between themselves. I'm not the last. Plump Michelle and top-heavy Linda walk behind me, chatting animatedly together.

The fifteen 3B boys soon catch us up and streak past being led by Mr Willis. 'Briefcase Boy' is right up in front, thin, bony legs pumping, his long black hair for once off his face, flowing behind.

'No Bag Boy' and his gang of three arrive parallel to us tail-enders.

"Nice bums girls. Cor, what I'd give to get me hand in them shorts…" Is he looking directly at me? His comments produce snorts of laughter from the girls around me. Pleased with the reaction to his apparently witty comment, he shows off by managing to run backwards whilst doing a crude masturbating gesture in our direction, then turns around and accelerates off to catch up with the rest of the jogging boys.

Can this afternoon get any worse?

'Miss Barker' jogs exaggeratedly on the spot waiting for us at the metal gated entrance to the park.

"For heaven's sake girls, hurry up. Some of the other girls are already on their first circuit. What is the matter with you lot?"

Obviously, a rhetorical question, as she immediately sprints off to catch up with the front runners.

I have absolutely no intention of running twice around the park, or even once for that matter. I bend down on the pretence of adjusting my shoelace and let Michelle and Linda manoeuvre around me. Then, when everyone has disappeared around the first bend, I slip into the hedge on my right just next to the park entrance. Not many leaves left in November for cover. I will have to push my way further into the denser, shrubbed evergreen area. Unyielding bare branches and twigs scratch my legs. I spot a yew tree further back and lean against the tree trunk silently waiting. A robin cocks his head to fix me with one inquisitive eye.

Scuffing footfalls and scrunching stones herald the first enthusiastic competitive boy and girl groups passing by with Mr Willis and 'Miss Barker' shouting encouragements. The next twos and threes of bobbing runners pass. That's all the boys of my form off around the park again. Even 'No Bag Boy' was running and seemingly enjoying the activity. Julie and Mary are now walking past, enjoying a promenade in the park, arms linked, they pass by me so close I hear their chattering, then Michelle and Linda amble past. Are they really all going to bother with a second circuit? Why does everyone mindlessly do what they are instructed?

I'm getting very cold though, in my dank, dark hiding place.

I'm just starting to shiver when, thank goodness, I hear the front runners approaching again and this time they turn left and head off back out through the green, ornate metal gates. I'll just wait a while and then 'reappear' with the last of the girls back out on the path. I make a mental note of who is passing. Just six girls left now. 'Blonde Hair' girl has slowed down and is clutching her side in distress. Julie and Mary pass again and here comes Michelle and Linda, now joined by Lorraine, the three of them deep in conversation. I wrestle my way out through the branches and begin a sort of slow stiff loping. My leg muscles protesting after the cold wait.

The school buildings appearing ahead prompt us all to increase our pace a little. We must appear to be a little red-cheeked and out of breath. 'Miss Barker' is standing waiting for us, arms folded, at the sports hall entrance, probably preparing her most sardonic, derisory comment.

Michelle, Lorraine, Linda and I lumber towards the door. 'Blonde Hair' girl is crying, slumped against a wall.

"Just where have you last girls been? So very disappointing."

Is it my imagination or is she looking especially at me,

"You really must make more of an effort. I will be expecting something much better next time and don't you worry", her forefinger waggles close to our faces, "I will definitely be keeping my eye on you lot. Now, for goodness sake, hurry up and get changed. The bell is about to go. There won't be time for you to take a shower".

Well, that's music to my ears at least! We edge past the volatile teacher and jostle our way into the changing room. There is a strange silence as the other girls continue with their dressing, bundle clothes into carrier bags, brush their hair, tie up shoelaces. I detect a quick smirk between two of the 'Village Girl' group. Arriving in front of my clothes pile, I know immediately it has been disturbed. I'd left everything folded; shoes placed on top. Now my clothes are rumpled, one shoe upside down on the floor. My heart thuds. I can't believe it; my skirt is missing. I rummage through the pile again and behind me the room erupts into shrieks of laughter.

"Hey, Miss clever clogs, you missing something?"

"Where. Is. My. Skirt?" I'm panicking, voice cracking, cheeks burning.

"Well, you think you're so bloody brainy don't ya? Mrs *I'm in the fuckin' top set for everything* now. Let's see if you can find your manky skirt ……or you'll just have to go to your next snooty lesson wearing your shorts!"

This is awful, I'm going to cry. Why are they doing this to me? The bell reverberates through the changing room. 'Miss Barker' puts her head around the door,

"Come on girls, get a move-on. You should all be out of here by now" The girls, still laughing, push past me and disappear through the door. I spot my skirt straightaway, laying crumpled on the bench. Someone had been purposefully sitting on top of it.

I've got maths next. I'm going to be late. I'll have to run all the way to the classroom. I'll have to walk into the room by myself, I'll be red-faced and flustered, my skirt will be all creased.
I can't do it.
It's quiet when I leave the sports hall. I make a quick left turn and slip into the music block. The two classroom doors are already shut, voices filtering through.
What luck! Practise room N° 2 is empty. I sidle in quietly shutting the door behind me. Pushing the upright piano a little bit to the left opens up the space behind. I clamber into the gap, collapse down to the floor, my arms around my pulled-up knees and burst into tears.

The next morning, after registration, Mary purposefully lingers next to me as we wait to file out of the classroom door.
"Wotcha!" She thumps her fist gently against my upper arm and whispers to me, "Just wanted you to know that it wasn't my idea to hide your skirt, okay? It was kinda funny though. You got so red and upset."
I smile briefly at her but quickly move away, heading off alone towards my next lesson.

The next week I didn't even bother to turn up for the double sport lesson. As soon as lunchtime choir practise was finished, I walked out of school and spent the whole afternoon, missing maths too, sitting, shivering on my log in the woods.

Chapter Thirty- Five

1976 was the year when all the opposition to the progressive movements in education reform during the previous decade finally became overwhelming. Criticism and doubts began to be increasingly voiced in public. Employers were denouncing the standard of secondary education and the media launched a campaign against comprehensivisation.
In January, the Times Education Supplement published an important article by Sir Arnold Weinstock, managing director of the General Electric Company. Entitled *'I Blame the Teachers'*, it argued that the shortage of skilled workers, particularly in engineering, could be attributed to the failings of the education system:
'Last year, in more than one of our major cities, the engineering employers failed to recruit as many apprentices as they wanted because not enough school leavers achieved adequate educational standards. This is a remarkable indictment of our educational system and one which raises disturbing questions.'
According to Weinstock, one of the questions raised was the whole issue of accountability of teachers. Couldn't ways be found of removing teachers who were struggling at their job?

A further onslaught continued in the newspapers, creating the idea that schooling in Britain was undergoing some sort of crisis, with teachers unable or unwilling to uphold standards and governors and inspectors incapable of correcting the problem.

In April 1976, the Daily Mail published an article stating that *'millions of parents are desperately worried about the education their children are receiving'*.
There I was, stuck in the middle of a raging war of discontentment and indignation concerning the current state of my secondary education.
It must have been an extremely difficult time for the teachers, the 'old school' grammar school teachers trained in formal teaching methods, but currently struggling with the challenges and

attitudes of the less able pupils. And now, even the young and enthusiastic newly qualified teachers embracing the comprehensive educational reform were being engulfed by all the negative and critical atmosphere swirling around in the media.

It was so wretched for me to be expected to sit in classes and watch some of the older teachers have their confidence and self-worth continually undermined and eroded. It made my stomach writhe with anxiety and anger. These were grammar schoolteachers being expected to teach mixed ability classes. It was obvious to me (but apparently nobody else?) that some of the teachers at my school simply could no longer control their classes of thirty mixed ability pupils.

I was incredulous. How had these established, respected and highly intelligent teachers not been sufficiently prepared for the comprehensive intakes? For the first two years I endured sitting in their lessons in silent shock, horrified and distressed by the rowdiness and disrespect around me, indignation simmering in my guts and causing me physical discomfort. I must be too sensitive. Everyone else seemed to be coping! But by this, my third year, I've had enough and simply choose to stop attending some of my remaining mixed-ability classes.

Sending disruptive pupils out of the class rarely resolved the situation. Their audacity would be cheered by the others, and it is doubtful the threat of punishment caused them any concern. By the time my school had five years of comprehensive pupils, it was rumoured that the Head and Deputy Head of these years, the Lower and Middle school, were having to spend <u>two-thirds</u> of their time dealing with the problems and misdemeanours of about 5% of their pupils. Such a waste of resources, time and energy.

One dignified elderly gentlemen teacher taught religious education. Mr Fleming was the quintessential grammar schoolteacher. Always clad in an immaculate but slightly worn three-piece suit, handkerchief folded triangularly into breast pocket, diagonally red and blue-striped silk tie, polished shoes. Thick white hair, matching bushy eyebrows, whiskery ears, liver-spotted skin. He couldn't control my form. He had no understanding or experience of coping with or engaging a mixed-ability class.

What on earth was being expected of this respected schoolmaster accustomed to only teaching academically selected grammar school pupils? How could he possibly comprehend the demands and skills now required to modify his established teaching method? He couldn't of course. He and other similar teachers would be one of the many overlooked and side-lined problems, forgotten in the fervour and excitement of the social and educational reform experiment.

Mr Fleming expected his lessons would carry on in the same well-established formula. Bibles would be handed around, passages would be read and studied, actions of biblical characters would be assessed, parables would be analysed. That simply no longer happened and if religious education was going to continue to be included in the comprehensive curriculum, then it seemed obvious that a drastic review needed to take place on what would be more suitable teaching material to offer to this new diversification of pupils' backgrounds.

I went to church with my parents a couple of Sundays each month, this was expected of me and non-negotiable, and I was, in fact, preparing for my Church of England confirmation. During my primary school years, I had also attended a Sunday School. I wonder how many of my year's intake regularly went to church.

Most of my class never bothered to pay attention to Mr Fleming. Bibles would be distributed but left unopened on the desks. Form 3B was definitely not interested in studying biblical texts or participating in religious or moral discussions. Group conversations continued, giggles amongst the huddles of girls, ribaldry thrown across the room, boys shouting to each other, immature sexual mutterings passed along the desks like a sleazy game of Chinese whispers. Nothing would ever be achieved. The class made no effort. I learnt nothing. It was heart-breaking and sickening for me to observe his panicked, uncomprehending yet resigned face. I could only feel sorry for this gentle gallant man.

Twice yearly my report came home with an **A1** next to religious education. A beautiful, copperplated, inked **'Excellent'** written next to it. I wonder if everyone in my form just received the same mark and comment.

This strangely mild, early February morning I have no wish to go to my next scheduled lesson of religious education along with the rest of 3B. I'm now finding it too distressing to spend the hour-long lesson sitting silently in the classroom witnessing the despairing anguish of the struggling Mr Fleming.

I've just come out of French. Miraculously, Emma still chooses to sit next to me. We manage to somehow scrape through with our weekly, barely rehearsed 'conversations'. I only ever see her in the French lessons. It's simply too difficult to try and get together with her at other times. We don't mix during the morning break times. She stays busy with her form friends in their own room, I don't have the confidence to walk into her classroom and drag her away. Lunchtimes for me are now always filled with music activities.
How different classroom friendships might have been, working partnerships more successfully forged, if we had been placed together in roughly compatible ability groups during the first and second years. How much further advanced academically we might, perhaps, also be!

Leaving the French classroom, of course 'Briefcase Boy' is striding along way ahead of me in the corridor. I can't bear the thought of following him up the staircase towards the R E classroom. The blue sky and precocious spring warmth taunt me. I need to feel the sun on my face. Pressing down on the metal bar, I slip through the next double swing doors along the corridor and head off across the tarmacked area towards the terrapins.
An anagram clue from that morning's Times crossword is still buzzing, unsolved, in my head: School master (3, 9).
I need to sit quietly somewhere and work it out, juggle the letters around on a page in my rough book. Maybe it is too poignant a clue today, considering how my emotions are flitting around all over the place.
I edge sideways through the shadowed gap between the two terrapins that Jane had showed me last year when we were sent out of our German lesson. I just intend to spend an hour here, in the calm, the peace and quiet, the unconfrontational, missing an hour of an horrendous 3B class and then I will re-enter back into the comprehensive school environment.
As I approach the small hidden area, I spot a grey- blazered figure bent over, grinding out a cigarette underneath his black scruffy shoe. He turns towards me, Oh no! it's 'No Bag Boy'. I can't turn back, he's seen me. He's grinning, but this time I can tell straightaway it is genuine, and not at all lecherous. He tilts his head in a questioning manner.
"Wotcha"
"Wotcha", I reply.
"You skiving too, then, Miss Brainbox?" I give a quick nod of my head. Interestingly, I don't feel threatened at all by this unexpected encounter. There's no conflict between us, we are both doing the same thing, hiding away, truanting.
"So, what you skiving then?" asks 'No Bag Boy'.
"Religious education, and you should be there too". We both suddenly burst out laughing realising the absurdity of it, two members of the same form keeping out of sight. Here I am admonishing him for not being in a class, I'm not there either. We continue in relaxed, light-hearted laughter for several seconds. Somehow united. We only have to look at each other and off we start giggling again! His laughing ends in a phlegmatic, tobacco- choked cough.
"That bloody lesson don't do nothing for me. He's a nice bloke though, that old geezer."
"What? That's not fair, why do you boys give him such a hard time?"

"Oh, that's just me and me mates having a laugh together. We don't mean no harm. It's just cos none of us want to know about that bible stuff."
I don't how to reply, I'm cross at him for his insensitive behaviour in the classroom, but I've chosen not to be in the lesson too, so we are equally guilty of disappointing the teacher. Silence descends between us for a few minutes as we stand together hidden in the gap between the two grey terrapins, listening to the muffled voices, the chairs scraping, the distant shouts coming from the sports field. Both lost in our thoughts, then I hear his now scratchy, gruff voice.
"Sometimes I really hate this place".
What? Did 'No Bag Boy' really just say that to me? The angry, aggressive and often lewd boy in my form just uttered something very sensitive and revealing. I'm surprised but honoured. There haven't been many occasions when someone in my year group has discussed with me about how they feel.
It's escaped my lips before I realise,
"So do I". I reply.
We were purposely not looking at each other, but I could sense he wasn't surprised by my comment. Out of the corner of my eye I perceive a small nod, understanding, no need for me to explain further. Maybe he just thought that everyone hated the school?
"You know, I don't know how to fuckin' explain it, you're clever than me, I can't do the fancy words like you, but sometimes I just get so bloody cross with being here."
I shrug my shoulders and lift my eyes to look at him.
"I get angry too. Can you believe that? It's all gone wrong for me as well". We do a synchronised half smile. Worlds apart, we couldn't possibly be more incompatible in social spectrum or academic ability and yet at this moment we are strangely connected and comfortable in each other's company.
Strangely, I am enjoying our conversation and don't want it to finish.
"Why do you get angry then?" I ask, just to keep us talking together but I think I already know the answer.
"Fucking obvious innit? I can't be arsed doing all this bloody writing and stuff. I don't want to be here. This ain't for me. I knows I don't fit in."
Well, I could actually do all the '*bloody writing and stuff*' and more…. but for many different reasons to his, I didn't want to be here, this wasn't for me. I didn't fit in either.
It was like the two of us standing there together skiving a lesson, hidden between the ugly, grey temporary buildings, epitomised the microcosm of the whole comprehensive education programme, highlighting some of its flaws. The experimental academic reforms, the misguided belief of fluid, unhindered social mobility had completely failed both of us. We were equally unhappy and struggling in this new system. Neither of us fitted in.
'No Bag Boy' broke the disheartened, morose atmosphere in his typical succinct manner.
"You've got nice tits by the way…. any chance of a squeeze?"
"No way, bugger off you!" I laugh and refuse him the pleasure, but what an exquisite brief few moments of acceptance. He gives me a wide harmless grin and it feels for a fleeting moment that we are friends.
I knew it would all change though, as soon as he was back amongst his cocky, insolent gang and I would be walking by myself, yet again, to the next academically selected lesson I had been placed in.
The bell clangs for the change of lessons. I haul my satchel over my shoulder.
"Right, I'm off, I'm supposed to go to maths now, you going to your next lesson?"
"Nah, I've had enough for today. Too early for me bloody bus though. I'll walk out to the main road and hitch a lift back to me village. A van or summat will pick me up, no prob. See ya then!"
"Yeah, see ya!"
I walk by myself, head down, to classroom n° 5 and top set maths, the answer to the morning newspaper's crossword anagram suddenly materialising from nowhere in my head as I slowly climb up the staircase to the first floor. My mouth contorts briefly in a sardonic smirk.

School Master (3,9)
Of course: The Classroom!

Chapter Thirty- Six

The month of March arrived with the docility of a lamb, contrary to the popular children's verse rhyme likening the weather at the beginning of the month with a lion and then ending with the predictable simile of a gentle young sheep. The first weeks were dry, sunny and mild. I did a lot of hiding behind the terrapins, skiving lessons or walking out of the school to sit alone on my log in the nearby woods, watching the horse chestnuts and willows unfurl their green leaves. Maybe if the weather had been more inclement, an icy blast from the north or persistent spring drizzle, I would have been forced to stay more within the school buildings sitting through my lessons! My truanting was becoming too easy to do, I was missing too many lessons, particularly some of those in which I was still expected to be back with my original form group.

For the sport lessons, I simply handed over fake letters with forged signatures, purporting to be from my mother or my cello teacher, even my piano teacher Mrs Williams (she would never know about the deceit!) stating that I would be absent from the lesson due to scheduled extra music practises, necessary chamber music rehearsals, important but utterly invented Associated Board of Music examinations.

I completely avoided the class music lessons. Mr Digby never mentioned my absences. Either he was too distracted trying to control 3B or he had come to the same conclusion as myself, that my presence in the classroom was a complete waste of time. He saw enough of me during orchestra rehearsals, quartet practices, music examinations and Saturday morning music school to know that I was still around!

I do still enjoy the art lessons though, the creativity, the patterns. I've got an accurate eye, consider myself a fairly proficient artist and childishly revelled in the praise of the teacher at my efforts. The laid-back, bohemian Mr Irvin skilfully maintained a successful class atmosphere. We all worked at our own standard, our own pace. No one was criticised, ridiculed and all effort was applauded. Mr Irvin had somehow discovered the calm yet entertaining platform required for a non-confrontational hour teaching thirty mixed ability fourteen- and fifteen-year-olds.

I invariably arrived late for art afternoon periods, always coming directly from the music block and quartet rehearsal, but there would usually be the empty fourth place besides Michelle, Lorraine and 'Blonde Hair' girl. They accepted me joining them at the rickety metal table. Sometimes we laughed together, and I could help them with the set tasks but mostly I was excluded from their conversations. They flitted from subject to subject discussing topics about which I knew nothing. Was the latest David Essex song absolutely his best ever? Who had seen the film Jaws? Had Clive Wilson of 4M really winked at Lorraine as they passed in the corridor? Was anyone going to be arsed to do the parentcraft project homework? (apparently, they were together in this class) and what were they all going to wear to Julie's birthday disco? I hadn't been invited.

'No Bag Boy' occupies the same table each week in the cramped terrapin, next to the window, watching the sports lesson going on outside. No more dirty gestures in my direction thank goodness. Sometimes just a conspiratorial smile if he catches my eye.

My favourite lesson during this third year was English, the pace exciting and demanding. My good knowledge of language enabled me to keep up with the grammar exercises. Reading the set books presented no problem. We had just completed George Orwell's Animal Farm. My mother had thrown a quick glance at the book on my bedroom desk and announced her opinion that it was *'probably a lot of modern made -up twaddle. Why on earth didn't we study something more traditional and classical'*...My three older siblings in their grammar school days had apparently all

written essays on far more *'suitable'* books. I didn't bother to contradict her or argue. My thoughts or judgement wouldn't be encouraged, and it was obvious she had never read the book so there would be nothing to discuss anyway. I doubt she even knew that Orwell's real name was Eric Blair and that, he was, in fact buried in a village churchyard not very many miles from our town.
During a recent class discussion about the differences in characterisation at the beginning of the novel of the two pigs Napoleon and Snowball, during which, of course I wasn't confident enough to put my hand up and join in, I worked on an anagram in my rough book: Animal farm: pig drama? (8). Would that have been good enough for the Telegraph crossword or even the Times!

My inability to express my viewpoint was now making it a struggle for me to write essays in my top set classes. I had no argumentative skills, so accustomed was I to always silently and unquestioningly accept what I was presented with. At home I had never been encouraged to verbally express my feelings. Discussions weren't permitted, my father's oft repeated, annoying Victorian phrase citing "children should be seen and not heard" predictably quoted most mealtimes particularly to visiting scientists, remarking at the dining table how polite and quiet we were!
I excelled at tests, remembering facts, doing research from reference books in the house or in the town library but structuring a critical analysis defeated me and infuriated the English, history and French teachers accompanied by my continued refusal to take part in class discussions. This was succinctly noted by Mrs Jacobi on my third-year history report,
'She has worked fairly well during the term, but an excellent examination result shows much higher potential.'
I puzzled over her remark. How was the teacher expecting me to reach this mysterious higher potential if it was not being attained by her class lessons? I could only be at the level of her instruction, the facts I copied from her writing on the blackboard, the information I read from the textbook. Before third year, trudging through our interminable worksheets, there had been no encouragement to think for ourselves, do any extra deliberation.
Why then, should I bother to make the effort now? I am filled with too much resentment for how I had been treated for the past two years, being purposefully ignored, academically held back and prevented from reaching my full potential. Now that my academic ability is finally recognised, and I am placed in a suitable classroom environment, it is purely my petulance and ill humour that prevent me from making that desired extra effort.
Was Mrs Jacobi suggesting and expecting that I should suddenly be inspired to do endless further individual research now that I have been released from the tedium and frustration of mixed -ability teaching and promoted to the top set? She was probably hoping I would immediately have profound analytical insight and wish to embark on discussing historical events. That wouldn't happen! I was just someone with no personality who sat obediently and silently in her classroom, looking out of her window too often, observing the birds, the clouds and people waiting at the bus stop.

My end of third year report card would, as usual, be dominated by comments on my lack of participation in class discussion and my refusal to contribute during lessons. I suspect that maybe the teachers were just having trouble remembering me being in the classroom, probably for the simple reason that I often wasn't actually present! No doubt I was standing hidden in a gap between two terrapins, huddled up behind a piano in music practise room n° 2 or sitting on a log over in the nearby woods.
What exactly am I now anyway? A third-year pupil trapped in this education reform programme that's for sure, but does the school want me to be an O level curriculum candidate blinkered to the fact I am surrounded by a less academic climate, or does it want me to continue being a mixed ability comprehensive intake pupil, simply expecting me to handle the vilification of segregation by aptitude? It's very confusing and I am struggling. I can't be both and I am unable to glide effortlessly between the two. I have failed miserably the social mobility experiment part. I have very few friends now in either my top set classes or my mixed ability classes. Maybe the other 200 or so pupils in my year group are coping splendidly but I have lost my way.

In my maths lessons I now sit by myself at a two-person table at the back of the classroom, making as little disturbance as possible to ripple the class dynamics surrounding me. The initial excitement at the pace and standard required has completely vanished. If I do attend a lesson, I slip in silently by myself, do the problems required and simply slip out again when the bell sounds.

The maths wasn't difficult, I still loved solving equations, and could quickly scribble answers. Coordinates, fractions and negative numbers didn't cause me any problem. By now I have perfected the construction of the most perfect circles in my rough book, divided meticulously into the twelve segments each with the precise inner angle of thirty degrees which I then shade in to mark the passing of each monotonous five minutes of the lesson. I even embellish my 'hour' circles with elaborate tangents, chords and radii! But, as expected, my lack of class work presentation, non-participation in debates about problem solving and refusal to *'show thoroughly all of the stages worked through'* was beginning to become a bit of an issue between Mr Evans and myself. There was even the insinuation that I was copying the answers for the classroom tests from others around me. Had Mr Evans not registered the fact that I sat alone!

Mathematics: Effort **4**   Grade **C**
A very disappointing term's work. She must not rely so much on her friends but must make a real effort herself.......

The second week of March I performed in a small concert featuring pupils who took music lessons with the peripatetic teachers. It wasn't programmed specifically as an upper school or lower school showcase concert, but a quick count of the performers revealed twenty-one upper school musicians and five of us from the lower school years three and two. No one from a first-year form was involved. I performed four items. As part of the small string orchestra playing two pieces of Baroque music to open the concert, then a movement from the Haydn quartet with Alexandra, Jane and Suzanne the viola player. After the interval I was part of a trio with my Saturday music school violinist acquaintance, Verity, from form 3S and Miranda, a fifth form flautist. We scraped through a barely rehearsed Mozart chamber piece (no one seemed to notice) and then for the penultimate item on the programme I performed the solo of Gabriel Fauré's 'Après un rêve' accompanied by Mr Digby on the piano. This is quite an advanced piece for cello in C minor with some tricky passages playing high up on the fingerboard. I had my sheet music placed on the stand in front of me but in order to effortlessly achieve the graceful, drifting triplet rhythm crisscrossing the accompanying rigid quavers of the piano I found it easier to shut my eyes and let the pensive phrasing take over as I wove the bow across the strings.

I missed my mother's perfunctory wink of encouragement, but anyway, on the walk home, she informed me that she felt the whole concert had been ruined by the final item. Three sixth form boys performing a couple of jazz numbers on piano, clarinet and trumpet. It certainly had us tapping our feet and smiling as their joyful, jokey music lingered on around us as we packed up our instruments. According to my mother *'it had been a discordant abhorrence which had spoiled the rest of the concert and completely ruined her evening.'*

Goodness only knows what she would have made of the catchy but irritating song lyric which was constantly being sung around me at school during the last few weeks. A request to 'Save all your kisses for me" seemed to be erupting from everyone's lips. A group called Brotherhood of Man were apparently going to perform this song at the forthcoming Eurovision Song Contest.

On March 16th, the Prime Minister Harold Wilson announced his surprise resignation. James Callaghan defeated the five other candidates to be elected leader of the Labour party and was appointed Prime Minister on 5th April. This news arrived into our living room as I sat, smothered by the usual oppressive silence, with my parents watching the BBC Nine o'clock News. My mother's knitting needles continually clicking.

From our television screen discreetly closeted in the tan-coloured wooden cabinet, Kenneth Kendall informed us that James Callaghan was the first British Prime Minister born in the twentieth century who had not attended university,

"Heaven preserve us all from another Labour Luddite leading the country!" exclaimed my mother. My father made no reaction to her comment from his armchair on the other side of the room, totally engrossed in his sheets of paper, writing a speech for a forthcoming science conference in Japan whilst sipping his snifter of sherry.

Within only months of becoming Prime Minister, James Callaghan had publicly acknowledged the fact that apparently something was going very wrong in state education. Being aware of his poor upbringing, leaving school at the age of fourteen to start a job, he let it be known that he was passionate in the value of education and the necessity for rigorous educational standards to enable working class youngsters to rise above their circumstances.

Despite this innovative action of a Prime Minister becoming personally involved in the education matters of the country, presenting himself as a man who wanted to *'reassure audiences well beyond the Labour party'* that concerns were being listened to, the press continued its relentless attack. The continued theme being that British schools were now in crisis and the teachers were failing to uphold standards.

The previous year the fourth 'Black Paper' had been published. Encouraged by the propaganda crisis which had reached alarming and incomprehensible proportions, the educationalist and politician Rhodes Boyson and co-author Brian Cox produced their critical paper entitled 'The fight for education'. Boyson argued that *'widespread dissatisfaction and concern about falling standards of discipline and academic achievements in secondary, particularly comprehensive schools, must force educationalists and administrators to look for some means of improvement'*. This fourth Black Paper received extensive media coverage.

In the early months of 1976, even before Harold Wilson had resigned and James Callaghan became Prime Minister, the current state of secondary education in the country was frequently being discussed in Westminster debates.

After the reading of the new Education Bill of 4th February by, the then Secretary of State for Education and Science, Mr Fred Mulley, a Conservative member of parliament Mr. Norman St John-Stevas took the floor and questioned whether this proposed education bill was *'an insult to the intelligence of all parents and was contemptuous of the anxieties that they feel? Parents were concerned not with how schools were organised but with how their children were taught within those schools. Did not this disquiet suggest a collapse of confidence among millions of parents over the standards of learning and discipline in our schools?'*

Was it just the parents who were worried about the quality of education currently being offered in comprehensive schools? What about us, the pupils, trapped in this disintegrating and now publicly despised nightmare? Surely, I couldn't have been the only cynical and distressed adolescent experiencing the failures? We had had no say in this radical experiment, simply propelled along into a system over-emphasising the importance of preparing us for roles in society above the need to maintain adequate academic standards.

Further discussions in Parliament recorded in **Hansard** during those months of Spring 1976 reveal just how unenlightened the government ministers were on what was happening in their country's secondary schools. In an Education Bill debate recorded to have taken place on 30th March it became clear how little uniformity there was for the entire country's comprehensive education reform programme and how little understanding there was for the policies currently being employed to educate the nation's youth. Asked if it was the government's policy to allow grammar streaming in the new comprehensive years, a Labour Minister of state for Education and Science, Mr Gerry

Fowler replied that the internal organisation of individual schools was apparently being left to the *'professional judgement'* of the teaching staff within.

The same Mr Fowler is then also recorded as stating that, personally, he regarded **'experiments with mixed ability teaching** *as providing a great deal of evidence about future forms of organisation'.*

So, no surprise then, I had been ensnared, frustrated and betrayed by a government organised, educational reform *experiment*!

The Labour government up until April 1976, had had no real discernible polices for the comprehensive education being received by a now incredible **70%** of their country's secondary school pupils! During those transition years of reform, they had been content to let the schools themselves decide on curriculum planning and content.

Comprehensive intakes, setting, streaming, exam-taking, mixed ability classes and curriculum conformity were all issues that needed urgent and drastic consideration. Government policy reform needed to be centralised.

How long would this 'comprehensive experiment' based on inadequate, ill-prepared ideals have continued if James Callaghan and his advisors hadn't been perceptive enough to listen to the discontentment of the educational professionals, the warnings of the industrialists and the harassment of the media?

On 21st May, 56 days after taking over as the Labour Prime Minister, James Callaghan met Education Secretary Fred Mulley to raise four areas of concern:
- the basic teaching of the three R's
- the curriculum for older children in comprehensive schools particularly science and mathematics
- the effectiveness of the examination system
- the provision of further education for 16–19-year-olds

The Labour Government was even prepared to announce a sudden *'halt to the forward march of comprehensive change'*. It was declared that the Department of Education and Science would now be focusing on curriculum reform and teaching methods.

My mother's derogatory remark about a continuing ineffectual Labour Government under the newly appointed Prime Minister had been inappropriate. James Callaghan was about to inaugurate a monumental revision of the education system. The reform to comprehensive education would come under the greatest scrutiny and reconstruction during the Labour administration of the years 1976 to 1979, more so then ever achieved by the previous Conservative government.

Chapter Thirty- Seven

Easter was late in 1976, Easter Sunday fell on April 18th. The spring term seemed to last forever. I prepared for and passed another Associated Board of Music exam. My mother and music teacher were pleased with me. It's just what I could do, keep them satisfied and they would think everything was perfectly all right. It wasn't of course, but if I just continued to set off for the school day at 8.50 every morning and return to the house at 4.10 each afternoon, pass consecutive music exams, perform in school concerts, bring home good scholastic results then who on earth would suspect that anything was going wrong? There had been a bit of a downward spiral noted in my twice-yearly reports about *effort* in the classroom, but excellent exam results always overcompensated and really, the only thing that interested my parents now, was how many O levels I would pass at the end of the fifth year.

Who on earth would be interested to know what was actually going on in my head? The despondent sadness that engulfed me, the loneliness that dragged me down as I walked by myself around the school building, the frustration and fury that curled caustically in my stomach. The naïve, but acute disappointment of being so misunderstood, so let down, so failed by the current education system.

If I was disappointed in the school, the way I had been treated for the last two and a half years, then I'm sure the teaching staff were equally disappointed in me. They had been adhering to experimental, and uncharted for their school, comprehensive education reform guidelines. It had obviously been necessary that I was to be purposefully unrecognised as an individual for the first two years of obligatory mixed ability class lessons. What most of the teaching staff couldn't understand about me was: Now I had been correctly channelled into third year top academic ability sets, why on earth did I persist in continuing to be so petulant, aloof and scathing? If the other 60 or so pupils who had arrived with me in this intake as *'the top 20% academic achievers'* were all coping and flourishing in their new classes then why was I, an unfathomable yet musically talented girl, being so uncooperative?

The teachers are disappointed by my querulous, sulky comportment. I'm disappointed by the fact that I no longer seem to fit in anywhere. Disappointment all around then.

It was the penultimate day of the spring term. Typical that the weather had turned colder, the days of enticing balmy warmth during the many recent days of missed lessons had been replaced by a cold snap just as the two-week school holiday was about to begin. The metallic blue sky above was deceptive, it didn't have the warmth it promised. Easterly winds constantly blew in brisk grey clouds heavy with hail which departed as abruptly as they arrived, returning to the weak, watery sunshine. "April showers bring forth May flowers" my mother had chanted pointlessly at me as I had turned my back on her that morning, "Why don't you wear your anorak?"

I am no longer interested in listening to her incessant proverbs and poems. That prophetic meteorological rhyme heralds from the 1600s. Annoyingly, and pointlessly, I can recite all those ridiculous month verses by heart. I give a backward wave and shut the back door behind me, immediately metamorphosing from the teenager who lives at home, silently screaming "you will never understand what is going on in my life" into the teenager who must cope with life in a comprehensive school. Never mind those silly 300-year-old childish ditties, I've got far more contemporary and realistic problems to cope with once I walk into the school buildings.

My second lesson of the morning is music with my form 3B but, of course, I'm not going to go. Walking slowly by myself towards the music block I make a surreptitious move sideways to the left and slip silently into the gap between the two terrapins, manoeuvring through to the tiny hidden space at the back. A hunched, grey-blazered body is already filling the space, back towards me, cigarette smoke spiralling up above his head. I know immediately who it is. 'No bag Boy'!

The change of air current in the narrow passage alerts him to my arrival, he turns to face me, "Wotcha!" His face changes instantly from hostile to friendly.

"Wotcha!", I reply, and we grin at each. He drops his finished roll-up onto the ground and grinds it into the soil with his grubby, stained trainer. Still smiling he forms his right-hand fingers into a gun shape and, *pow,* pretends to shoot me.

"Hey, Miss Clever-Clogs, let me guess, you're skiving a bloody lesson?" His voice has got smoother, more baritone, since I last heard it.

"Got it in one", I giggle back. I'm feeling unthreatened and relaxed about carrying on a conversation. I'll try and get a swear word into my next sentence.

I lean towards him wagging my forefinger comically like a reproachful old woman, "And I bet you don't even know what bloody lesson you're meant to be in either, do you?"

He bursts out laughing, flexes an arm muscle and pointedly feels the taut bicep with his other hand, knowing I am watching this display of masculinity, then scratches his head in a mock confused gesture. The black hair has returned thick and curly after the drastic number one at the beginning of the school year.
"Nah, haven't an effing clue. I've only just arrived, got in late didn't I. Was at me bro's house last night, only bloody overslept didn't I. Got a lift on the back of his bike. He dropped me off on his way to work. He's got a new bike, wicked it is, a Honda. Mostly black. Got it from that bloke out on the ring road. You know the one, bloody good deal an' all".
That's the most I've ever heard him say. It goes without saying I know nothing about motorbikes, but it doesn't matter. It is just a good feeling to be chatting with someone. I let him continue explaining engine size, chrome, speed, as we stand there together wedged in the cold shadows of two grey terrapin walls. On either side of us the screech of furniture scraping, bangs, knocks, muffled children voices, the rumbling bass of the teacher.
The gloom intensifies and heavy drops start to hit us.
"Bloody 'ell, raining again", 'No Bag Boy' moves closer to me, "Here, get under me blazer", he raises one arm for me to apparently snuggle in next to his body. I'm only wearing a thin grey zip-up jumper over a white shirt and involuntarily give a shiver, but the sudden stench of his perspiration, musty male unwashed body smell repels me.
"Oh no, it's okay thanks, I better be going". I stare up at the sky to avoid his eyes which I can sense are pinned on mine. "It won't last, I've got to go anyway" I bend down to swing my satchel up onto my shoulder, I'm flustered, pink-faced, embarrassed. Hastily stumble off through the gap.
"Hey, by the way", he's shouting after me, "You fancy doing summat in the hols, meet up, have a laugh together, stuff like that?"
Oh, my goodness, no, no of course not, what is going on? I would never be allowed to meet up with a boy in the town, especially not this boy! but yes, yes actually I do! Have I just been asked out? I have a weird tingling feeling in my stomach, an unfamiliar fluttering sensation, my heart is racing.
"No, it's okay thanks" I call back. Stupid, stupid me. I'm just repeating myself; I have no idea what to say. "Sorry, I've got loads organised this holiday, orchestra course and all that……" My excuses disappear into the icy sweeping rain as I run back across the playground towards the main school building.

It's true, I do have an orchestra course to attend!
As always, my holidays will be meticulously organised by my mother. Even more need to regulate my activities, my contacts, now that there is the possibility I might be spending my days with salubrious characters from my comprehensive school classes.
There will be the week-long residential orchestral course to attend, a concert to perform in, maybe rehearsals with an impromptu orchestra within the town, haphazardly organised by ex-grammar school pupils returning from university. There will be music lessons to continue with, daily instrumental practise and, squeezed in somewhere between all those other activities, a mind-numbingly, boring but obligatory stay with my grandparents in their claustrophobic, knick-knack filled, damp bungalow in Burnham-on-Sea.
Of course, there will be no time to '*mooch*' around the town centre, meeting up with undesirable characters from my school, or, if you add an s '*smooch*'!

Actually, I am really, really looking forward to the county youth orchestra residential course taking place somewhere down in the New Forest this Easter holiday. For two reasons: this April we are going to be rehearsing and then performing Brahms's fourth symphony, my favourite composer, my favourite symphony of his which he wrote just ninety-one years before AND I have been chosen as the leader of the cello section for this concert, all the nine other cellists following me, responding to my direction, my phrasing, my bowing. I'll have to oversee the sectional rehearsals, practise the fingering necessary in the trickier cello parts, check the sheet music has the correct bowing notation. Always lethal if you and your seating partner's bow move in opposite direction, the risk of wood clashing, entangled horsehair. The worst-case scenario being actual physical damage to instrument or person!

My selection as *'leader of the cello section'* was announced at last week's evening orchestral rehearsal. I realised the news wasn't welcomed by everyone. A few string instrument players raised their eyebrows, muttered quietly their disapproval, including some of my fellow cellists. No surprise and it doesn't bother me that much. I'm sure I can shrug it off.

How many rehearsals have I sat through, waiting whilst the conductor demonstrates the certain rallentando he is searching for, watching the brass section practise a certain passage, and looked around all the faces in the vast orchestra semicircle and tried to work out which schools they all attend. The majority come from the private schools, not just the two elite schools in my town but now from the prestigious schools in the nearby city since the county boundaries have been changed. There are only four of us from the comprehensive years of my school. From the third year, Verity, the violinist. Philip, the conspiratorial, worldly-wise piano pupil and myself. Another violinist, Caroline from the year below us and that's all in the orchestra of over seventy youngsters.

My friendships with Patricia, my red-haired cello friend and other musically talented youngsters from Saturday morning music school have certainly diminished. Girls from the private paying schools, and the grammar school selected years keep themselves to themselves. I'm from the comprehensive school. *'Something vaguely offensive'*, unknown and feared in the eyes of parents and privileged pupils. I'm sure that's why the announcement of my leadership of the cello section met with some surprise and resentment.

The last day of term and the customary school bulletin is handed out to all of us to take home. As always, I scan quickly through it to make sure there is no mention of me, none of my English writing included without my consent.

Oh yes!

That was going to happen again to me in the following school year, my fourth year. A creative writing piece I submitted for the mock English language O level was printed, word for word, in the termly bulletin. How could they do that to me again? My sister had handed the bulletin to my mother before I had had the chance to look through. The story I handed in to the invigilator, I believed confidentially, at the end of the mock exam time limit was realistic and modern, set in a television recording studio. I used colloquial speech capturing the everyday conversations and experiences that surround me and included a swear word. Unadulterated, there it was in print. I was mortified, my parents horrified.

My mother hissed at me through pinched, bloodless lips. *'How embarrassed she and my father had been at seeing my work in the school bulletin. All the parents reading that! Whatever would other people on the housing estate, colleagues of my father, think of my use of the English language? What had possessed me to write in such a style, use such despicable words? They were so very disappointed in me.'*

Just more disappointment surrounding me then.

However, that dreadful incident was still in the future.

This school bulletin dated **April 1976** was curiously titled *'A look at the future'*. I'm not sure what this phrase could possibly be referring to. An optimistic dream or, more likely, my cynical, dispirited self was wondering, if someone was having a wry and hopefully undetected observation of the current state of secondary education!

Of the four printed A4 pages only one article referred to something accomplished by the Lower School – the comprehensive years, the six hundred plus pupils who now made up the majority of the entire school. The rest of the bulletin featured paragraphs praising events and achievements that had involved the grammar school years. In my eyes, something was not quite right. Wasn't anyone else seeing this?

The front page of the bulletin, under the enigmatic black inked *'A look at the future'* was then completely filled with school uniform information. Obviously intended for the comprehensive intakes....

'It is important that pupils come to school properly and smartly dressed and we rely on parents for making sure that their children do this.'

Apparently, there must have been a lapse in correct adherence, but hadn't that already been predicted two years before, when the National Youth Employment Council reported that young people are now more likely to *'resent guidance about their appearance'*. Was our headmaster vainly attempting to maintain the pride that was once synonymous with wearing a grammar school uniform.

The front page carried on pronouncing that *'shoes must continue to be sensible; extremes of fashion must be avoided. Boys' shirts must be plain white or grey. Girls' blouses must be plain white too and not patterned or coloured'*. I really doubt that will put a stop to the Bay City Roller style tartaned collars which are now omnipresent in the corridors.

'Boys' trousers should be grey', and the same stilted phrase again, *'avoid extremes of fashion. 'Baggies' are not allowed'*.

'Boys' ties should be neatly knotted' is followed by the cringingly condescending sentence to *'please teach your son if he has difficulty with this!'*

The last point is that *'jewellry and make up are not allowed in school'*. I loved the fact that jewellery had been spelt wrong on the school bulletin, but I didn't have the courage to tell anyone and, besides, the girls in my school year who had worn make up and jewellery every day since that first day in September 1973, would they really care? A few of them were now quite unapproachable, hostile and feared by some teachers.

I doubt this desperate attempt at controlling standards and attitudes would have happened during the grammar school years. I had never seen a school bulletin come home whilst my two older sisters were at the grammar school decrying the state of the pupils' clothes.

At the bottom of the first page, after the pointless and provocative school uniform information was a slip to be signed by every parent and returned to the school as evidence of receiving and reading the bulletin. It's like we are back in primary school. I wonder just how many signed bits of paper will be handed in on the first day of the summer term!

The one (and only) paragraph relating to a lower school event mentioned the recent *'enjoyable'* junior concert. The junior choir had performed *'with enthusiasm'*……. and that completed any acknowledgement of the entire six hundred pupils in the first three years. Just what percentage of those six hundred pupils actually participated in the music activities offered by the school? Probably less than ten per cent!

Was there really nothing else currently happening in the comprehensive years worthy of a mention? The remaining three pages of the bulletin contained paragraphs reporting on upper school grammar school pupil achievements:

An upper school play had been a *'remarkable production'* with *'excellent acting'*. The date was given for an upper school concert which *'promises to be a really worthwhile evening'*. There were write-ups on successful fourth year exchange trips to France and Germany and a visit by the fifth form classes to the recently opened National Theatre in London to see Hamlet. There had been a *'thought-provoking'* sixth form A level visit to an Oxford university to hear a lecture on *'Whatever happened to the positive hero in Soviet Literature'*. A group of sixth form historians had spent a fascinating day at the National Army Museum. The chess club needed new players. There had been successes for the under 19 girls badminton team and the under 16 boys rugby team and, oh, there was a school uniform duffle coat, size 36, for sale!

The imbalance between the remaining grammar school years' activities and achievements and the three new comprehensive years was unmistakable and shameful. I wonder who else spotted it?

Chapter Thirty-Eight

I was probably enjoying playing the Brahms symphony n° 4 during my youth orchestra residential course when the next damning report on the failing state of education in Britain was swooped on by the media and given mass exposure. Towards the end of April, Neville Bennett, a professor of Educational Research at the university of Lancaster produced a report called *'Teaching styles and Pupil progress'* claiming that formal teaching methods achieved better results than informal teaching.
The British media, continuing its unrelenting campaign to discredit current educational standards brandished this latest report as a *'scientific study of progressive teaching methods which proved that they simply did not work'*.
There was immediate criticism of Bennett's findings, but this was mostly ignored by the press, the damage had been done.
Neville Bennett claimed he had found that *'pupils of formal and mixed teaching were <u>four months ahead</u> of those taught using informal teaching methods in reading, English and maths.'*
Formal teaching indicates a passive role for pupils, regular testing and an accent on competition. Informal teaching leans towards integrated subject matter, an active role played by pupils using discussions and very little testing. The teacher's role in formal teaching was to lay more stress on the promotion of a high-level academic attainment. A teacher who preferred using informal teaching methods would emphasise the value of social and emotional aims, the importance of self-expression, and encourage creativity.
Bennett's findings came from his study of primary school -aged children, but the comparisons to the teaching in the new comprehensive schools, the decline in academic standards, the constant criticism of attitude and behaviour was obvious and not lost on many people.
I had just experienced two years of *'informal teaching'*. Tables and chairs arranged in supposedly unthreatening quasi semi-circles. Endless tedious class discussions involving irrelevant subject matter. Blurred, integrated mediocre projects, decorating margins, a lot of colouring-in.
Now I am third year, and selection for *'top set'* means straight back into traditional formal teaching methods. It's just so obvious! In most of my classrooms the tables now all face the front of the room, the teacher and the blackboard. We respond to given instructions, copy unquestioningly what has been written, work in silence. Class discussions are focused and intelligent, relating to subject material. No longer aimlessly meandering along, listening to attention-seeking individual's likes and dislikes, constantly interrupted by irrelevant chatter, immature giggling and disciplinary issues.
If this transition to simply move back into the traditional *'formal teaching'* environment of O level examination preparation, after the first two years was preordained for the top ability 20% pupils then, why, oh, why, were we ever expected to endure those first two years of informal teaching? Was it purely to observe whether it was indeed possible for the more motivated pupils to pull up the average and lesser academic amongst us in the mixed ability classrooms? Was it to study the social mobility experiment of improved integration and thus offering better educational opportunities for the late developers? Sadly, for me, the whole experience had been an unforgiveable affront to my intelligence.

Never mind the four-month ability difference that Bennett exposed. For those of us with O level exams to prepare for, apparently, we've got the whole first two years of informal teaching to *'catch up'* on now!

Five years later, Neville Bennett would withdraw his original findings. Thank goodness, though, that they had thrown yet more fuel onto the fiery debate and prompted the Labour government into taking a good look at what was currently happening in secondary education.

My school's obsession with maintaining its grammar school reputation for gaining good O level public examination results continued. English teacher, Mrs Matthias announced to us in her usual husky contralto voice during a lesson in May, that *'if we keep up, moving along quickly, continue at a good pace, we would be taking O level English language a year early, at the end of our fourth year instead of the usual fifth year'*. A buzz of excitement surges around the room. At last, we have been recognised, our ability acknowledged.

I can imagine the headmaster and various members of staff already visualising the probable headlines in the local newspaper:

'Good results at O level for first comprehensive intake'……. or **'Success for comprehensive pupils achieving O Level English one year early'**……

Even after the horrendous incident of my mock exam essay being printed for public viewing without my permission, I still somehow managed to keep going, put it behind me. Although I would never forgive the school, I concentrated on the actual exam (it wasn't too difficult) and I achieved the top mark, an A grade.

I must admit, most English lessons I sit and watch 'Briefcase Boy'. He is always so animated in the classroom; Mrs Matthias adores him. She smiles at him, claps her hands together, bracelets jangling, when he says something entertaining. He sits at the front, his hand always up to answer questions. I want him to look at me, acknowledge me, but he doesn't. I am jealous of how he is coping. We are the only two from our original form who have now ended up in the top set classes, but we never walk together to a classroom. He is surviving, he seems happy, he laughs a lot, he talks to anyone sitting next to him. I wish I knew how he managed. He must have some inner resilience that I don't possess. It's SO infuriating, why won't he like me!

"Hey, hey!" someone is shouting in the corridor behind me, I turn around and see Alexandra waving, trying to get my attention, walking quickly to catch me up.

She is not in a good mood.

"Where the hell have you been?" She's waving some music at me, "I need to give you this. Mr Digby wants us to start rehearsing this quartet, here's your part", she shoves the manuscript towards me, "I waited outside the music room, I thought you had a music lesson period three, but you weren't there? Why weren't you in the class? What IS going on with you?"

Oh, oh, my stomach cramps and folds in on itself. Someone actually cares about me, wants to know what is going on in my head? I can't begin to explain to anyone just how I feel though. Where would I start?

I take the music from her and begin the lies,

"Thanks, Alex, for the music. Everything's fine, just had a dentist appointment, no worries, see you at the next rehearsal".

Chapter Thirty-Nine

A cuckoo has started to timidly utter its woody, clarinet-like two note phrases somewhere above me as I sit alone on my log in the wood. I listen to the falling major third interval. The bird sounds very mournful, I hope it will find a mate this summer. The trees hiding me are now verdant and dense. A dog-walker passes close by, but I keep motionless. The spaniel detects me though, wriggling its nose and sniffing in my direction as I perch cross-legged in my special place beside the shallow stream. I must keep an eye on the time, make sure I synchronize my appearing back into school just as the bell clangs for change of lesson.

I'm skiving double maths, just couldn't face it this morning. We're doing **probability** at the moment. It isn't that difficult, just common sense really, patterns and fractions. I always get the homework correct. Of course, I should be in the classroom, throwing dice and pulling coloured counters out of a bag. Laughing along with everyone else at predictable outcomes or unexpected results, but as soon as I heard Mr Evans utter the wretched words that we would be *'working with a partner'* I knew I couldn't be in that lesson. I sit by myself; I have no friends in the top set maths classroom. Mr Evans dislikes me enough already, I hardly want to give him any more reason by appearing pathetic and partnerless, non-participatory from my solitary position at the back of the room.

Just two weeks ago he had towered above my table, menacingly stabbing his nicotine-stained forefinger on my exercise book, threatening to put a red line through my answers because I had deliberately shown no stages of working out for that day's test of problems in finding a percentage increase or decrease. I'd just written the answers. His tobacco-tinged, yellow spittle rant had ended with asking me *'why am I being so incongruous?'*

Now, that's a good word. Apparently, I am incongruous in his maths lessons. Is there an anagram? *Goons ruin* as well as *cu*. I need to jiggle it all around in my head, hint that the chemical symbol for copper needs to be included in the anagram. I'll work on a good cryptic clue. Plenty of time to scribble in my rough book whilst I skive other lessons.

How many synonyms for the word incongruous, and would not each synonym sum up exactly my difficulty with coping with the previous two years at this school and my inability to fit in now?

My refusal to cooperate in the maths classroom was complete bloody-mindedness although this was an expression I had never yet used about myself! Who would have thought I had such rebellion in me!

If I could do simultaneous equations, manipulate algebraic expressions, factorise, work out percentages in my head, then why should I NOW bother to demonstrate my ability to the teaching staff who had refused to acknowledge me for the first two years.

When I arrived at the school aged 11, I could analyse a Bach fugue, dissect the strict framework, understand and unravel the complex and rigid rules, (not dissimilar to solving equations?). The total encapsulation of the two things I loved the most: music and maths. All those patterns, sequences, subtle nuances and codes to be studied and deciphered, but no one wanted to know, and I was naive and compliant.

My previously immature indignation has now erupted into much more serious detrimental petulance. As my skiving of the mathematic lessons escalated, I would later discover that I had totally missed out on learning some of the principal rules of trigonometry. Therefore, two years in the future, I would be unable to answer correctly that traditional, omnipresent question on the O level maths paper concerning the angle of the ladder placed against the wall!

My personal self-destruction had begun, I was on a downward spiral ruining my own chances, but it transpired that, at least, some girls from 3B were profiting from their maths lessons. Three other girls from my original form had been selected to be in set n° 2 or n° 3, although I didn't know this at the time, I never chatted to them about maths lessons. Their lessons were less intense, they combined basic maths studies for either the O level or the CSE exam. Two of these girls went on to

pass maths O level with a **C** grade. The third received an equally respectable certificate grade 1 at CSE.
I had no idea that girls from my form 3B were studying equivalent maths albeit in a different classroom to mine. The third-year setting had kept us too alienated, but the education reform had indeed worked for these girls in their mathematic exam preparation. They had coped admirably as they flitted between the two separate exam syllabi. Was this a vindication of the original 1964 Labour government manifesto offering *'a grammar school education for all'*?

So now I can't seem to fit in to any lesson at the school anymore. I have no friends in the top set classes and I have no friends in the lessons I still endure back with my original form members. I feel like a transient, invisible being floating unrecognised between grammar school predisposition and comprehensive reticence. And unrecognised I still seem to be as, still not yet, has any one teacher commented on my absence in lessons. I'm sure the teaching staff have far more pressing issues at this present time than worrying about just one ill-tempered sullen teenager.
I do wonder, though, whether Mr Digby has started to realise I seem to be in the music block an awful lot. I was coming out of practice room n° 2 one afternoon last week, skiving 3B sport, and walked right into him as the bell was ringing for change of lesson. I'm sure he registered my somewhat blotchy face and involuntary sniffing,
"Everything alright in there?" he had asked quizzically, staring at me. Both of us a bit flustered by this sudden close encounter.
"Yes, Sir, fine thanks" I manage to splutter, fumbling, head down, within my satchel and heading off on some pretence towards the instrument cupboard. Maybe he just thought I had got a bit emotional, lost in instrumental practise, but I can sense his concerned eyes following me.
I had been playing the piano in room n° 2 for some of that skiving hour. I'd found a book of Chopin preludes in amongst the abandoned O and A level set music scores in the cupboard off the main music classroom. My goodness, these piano pieces were a whole new challenge and I have enjoyed trying to sightread them, some of them are so difficult! But I'm quite excited. I've realised that Chopin's prelude op 28 in C minor is the very music that Barry Manilow based his recent pop hit on. I loved listening to him singing "Could this be magic". I've played through this prelude a lot in the practise room; I can just about get through to the end!
For one brief minute I believe I have found some sort of connection between my freaky self and the rest of my year group and then it dawns on me, I'm sure hardly any of them ever actually listen to Barry Manilow anyway. As always, I am pathetically way behind my peers. They are now all listening to far more exhilarating, anarchist and provocative sounds. Shrieking, multi-pierced, stiff pink-haired punk pop groups are inciting everyone to rebel. Most of my school year group is loving it.

I linger in the dimly lit music instrument cupboard, waiting for the short corridor in the music block to be free from other children and Mr Digby, so I can exit discreetly.
Then suddenly the doorway darkens, and Mr Digby is right there, standing in the shadows, blocking my way out.
"Ah, there you are! Just wanted to catch you for a minute…." Oh no, please don't say anything about me crying, hidden away, I'm fine, really, I'm fine.
"Heard you playing some Chopin just now, very nice". Oh dear, maybe the two practice rooms aren't as soundproofed as I initially thought! I hope nothing else has been heard.
"You're doing really well on the piano. One of the best we've got in the lower school years, so I just wanted to throw an idea at you for next year …., you will be fourth year and all that!" He does a strangulated chuckle as though it is totally beyond belief that I have somehow already survived three years at the school.
"The music staff, and the headmaster, wondered if you would be interested in playing the piano for some of the upper school assemblies in September. It would just be the hymns of course and, if you wanted, at the end, a little classical piece as they all troop out of the hall. Something by Clementi or that Beethoven I've heard you practising. Maybe the Debussy, the girl with the flaxen hair, that

seems to be coming along nicely? Devilish key to play in with all those flats, excellent achievement though. Well done."
Oh my god! How much going on in practice room n° 2 has he actually been overhearing?
"It would really help us out. We're going to be a bit short staffed next term, what with Miss Smith leaving us". That's news to me, I didn't know Miss Smith was going, I keep my head down, nodding slightly as though I am thinking deeply about his suggestion, he continues,
"Anyway, jolly good, have a think about it why don't you? As I said, we would really appreciate it. You won't find it too difficult. Just arrive a few minutes earlier in the morning to collect the chosen hymn number from the headmaster's secretary. Right off you go then".
I have been dismissed. I manoeuvre around his body in the doorway,
'Oh, and by the way," he calls after me, his voice quieter, gentler "You know, if you ever want a chat about anything, you can always come and see me".
I feel like my heart is going to thump out of my chest, I can hardly breathe. I'm shaking, my face burning. I can't possibly go to my next lesson now! It was supposed to be biology, but I divert behind the terrapin. Thank goodness there is no one else there. I need to be by myself and sort out these baffling, swirling emotions.
I could never, ever talk to anyone about all these confusing feelings that constantly churn inside of me. Especially not a male teacher! How embarrassing that his perceptive eyes have burrowed into my inner self. I will have to become more devious, more uncommunicative.
I cannot believe the absurdity of that last conversation. They really have no idea, do they? Here is Mr Digby, one minute, trying to be sensitive, asking me awkwardly if some *'things'* are not going quite right for me. Perceptively picking up that my musical precocity might be causing me some emotional problems, and then, in the very next breath, he is incomprehensively and naively asking me to put myself in a position that would exacerbate my acute struggle to fit in with the rest of my year group.

Somewhere burrowed deep beneath my ribs is a warm curl of satisfaction that my piano playing has been recognised but ...
No, no, no. I will never play the piano for the school assembly hymn singing. Could there be any more obvious way of proving to everyone else just how incompatible and weird I am? What perfect fuel for further ridicule, mockery and rejection.

The cuckoo continues its staccato major third repetition B down to G. Checking my watch, I realise the bell will be sounding in a few minutes, so I need to start walking back towards the school. It's English next so I'll just walk down the side entrance past the dustbins and the back of the kitchens and slip in through the double doors nearest to the staircase for the first- floor English classroom. I must remember to brush off any moss or bark clinging to the back of my skirt!

Now what's going on? Everyone is still lined up along the scuffed brick wall outside of the classroom. Mrs Matthias is clapping her hands, we are not allowed to enter her room, everyone has got to go back down the stairs to the hall instead. She doesn't look very pleased. Obviously, we will be missing some of her lesson and, even worse, losing some of that precious 'catching up on the coursework time'! I had even been looking forward to her lesson too, wondering what mark I had achieved for my last piece of handed- in homework on Chaucer.
We trudge back down the stairs and join the rest of the grey surging mass heading towards the main hall. Heads are being shaken in bewilderment, shoulders shrugged, mutters, whispers. Julie and Mary emerge side by side from an adjacent corridor just as I am turning a corner. We jostle together, Mary raises her eyebrows at me in a brief shared 'what is this all about?' gesture. It would seem that all the third-year forms have been summoned to the hall. The crowd grinds to a halt as approximately two hundred curious yet disgruntled pupils attempt to squeeze through the double doors.

A surge from the back of the horde makes us all jolt forward, bumping into the back of the person in front. John, Kevin and 'No Bag Boy' elbow their way through and stop next to Julie, Mary and myself. 'No Bag Boy' surreptitiously winks at me and I quickly smile back.
"Wotcha girls! What the fuck is it now? Me and me mates have had to walk all the soddin' way over from the bloody woodwork room. Come on guys, let's sort this out….". The three stocky lads push on through towards the swing doors. They don't look back but I'm sure I felt a hand rest on my shoulder and pass lightly down my back. I know who it would have been.
Inside the hall, conversations hum around, rumbling low voices, a burst of shrill laughter, shoes squeak and the dinner ladies laugh behind the closed, wooden-panelled concertina doors. The headmaster is standing on the raised stage, clad in his usual baggy brown suit, arms folded across his chest, watching us trickle in, perfecting a *'very annoyed'* stance.
The teachers of the classes we are all supposed to be in shuffle along in a line behind him.
Mrs Matthias has her hands on her hips, glaring at something above us, annoyance shimmering off her body like electric waves. She doesn't remain long behind the headmaster, but strides off, exit stage left, in a dramatic flurry of having *'far more important things to do'*. Two CSE English teachers chat casually together. The woodwork teacher strolls in, a helix of wood shaving still dangling from his brown corduroy jacket sleeve. A young teacher I don't recognise stands stiffly, eyeing us all. Long brown hair held back in a ponytail with a flowery scarf. White blouse and calf length patterned Laura Ashley skirt. She doesn't know what to do with her hands, one minute clasped in front, then by her side, then nervously behind her back. I wonder what she teaches, parentcraft, home economics, needlework? She looks a non-academic, hands-on, creative CSE sort of tutor.
For some inexplicable reason the sports teacher 'Miss Barker' is already in the hall, maybe she was talking to another teacher or just taking a short cut through from the doorway leading off the stage into the old gym. She has sensibly decided not to attempt to push through the contraflow of the mob squeezing through the hall entrance and is waiting impatiently to one side, agitatedly swirling her neck whistle on its blue rope round and round in a circular movement. Eyes narrowed, she watches us one by one as we tumble through the door, glaring at anyone who makes the mistake of looking at her. I mistime a glance in her direction and our eyes lock for longer than is necessary. Oh no! Now she has registered that I am in the school building today. I was intending to skive the form 3B sport lesson later, but I think I will have to show up now that she has spotted me.
The last third formers trickle in. The headmaster claps his hand, a lot of exaggerated shushing hisses around the vast space. One of the CSE English teachers unsuccessfully stifles a yawn. We are commanded to sit down.
Sit down? What on earth is going on? This must be serious, the headmaster wants to accentuate his dominance, increase the height difference between himself and us. The grey mass surrounding me lowers itself reluctantly down. Ripples of disgruntlement oscillate. The boys spread themselves to take up as much space as possible, legs stretched out in front, chests thrust forward, leaning back on arms splayed out behind. Brazen hostility. The girls fold themselves into delicate and secretive curves, legs curled around close to the body, grey skirts pulled tightly over knees.
The headmaster clears his throat and begins. He wishes he didn't have to tell us this but apparently there was *'a very serious incident on one of the buses involving third year pupils returning to the villages the previous evening'*. The headmaster will *'not go into details',* he tells us in a voice suitably sombre, but *'police have been involved'*. This sentence provokes a derisory guffaw from a male group somewhere behind me. Maybe they have already experienced police intervention!
The headmaster continues with sentences expressing *'his disappointment'* and *'unacceptable behaviour'*.
More disappointment, as always, surrounding me and the whole of this experimental intake then, but the buzzing of low speculation has become far more interesting. I attempt to discreetly tune into Julie and Mary's conversation next to me. Julie thinks that someone started a fire on the back seat. Mary heard that a gang of rough third -year boys attacked a first -year boy, making his nose bleed staining a bus seat.

A group of girls from 3W on my left is saying something more thrilling, I lean a bit towards them to hear better. Karen thinks that Steven and Trudy *'went a bit too far'* on the back seat and that Trudy's blouse got ripped, she became upset because others were watching and told her mum, now the police are involved. Tracy from my form shakes her head and whispers to the group. I can't catch what she is saying but I expect she has a far more accurate version of events. She was probably on the same bus.

Actually, I've had enough of this. I am SO fed up with this entire school year being dragged down and punished for the disruption and misbehaviour caused by a small percentage of its pupils. How dare the staff of the school treat us as all being of the same ilk. Our mixed ability intake contained 210 pupils of vastly different academic and social standards and principles. Is it too much to ask or expect them to respect our individuality?
Really, couldn't some of the teaching staff have had the intelligence to determine that the pupils who don't go on the school buses to the neighbouring villages might not be involved? Why is it necessary for us all to be implicated, the whole year group included in the criticism, continual humiliation and displeasure?
The most infuriating yet ludicrous issue for me to cope with, is the fact that one minute I can be individually recognised by a member of the teaching staff, even the headmaster, have a one-to-one conversation respecting and acknowledging my academic and musical abilities. Asked, even, to play the piano for school assemblies, but then, the very next minute, I am completely disregarded, slighted. Brutally ignored and treated as just another of the dissatisfying comprehensive intake pupils in the experimental education reform programme.
I should have stayed in the woods.

I walk by myself reluctantly towards the sports hall, it's the last lesson of this warm but frustrating May day. I'm only turning up to 3B sports because I know 'Miss Barker' spotted me in the hall earlier in the day and it would be so typical of her to wonder why I am not in her lesson when she now knows I am on the school grounds.
We are going to be playing rounders out on the field. Once changed, the girls huddle at the door waiting to follow 'Miss Barker'. I hang back, keeping an eye on my clothes pile, planning to be the last out of the changing room door and then the first back in, once the lesson is finished. The teacher arrives, clapping her hands, jogging on the spot, counts us (everyone present today!) and expects us to run out briskly into the sunshine. There's no immediate rush or enthusiasm, we amble out, arms folded protectively over newly developed breasts, cardigans tied around our waists hiding buttocks and thighs squeezed into unflattering tight, blue cotton shorts.
Julie and Mary are walking with Tracy. I hear her recounting to the two of them the happenings of the previous evening's get together outside the Red Lion pub in her village.
"So, it was bloody brill, wasn't it? Mike and Pat turned up an' all. I didn't think they was gonna come cos I heard summat had happened with Mike's mum but anyway…. John and Kevin were there, and you know what?" They shake their heads. "Go on, tell us then" implores Julie.
"Kevin only had his arm around Joanne, didn't he!" Julie was impressed with this important nugget of information, wide-eyed and shocked, but Tracy wasn't going to be stopped mid-flow, "So, I reckons he must have chucked Debs then, I'll have to find out from her sister, casual like. And listen to this, Matt only disappeared round the back with Liza, didn't he. And it was for bloody ages, wasn't it?" There are nods of agreement from the 'Village Girl' group. Julie wants to know if anything happened,
"Well, I asked Liza later, what they done. She said nothin' much. Just hands on the tits and then he kissed her and put his tongue in her mouth and she nearly fuckin' puked cos he had just finished a fag". The girls giggle horrified yet excited. Tracy fiddles with her hair but it doesn't budge, sprayed stiffly into flicks either side of her face, primping herself for the next and best revelation. "Then Pat only went and got me a lager and lime didn't he. I reckon he fancies me".

That same evening, whilst some of the girls from my form and other third formers were out 'having fun' at a village pub, I had been sat in front of the television in our living room adhering to the expected family tradition of watching thirty minutes of Magnus Magnusson asking specialist and general knowledge questions to the four contestants on Mastermind. I usually mange to answer quite a few before the programme finishes and I can escape the suffocating atmosphere and disappear up to my bedroom.

"Hurry up girls" shrieks 'Miss Barker' for about the fifth time. Tracy is still chatting to Julie and Mary.

"Anyway, we're probably all meeting up again at the pub Thursday evening, you two want to come and join us? You could get on the bus with us, we'll hand you our passes out of the window so you can show 'em, but if it's Don driving, he don't give a fuck who he lets on……. then we'll get chips or summat like that to eat and hang around the green until the pub opens". Tracy turns eagerly towards the two girls. Julie is a definite yes. Mary isn't sure.

Obviously, I'm not included in the invitation. Anyway, Thursday evening is youth orchestra rehearsal night for me. This summer term we are rehearsing Rachmaninov's symphony no 2. Such emotional, powerful and technically demanding music for us teenage instrumentalists to get to grips with. The haunting clarinet theme in the third movement, the adagio, gives me goose bumps every rehearsal. How is possible for someone to write such exquisite and heart wrenching phrases?

It feels like a completely different person in a completely different life who, only a few years ago, during a primary school junior maths class, announced she aspired to be a music composer too. Whatever happened to that little girl!

Chapter Forty

Six more weeks left now until Friday July 23rd and the end of my third year.

'The most important thing we have to do', Mr Bradshaw informs us during a morning registration in our 3B form room, flicking through the pile of papers in his hand, *'is to take these forms home and very carefully decide with our **parents** (*that got several sniggers) *on our chosen subjects for the fourth year and the beginning of exam preparation'.*

Ignoring the factiousness, an art he has perfected over the last three years, Mr Bradshaw continues his prepared spiel, wanting us to realise how important these choices are. *'These will be the subjects that you choose for exams whether they are GCE O level or CSE'* and *'after the parent/teacher consultation evenings, he is sure most of us will have been advised which courses to follow.'*

I hadn't come to any evening consultation discussion with my parents. What a ridiculous idea thinking you might need to talk over exam choice! No question of what lay ahead for me over the next two years. Preparation for O levels, following in the footsteps of my older brother and two sisters.

Holding up one of the 2-page stapled forms Mr Bradshaw points out the format of the printed papers. Although the June sun is sending dazzling diagonal shards across the classroom, from my place in the back right-hand corner I can just about pick out typed columns. We are to choose **1 subject** from **each column** noting carefully if the heading at the top of column says **O level** or **CSE**. 'Briefcase Boy' is nodding earnestly, I don't think there's any doubt which columns he will be selecting.

He went on to achieve 9 O -level passes, 7 of them with the highest possible grade A.

I observe that 'No Bag Boy' has tuned out of Mr Bradshaw's explanation, he winks across the room at me and then, with an exaggerated backward arm stretch and disrespectful yawn, gazes up at the ceiling.

At the end of the fifth year, he walked away from secondary education with one certificate at CSE grade 5 in woodwork.

I never knew what happened with the remainder of Mary's schooling. She left during the first term of the fourth year when her father abruptly changed his job and they moved away to the West Country.
I heard that Julie was delighted with her two CSE certificates, a grade 4 in French and a grade 5 in needlework.

"Jolly good then", Mr Bradshaw seems relieved to have finished his discourse after twice reassuring us that further help and consultation would always be available for those who need it. It seems straight forward to me, but I can appreciate how it will be a bit more complicated for those pupils who are in the dual exam classes, for subjects such as maths, English and French. Do they select from the O level column or the CSE column? As it happened, most of them were then offered the opportunity to sit <u>both</u> exams getting a *certificate* for each attempt, whether it was an A to C pass at O level or a D to E failure at O level or, indeed, a grade 1 achievement at CSE or a grade 2 to 5 certificated result. Other pupils would have been advised to choose CSE exam option for academic subjects and maybe try for an O level certificate in the more creative subjects of art, home economics and needlework. The rest of my school year would have been advised to choose subjects from the CSE columns and try for CSE certificates.
All those certificates being awarded! Every single O level attempted resulted in an A to E grade certificate and every single CSE attempted resulted in a grade 1 to 5 certificate. No wonder the school bulletin could later boast that 189 pupils out of 205 in my school year had **'*achieved at least one certificate*'**!
How many parents, townspeople, county education advisors were taken in by this statistic issued from the former grammar school implying that educational standards were being maintained, when gaining a 'certificate' no longer represented the previously accepted academic criterion?

Watching Mr Bradshaw holding the forms to be filled in, I can't help wondering just how much of the exam choice decision is actually being left to the individual pupil to take during these last weeks of our third year and how much has already been predetermined by the assessments of the teachers. There will surely have to be a fair amount of discreet last- minute undermining of pupil and parent choices in order to control class numbers, teaching availability and timetable constraints!
What an utter logistical nightmare of sorting out the fourth -year curriculum options for over 200 pupils in this experimental school year and what a daunting prospect for the headmaster and staff to keep it all under control, if indeed, they can.
In 1970 the grammar school ran smoothly with 720 pupils from first form to upper sixth. When I return for my fourth year in September 1976 there will be over 800 comprehensive pupils alone making up years one to four, the remaining three grammar school years numbering an eclipsed minority of around 230 fifteen- to eighteen-year-olds.
Mr Bradshaw hands us the papers as we shuffle past him through the classroom door. I push it down into my satchel and head off along the corridor to double French. As always, 'Briefcase Boy' is way ahead of me, striding hurriedly onwards with his characteristic awkward gait of someone trying to cope with unfamiliar longer legs and arms.
What none of us collecting our *'choices for exam preparation'* form as we leave the room that June morning realised was just how portentous a barometer it was going to be for the first three years of reorganisation to comprehensive education for the secondary schools in my town and indeed throughout the county. We, the first experimental intake, are about to begin preparations for public examinations. When subject choices are made now, two years down the line, what will be made of it all? It's not just the exam results that will be meticulously scrutinized. What about the foray into mixed ability teaching, equal education opportunities for all since our first day at secondary school? Were we, the guinea pigs, able to achieve what was hoped of us from this social mobility trial?

An intense study would be needed to ascertain if, indeed, the melange had succeeded. Had the more able pupils in my year group 'pulled up' the less able? It's true that the reform to comprehensive education principles offered fairer opportunities for the less confident and late developers. Pupils in my school year could prepare for previously unimagined public examinations. A far cry from R A Butler's edict circulating in the late 1950s that denied the majority of pupils who ended up in secondary modern schools the opportunity to study for GCE O level examinations.

Can a successful comprehensive education system succeed whilst two separate exam schemes still run concurrently within the same school? One set of exams for the more able and one set of exams for the less able……
"Hey, you, what set are you in for maths and English then?"
"The top set? Bloody 'ell! You can bugger off then, just don't come near me and me mates, got it?"

Our fifth -year public examination results would offer much material and significant data for future educational debates. We'd struggled, tried our best in unsettling trial conditions, most had coped with the shock of the third -year setting by ability, but the enormous stigma of the parallel academic ability exam courses continued to divide the year group mentally and physically, academically and socially.

Never mind us, though, the experimental pupils, it was our **exam results** that would provide sufficient information about what was currently working or failing in the country's schools? Was it now obvious that some subjects could be easily adapted for either O level or CSE course work? Others needed a drastic reworking before there could be compatible opportunities. There still seemed to be such a vast gulf between the academic expectancies. Biology O level or CSE biology studies, chemistry O level or CSE chemistry studies. Did adding the word 'studies' to the subject title imply it was bound to be less academic? Physics CSE was not a very popular choice in my year group, chosen by only eight pupils. Almost equal numbers of pupils tried for either French O level or CSE but studying German remained an O level orientated subject. Just three pupils struggled at the CSE exam. More integration between the two curricula was desperately needed. At least the concept of a national comprehensive curriculum was already being discussed.

I'm not looking forward to handing the exam choice form to my mother later in the day. Conversations about anything happening in my daily life between 9am and 4pm are completely impossible now. The schism between my school life and home life has become irreparable.

Sorting out a choice of one subject from each column proved more difficult than I expected! I decided to look at the form and make my choices secretly in my bedroom before showing the completed form to my mother. I just couldn't bear to have a stilted talk, reveal my thoughts, discuss my preferences and I certainly couldn't cope with a collision between my two separate worlds!
I only needed to choose from the O level columns, but the subjects listed in each column seemed bizarrely mismatched and vehemently adhered to the traditional grammar school division of choosing between science or art streams. Even in these early education reform years my school resolutely clung to its previous O level traditions. At aged fourteen we still had to choose whether to be a linguist or a scientist? History and geography floated vaguely around as secondary options and music was a minor periphery possibility. English (both language and literature) and maths were compulsory subjects to be continued by me at O level standard. I wanted to choose history (loved the classroom!) so in the column that contained history and geography as well as the three separate sciences, I circled around history for my choice. Geography appeared in another column but so did music which, it goes without saying, I would be doing. I circled around music of course which therefore meant I would not have the possibility of continuing with geography.

Music only appeared once in the many columns. Six pupils chose to pursue the subject to O level (music CSE was not even an option) and four of us achieved a pass A to C. By the time I sat the music O level there would no longer be a junior orchestra for school years one to three. Simply not enough pupils arriving at the school now with adequate musical instrument playing skills.

French was in a column with German and again the three sciences. This catered for choosing to be either the budding linguist or the scientist. I circled around French. That column decided. I was desperate to take art to O level. My parents had always been supportive of my artistic talent and Mr Irvin repeatedly wrote in my reports that I could gain an O level in the subject. The option of art was in a column including home economics, needlework, metalwork or woodwork and technical drawing. I circled around art.

Russian and Chinese language options only appeared in the O level columns. Parentcraft was purely a CSE choice. An enormous uncharted spectrum of ability to cater for.

My O level subject choices were made and *oops!* didn't include any of the science subjects! I doubted I would get away with this, once my parents realised! For many reasons, I had completely lost interest in biology, chemistry and physics over this past year. My end of term report understatedly pointed this out to my parents:

'This report is not as good as her previous report and there has been a noticeable decline in standard in science subjects'.

The strange groupings of the subjects on the form had enabled me to achieve a biased choice of subjects leaning towards the arts. I was guilty of the increasing criticism being expressed by the current heads of industry that youngsters nowadays were leaving school ill-prepared for jobs in industry and technology.

In retrospect, I know I should have been forced to follow at least one science subject, perhaps chemistry, simply to have kept my mind open to broader horizons and more varied career options, but in those early years of experiment whilst schools still controlled their own curriculum planning and public examination entries, we were simply able to choose unbalanced and not particularly profitable curricula. This problem would not be resolved until the introduction of a core curriculum.

It must have been a struggle for the school to maintain the equilibrium between the O level academic subjects whilst offering the more practical topics of CSE possibilities. Amongst the girls in my school year who followed CSE courses, home economics was by far and away the most popular subject. 29 girls prepared for this exam, only 11 girls sat it as an O level. The next popular CSE subject was parentcraft. The third most popular was needlework. For the boys CSE metalwork and woodwork featured high up in the table of certificates gained.

The formal teaching of Miss Roseau produced an excellent O-level French success rate but sadly it would become obvious that the school's renowned excellence in the innovative language department was already in decline. At the end of my fifth year, four girls and one boy achieved the remarkable feat of an O level pass in Chinese, 'Briefcase Boy' was the one boy of course, but only two pupils managed a pass in Russian, and two a pass in German. It would become noticeable that successful upper school German exchange visits and sixth form Russian language outings no longer featured in forthcoming school bulletins, still ironically titled *'A look at the future.'*

The subject art was the success story of my comprehensive intake! Thirty-eight pupils wanted to continue with it to fifth form public examination level. That was, incredibly, almost nineteen percent of the pupils in the whole year. There even had to be two separate classes slotted into the timetable. What a testament to the teacher, Mr Irvin, who handled mixed ability classes superbly, no conflict, no tensions, no divisions between social classes or academic ability. What a rare specimen he was. A teacher ensconced in grammar school tradition who transitioned perfectly to comprehensive mixed ability teaching. There was no CSE art course proposed on the *'choosing your exams'* form. Only O level. Of the 38 pupils who sat this exam; 21 achieved a pass A to C. Over a fifty per cent success rate!

I handed the exam choice form to my mother with the pencilled circles around my chosen subjects. She scanned it briefly,
"Hmm, I'm not sure your father will agree with this. I'll hand it to him this evening. Let's see what he has to say about it."
But strangely, my father had nothing to say on the matter and the next morning the form, signed, had been left on the breakfast table next to my cereal bowl ready for me to take back to school and hand in to Mr Bradshaw. Either my parents realised that my artistic-biased, science -less choices really couldn't have been avoided considering the peculiar arrangement of the options in each column and the confusion of so many different public examination possibilities within the two parallel syllabi, or it was proof of their miscomprehension and despair at the continuing decline in the standard of my education.

After the much-publicised meeting between Fred Mulley and James Callaghan on 21st of May to discuss the acknowledged concerns about the falling standard of secondary education and the announcement that the Department of Education and Science would now focus on curriculum reform and teaching methods, it was reported that the then Secretary of state for Education and Science, Fred Mulley was caught by surprise when he learnt that it was the Policy Unit and not himself drafting a major speech for the Prime Minister to deliver later in the year (the famous Ruskin College speech of 18th October). To save face Fred Mulley agreed to prepare a parallel lengthy memorandum on the issues Mr Callaghan had already raised. Maybe the Prime Minister was already looking further afield to appoint a new Secretary of state for Education? Within a week of starting my fourth year of comprehensive secondary education, on the 10th of September 1976, a Mrs Shirley Williams was announced as taking over the post of Fred Mulley.
The result of this hastily prepared memorandum by Fred Mulley was entitled *'School Education in England: problems and initiatives'* always known as the '**Yellow Book'** because of the colour of its cover. It was produced by the Department of Education and Science with input from the Downing Street Policy Unit. It was not intended for public viewing or scrutiny and was circulated to only a small number of people in July 1976.
However, just as I was trying to settle into my fourth year in the autumn of 1976, some sections of the Yellow Book were deliberately leaked to The Guardian. On the 13th of October, the newspaper produced a front-page article under the headline '*State must step into schools.* The newspaper continued its revelations with the (yet unconfirmed) details of a national curriculum for secondary schools, stating that a plan to introduce a basic national curriculum for Britain's secondary school had been put to the Prime Minister.
The Times Educational Supplement commented that the quality of education had become a major political issue and the Times newspaper welcomed *'the beginning of a government drive to bring back standards into teaching, concentrating on the basic skills of reading, writing and arithmetic'*.

When, exactly, had these standards begun to fall? At what point had it all gone so wrong?

I think I might be able to answer that! After all, I had been part of the comprehensive education reform experiment.
Since 1973, I've sat silently in classrooms observing the mayhem, the struggles, the failures. I've walked out of mixed ability lessons at the end of the designated hour with absolutely nothing learnt, nothing achieved. Just frustrated with the behaviour and frequent disciplinary interruptions caused by certain youngsters.
I watched the implausibility of attempting to unite such a vast spectrum of academic and social differences. I suffered those first two years of informal teaching methods supposedly offering equal

educational opportunities to the unprecedented large comprehensive intake of 210 eleven-year-olds.

I certainly don't think the brighter academic pupils 'pulled up' the less academic. On the contrary, I think that for the first two years at my school, the banal worksheets, the dumbed down integrated subject matter, the kid-glove approach to cater sympathetically for all education ability, impeded the academic standard of the average and brighter than average pupil.

The initial impetus of the symbolic move up to secondary education seemed to be side-tracked. It felt like we were simply being held back at primary school education level.

I considered the first two years of my secondary education had been a complete waste of time. Third year academic ability selection obviously meant that potential O level candidates in my school year were simply regrouped in the hope that they would now 'knuckle down', and CSE candidates in my school year were offered all the vocational opportunities previously found in a secondary modern school. Those with the determination and ability were expected to catch up on delayed course work, others didn't bother, but how much momentum, inspiration and, more importantly, actual academic achievement had been lost during those first experimental comprehensive years?

Is that when the educational standards started to fall?

I was one of the pupils in those first reform years. I watched everything. Could it have been that the desired conversion to egalitarianism was a contributing factor to the decline in academic standard during the first half of the 1970s?

Coda: My fifth year has finished

Thursday 25th August 1978. It's nine o'clock in the morning. I walk back towards the school buildings under the intermittent shade of the tall, leafy horse chestnut trees lining the road. It's the day to collect the flimsy, palely printed rectangle of paper revealing my O level results. Ahead of me, I spot several other pupils of my year group heading in the same direction, about to find out, too, how successful or not they have been in their fifth-year public examinations, whether GCE O level or CSE. I feel strangely calm and disconnected from the reality of the importance of the next half an hour or so. Completely numbed by my experiences of the previous five awful years of secondary education, I actually no longer care what I have achieved.

I've spent too long trying to create an impenetrable shell of non-communication that hopefully protected me from parental disappointment, teaching staff disappointment, loneliness, confusing incompatibility and the ever-present rage at being an unwilling participant in an embryonic and ill-conceived educational reform experiment.

Despite an awful lot of skiving lessons, preparation for the O level exams was not difficult for me. Reading, researching, memorising facts and figures meant I had revised accurately and knew what would be expected of me. My O level lessons (those that I attended) during the fourth and fifth year had been focused, traditional and correct. A visitor to the school, sitting in on one of the classes, shielded from the more contemporary and experimental teaching methods going on in other parts of the building, would, I'm sure, have been convinced he was back observing a normal grammar school lesson! Around him in the classroom would be the recognised top 20% academic ability pupils from whom the school expected good public examination results. We had been offered the opportunity to excel and maintain the ex-grammar school's reputation.

Maybe I could, or should, have done even better. The school was obviously trying its best to continue the O level programme whilst being overwhelmed by its larger, more complicated government-directed successor.

I stand by myself in the hushed, submissive queue. Ahead there are squeals of delight, expletives, and groans from pupils arriving at the table to be handed their results from the school secretary. Some teachers stand aside in a huddle as we shuffle slowly past. Their judging eyes follow us, hands held in front of their mouths as they quietly murmur to each other. They would have arrived earlier, flicked through the results, tutted at wasted effort, been surprised by unexpected successes. As I pass Mrs Matthias, she dramatically raises her eyebrows in a *'whatever happened? I wasn't expecting that'* sort of expression. Oh dear! Mrs Jacobi catches my eye as I walk past and smiles at me. That will be a first!

Nearly at the front of the queue now but some rumours have begun to buzz around me. Apparently, someone on my housing estate has failed all but one of the O levels they attempted...... A couple of faces belonging to friends from my primary school immediately turn to stare questioningly at me.

The insubstantial thin piece of paper is in my hand. I have passed 7 O levels of grade **A** to **C**. For English literature I achieved an **A**. That would explain Mrs Matthias's surprised expression. By the fifth year she was continually chiding me for my non-participation during class lessons and my aloof and petulant attitude:

'She has a sound knowledge of the texts but has not been giving the work everything she could….'
'Enthusiasm and effort will be needed to succeed at O level'.
'She continues to make little significant contribution in class ….'

I was probably her least favourite pupil in that top set English O level class! Why should I bother to hand in good work when I had repeatedly been betrayed by the teaching staff and my creative writing essays were printed, without my permission, in the school magazine? I'll simply save my best efforts for the public examinations.

Well, I did, and I have achieved an **A** grade!

For history I had obtained a grade **B**. I found out later that not a single pupil in my year group managed a grade **A**. Even 'Briefcase Boy' received the same as me, a **B**. Maybe Mrs Jacobi was just pleased that some of us had, indeed, managed to find our 'potential' and make the extra effort she was demanding from us, but I wonder if those first two years of integrated humanities subject material, the blurred boundaries for understanding specific topics, the uninspiring mediocre worksheets had held us back. Despite being top set, high academic ability prospects, we had just never been able to 'catch up'.

For Maths I had been awarded a **D**. Now, was that a **D** not far below the standard required for a pass **C!** Or was it a **D** for d̲esperately bad and my marks were way down near an **E**. I would never know, a failed O level but at least I'll get a certificate!

This maths result epitomised my personal failure at secondary school. I had arrived in the first form year full of enthusiasm, desperate to learn, loving all subjects but it wasn't long before boredom and annoyance began to ruin my prospective. When my academic ability and potential was finally recognised at third year and I was placed in all the top sets, I should have been ecstatic, suddenly being offered the opportunity to work as if in a grammar school environment. Now, I could race ahead working on all those maths problems and puzzles that had once fascinated me so much. The others in my academically selected classes responded well, worked hard, enjoyed the lessons, but I didn't profit. The downward spiral had begun. By now I was always lonely in the classrooms I had been assigned to, indignation shrouded my reasoning and cynicism choked my confidence.

Instead of revelling in maths lessons, working at a respectable, recognised high standard, heading towards an O level I was perfectly capable of passing, I chose to skive the lessons and hide in the nearby wood, missing out on learning important and necessary sections of the syllabus.

I wasn't personally upset that I had failed maths O level (although heaven forbid what my parents would say!) because I knew that I could easily have passed that public examination. Swept along as an extremely unwilling participant in an education reform programme, I felt that maybe I had finally been able to show a bit of rebellion. My refusal to cooperate, follow instructions, adhere to conformity was undoubtedly detrimental to my result, but did it expose the inconsistencies and fallacies of the new O level grading system. My awarded D grade with its certificate, what did it in fact indicate? Had I missed gaining a C, a pass, by just a couple of marks? I suspect I had probably provided enough correct answers to most of the maths exam questions but, maybe my refusal to show any of my workings for the exam paper had tipped the balance against the marker allowing me a **C** grade. My petulance and irritation had, once again, engulfed me and ruined my performance.

My answer to the simultaneous equation question would have been accurate. I loved doing those in my head but…. NO working out shown on the submitted answer sheet so: *'maybe this candidate copied the answer from someone else?'*

I'm sure I did well on the mean, median, mode question. How I loved handling data, frequencies, percentages and fractions. Dividing up music bars into compound quadruple time. Working out how many demi or semiquavers would be needed to play out a trill ornament and would a triplet be necessary before the final turn? Drawing all those clock faces in my rough book, meticulously partitioned into equal segments to mark the passing of each tedious five minutes. Perfecting the pie charts which recorded how many hours of lessons each week I spent with members of my original form 1B. During the first year it was a claustrophobic 100%, by the fifth year it was a mere 6%.

The trigonometry question: what was the angle of that predictable ladder against the wall? Was this the question which had failed it for me. I didn't know my cos from my sin or tan! Too many skived lessons. I never got my head around how to use that wretched little logarithm booklet!

When I return to the house, my sister Rosemary, home for the summer holidays from her south coast primary school teaching job is waiting for me in the kitchen, anxious to know what I had achieved. How many O levels had I passed? ……..

And is that really all that matters after my previous five years of secondary education? Which public examinations have been passed or failed whether GCE O level or CSE and now, since the government changes of 1976, how many *certificates* have been awarded!

Does anyone care what happened to me between September 1973, the day I entered secondary school as part of a reform programme changing to comprehensive education and the day in June 1978 when I put down my pen in the echoing gym, having finished writing the answer to my very last O level? I doubt it. We were always simply guinea pigs in an ongoing government trial. Individual pupils' experiences would be irrelevant.

Rosemary is impressed by my seven O level passes. "Well, you did better than me then!" she magnanimously admits. Rosemary had been a 1960s eleven plus selected, grammar school pupil. I had been part of a comprehensive mixed ability intake. I gained more O level passes than she had. Is this what it is going to be like from now on? Surprise at pupils attending comprehensive secondary schools achieving good public examination results!

My school had tried its best to encompass all that was expected of it in its transition from grammar school to comprehensive. During my time there, it continued its established O level syllabus courses whilst welcoming pupils who would be better served by CSE exams. All academic abilities were recognised and catered for. Most of my eclectic year group seemed to be enjoying their school days, benefitting from the extensive lesson options and having the 'time of their lives' but, for me the large intake had been daunting, the academic setting at third year disquieting and the parallel examination course curricula distracting.

Was it just simply me who failed within this 1970s experimental mixed ability comprehensive education system, or was it the comprehensive education system that failed me?

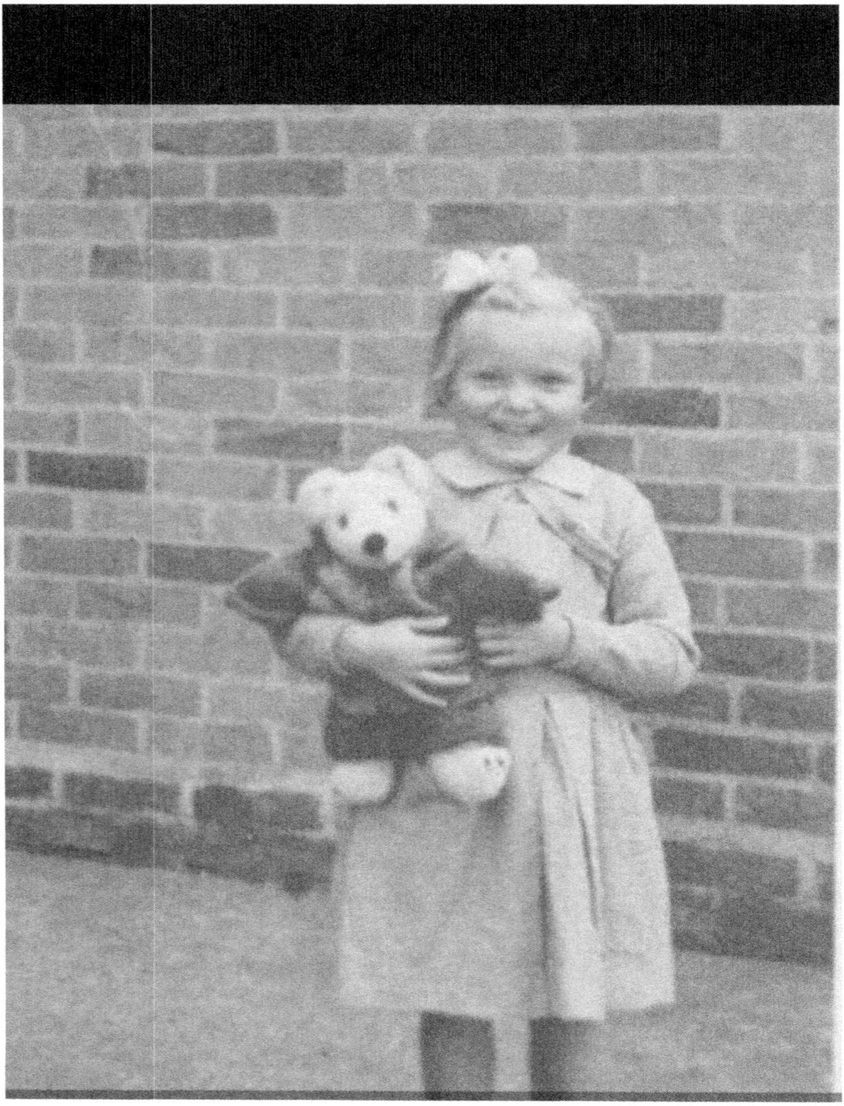

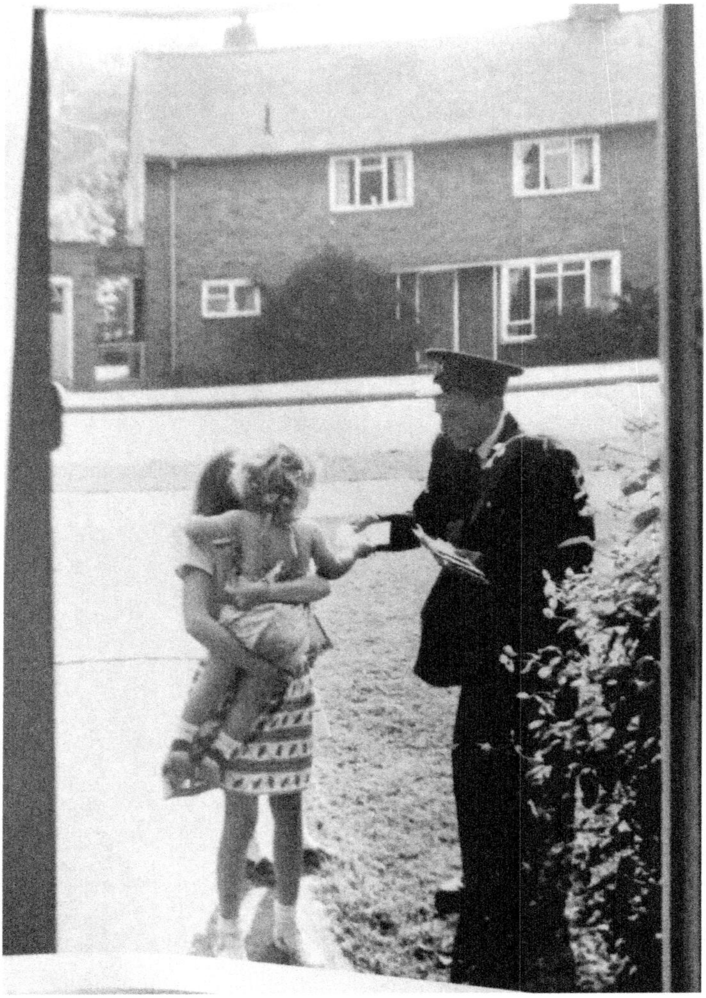

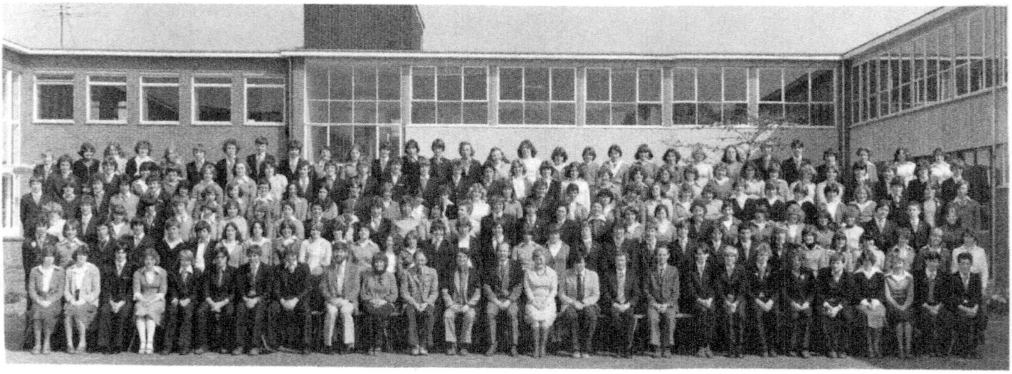

Printed in Great Britain
by Amazon